'Here is a learned and s ... instructs, and instructs ... ree million.' Sam Leith, *Gua...*

'David Crystal is one of ... authorities on the English language today ... *Making a Point* is a fount of good sense and entertaining example.' Christopher Hart, *Sunday Times*

'Professor Crystal leads us through this minefield with characteristic wit, clarity and common sense. He gives a fascinating account of the origin and process of every kind of punctuation mark over one-and-a-half millennia, and he offers sound advice on how punctuation may be used to meet the needs of every occasion and context.' *Telegraph*

'In his new book, the all-things-linguistic god Professor David Crystal explores the bizarre, wonderful, funny and adventurous stories of English punctuation marks ... At the end of the day, whether you are one who raves at the apostrophe in a Potato's or loves the serial comma, it's worth getting a copy of Crystal's *Making a Point*.' *Huffington Post*

'David Crystal's superb new book is packed full of illuminating examples ... With crisp, tight prose punctuated with self-conscious precision, Crystal provides not only a historical guide but an indispensable reference manual.' *South China Morning Post*

'Crystal will delight anyone interested in written language ... he brings scholarly acumen and gravity, as well as delight and good humor, to his subject.' *Publishers Weekly*

DAVID CRYSTAL is Honorary Professor of Linguistics at the University of Wales, Bangor. His many books range from clinical linguistics to the liturgy and Shakespeare. He is the author of *The Story of English in 100 Words* and *Spell It Out: The Singular Story of English Spelling*, both published by Profile. His *Stories of English* is a Penguin Classic.

Making a point

Also by David Crystal

The Cambridge encyclopedia of language

The Cambridge encyclopedia of the English language

The stories of English

The fight for English

Think on my words: an introduction to Shakespeare's language

Txting: the gr8 db8

By hook or by crook: a journey in search of English

A little book of language

Evolving English: one language, many voices

Begat: the King James Bible and the English language

Internet linguistics

Just a phrase I'm going through: my life in language

The story of English in 100 words

Wordsmiths and warriors: the English-language tourist's guide to Britain (with Hilary Crystal)

Spell it out: the singular story of English spelling

The disappearing dictionary

Words in time and place

The Oxford illustrated Shakespeare dictionary (with Ben Crystal)

Making a point:

the pernickety story of English punctuation

David Crystal

PROFILE BOOKS

This paperback edition published in 2016

First published in Great Britain in 2015 by
PROFILE BOOKS LTD
3 Holford Yard
Bevin Way
London WC1X 9HD
www.profilebooks.com

10 9 8 7 6 5 4 3 2 1

Printed and bound in Great Britain by
CPI Group (UK) Ltd, Croydon CR0 4YY

A CIP catalogue record for this book is available from the
British Library.

ISBN 978 1 78125 351 9
eISBN 978 1 78283 108 2

Mixed Sources
Product group from well-managed
forests and other controlled sources
www.fsc.org Cert no. TT-COC-002227
© 1996 Forest Stewardship Council

Contents

A preliminary dialogue

There are two extreme views about punctuation.

the first is that you dont actually need it because its perfectly possible to write down what you want to say without any punctuation marks or capital letters and people can still read it youdontevenneedspacesbetweenwordsreally they dont exist when we speak to each other after all and yet we nonetheless or should it be none the less understand what people are saying

The second is that it's essential because it aids legibility. It's much easier to read if there's punctuation. Also, the marks show us how to read aloud in a way that reflects the pauses, rhythm, and melody that we use in speech. They help us see the grammar of complex sentences. And they help us sort out ambiguities – otherwise nobody would ever have got the joke in *Eats* (,) *Shoots & Leaves*.

but that joke was funny precisely because its so unusual we dont encounter that sort of ambiguity most of the time when we write and its crazy to have to learn a complicated system that nobody agrees about just so that we can sort out rare cases of ambiguity

But punctuation isn't only about ambiguity and intelligibility. It also shows our identity as educated people. For historical reasons, society expects people to spell correctly and to punctuate correctly.

how can anything be correct if theres so much disagreement

about it theres an example already in what youve written you
put a comma in after the word rhythm in your first comment
thats something a lot of people including some ministers of
education would disapprove of

There are historical reasons for that, too.

what are these historical reasons you keep going on about

Read on …

A traveller's introduction

If you walk along the main shopping street in Belgrade, in the direction of Kalemegdan Park, and turn left just before you reach the end, you will find yourself in Kralja Petra street. Towards the bottom, opposite the Serbian Orthodox cathedral, is the oldest traditional *kafana*, or tavern, in the city. And its name is a punctuation mark.

A question mark, to be precise. And that is how everyone knows it. People say they will meet 'at the question-mark tavern' – *znak pitanja* in Serbian. You can't miss it, as on the outside wall is a prominent lantern with a large question mark on it. And inside you are surrounded by menu question marks. It is a typographical paradise. If there were a Question-Mark Protection Society, this is a place where its members would surely wish to end their days.

Behind every punctuation mark lies a thousand stories, and nowhere is a story more interesting than in the case of number 6 Kralja Petra. In 1892, the owner wanted a new name for his tavern and looked for the nearest landmark, which was the church across the street. So he called it 'By the Saborna Church'. But he hadn't taken into account the likely reaction of the Church authorities, who were furious at the thought of the name of their cathedral being associated with a pub. Temporarily at a loss for an alternative, he put a question mark on the door. And it stayed.

A question mark as the name of a pub. It's a function of

The author admires the question-mark tavern.
(inset) The tavern menu cover.

punctuation that would never have been dreamed of by those who first thought of adding marks to their writing to make it easier to read. But the story of English punctuation is littered with such personal preferences, unusual practices, and arbitrary decisions – as well as occasional linguistic reasoning. For such a tiny system – only a dozen or so marks in common use, after all – there's an amazing amount of uncertainty over usage.

And an even more amazing amount of personal involvement. What other area of language has generated motivation of the kind shown by the two enthusiasts who went hunting for punctuational errors all the way across America, correction-pens in hand, risking jail in the process? What other area of language has produced as specific an organization as the Apostrophe Protection Society? What other account of a language topic has achieved anywhere near the remarkable 3-million-plus sales of Lynne Truss's punctuation manifesto, *Eats, Shoots & Leaves*?

When a language is written down for the first time, the writer has to perform two apparently simple tasks: spell the words, and punctuate the sentences. Both turn out to be unexpectedly complicated. I've told the story of how writers solved the spelling task in *Spell It Out*. This book tells the story of how they solved the second – or rather, didn't entirely solve it, judging by the furious rows over what counts as correct punctuation which still surface in the media. One only has to write *potato's* to elicit an emotional reaction of biblical proportions.

There is something really special about punctuation, and its story needs to be told. Who were the people who introduced punctuation to the English language? Why did they do it? How did their invention evolve over the centuries? When did the enthusiasms and uncertainties originate? What is happening to punctuation today? And what is its future? That is what this book is about.

1
In the beginning ...

Up on the second floor in the Ashmolean Museum in Oxford, in a gallery displaying artefacts from early England, there is a beautiful teardrop-shaped object. A decorated golden frame surrounds a colourful enamelled design protected by a flat panel of polished rock crystal. It shows the picture of a man dressed in a green tunic, and holding a flowered sceptre in each hand, his wide eyes gazing intently at something we do not see. And around the rim of the object, just a few milli-metres thick, is an Old English inscription in Roman letters:

AELFREDMECHEHTGEWYRCAN

There are no spaces between the words. Inserting these, we get

AELFRED MEC HEHT GEWYRCAN

Alfred   me ordered   to make
= Alfred ordered me to be made

This is King Alfred the Great, and the object has come to be called the Alfred Jewel.

It was found near Athelney Abbey in Somerset in 1693, the place where Alfred launched his successful counter-attack against the Danes in 878. There has been much debate about the identity of the man, and what the purpose of the jewel was. An important clue is the base of the object, which

The Alfred Jewel in outline, showing (left) the location of the inscription on the object, and (right) the way the inscription surrounds the figure.

is in the form of a dragon-like head with a cylindrical socket in its mouth. What did that socket hold? Probably a pointer, used to help a reader to follow the lines of text in a manuscript, which would often be placed on a stand some distance away from the reader. It's now thought the large-eyed figure represents the sense of sight. His eyes are wide open and focused because he is reading.

For people interested in English punctuation, the jewel inscription provides an important opening insight. There isn't any. This is a sentence, but there's no full stop. All the letters are the same, capitals, so there's no contrast showing where the sentence begins or that Alfred is a name. And the inscription lacks what to modern eyes is the most basic orthographic device to aid reading: spaces to separate the words.

Sixty miles away, in another museum, there's another remarkable object from Anglo-Saxon times: the Franks Casket. This is an intricately carved whalebone box that was presented to the British Museum by one of its curators, Augustus Franks, in 1867. Each side of the box displays scenes from Roman, Jewish, Christian, and Germanic traditions, accompanied by an explanatory inscription in English and Latin. The English words are written in runes, and if I transcribe a few in their Roman letter equivalents, they would look like this:

HERFEGTAÞ+TITUSENDGIUÞEASU

Once again, there are no word-spaces. Inserting them, we get

HER FEGTAÞ +TITUS END GIUÞEASU

Here   fight   Titus   and   Jews

It is a description of the capture of Jerusalem by Emperor Titus in AD 70. (The letter Þ represents a 'th' sound.)

This state of affairs is common in the inscriptions of the period. Many have no spacing or punctuation marks at all. Today, word-spaces are such an obvious and universal feature of the written language that we can easily forget they are there, and ignore their role as a device of punctuation. But a word-space is just as much a punctuation feature as is its close relative, the hyphen. And one of the topics I'll discuss later in this book will be the uncertain trading-relationship between spaces and hyphens. Should a word be written spaced, hyphenated, or solid? Is it *flower pot, flower-pot,* or *flowerpot?*

Word-spaces are the norm today; but it wasn't always so. It's not difficult to see why. We don't actually need them to understand language. We don't use them when we speak, and fluent readers don't put pauses between words as they read aloud. Read this paragraph out loud, and you'll probably pause at the commas and full stops, but you won't pause between the words. They run together. So, if we think of writing purely as a way of putting speech down on paper,

The back of the Franks Casket, showing the Titus inscription.
The sequence of runes begins at the bottom left-hand corner
and continues across the top up to the mid-point.

there's no reason to think of separating the words by spaces. And that seems to be how early writers thought, for unspaced text (often called, in Latin, *scriptura continua*) came to be a major feature of early Western writing, in both Greek and Latin. From the first century AD we find most texts throughout the Roman Empire without words being separated at all. It was thus only natural for missionaries to introduce unspaced writing when they arrived in England.

Writing in antiquity was viewed by most people as a guide to reading aloud. Today, we tend to read silently, privately, rapidly. We can skim through text if we wish, omitting portions. In early Greek and Roman civilization, people routinely read aloud to audiences in displays of oratory, every syllable was valued, and eloquence was highly rated. No skimming then. A text would have been well prepared before being read in public, so that it became more like a musical score, reminding the reader what to say next. In such circumstances, experienced readers wouldn't need word-spaces or other marks. Some influential writers, indeed, poured scorn on punctuation. Cicero, for example, thought that the rhythm of a well-written sentence was enough to tell someone how to bring it to an effective close. Punctuation marks were unnecessary.

But without punctuation of any kind, readers would have to do their homework to avoid unexpected miscues. We would have to do our homework too, if we had no word-spacing today. Faced with the sentence

therapistsneedspecialtreatment

we need to know if this is a text about sex crimes or about speech pathology before we can correctly read it aloud. Early writers on oratory and rhetoric, such as Aristotle and Quintilian, often illustrated the dangers of misreading an unpunctuated text, and stressed the need for good preparation. Familiarity, they hoped, would breed content.

We can carry out an experiment to show how familiarity with a text helps our reading of it, even if it is unspaced. Take a text you know well, and write it down without word-spaces, then try reading it aloud. Like this:

tobeornottobethatisthequestion

ourfatherwhoartinheavenhallowedbethyname

jackandjillwentupthehilltofetchapailofwater

Our knowledge of the content enables us to read it quickly. But with a bit more effort we can do this even if we don't know the text in advance. In fact, this is something we're increasingly doing these days, as a result of the Internet.

Domain names don't use word-spaces. Consider the following addresses:

www.davidcrystal.com

www.iloveshakespeare.com

www.thisisanexampleofapossiblelongdomainname.com

It may take us a millisecond or two longer to read these strings, but we can do it. *Scriptura continua* is back!

In Anglo-Saxon times in England, inscriptions typically don't show any sign of punctuation. But not all. What is thought to be the very earliest sentence inscribed in English in fact does show word division. This is the Undley bracteate, a tiny gold medallion found at Undley in Suffolk in 1982, and dated to the second half of the fifth century AD. It consists of three words in runic letters, and the words are separated by small circles:

gægogæ ° mæga ° medu

The meaning is uncertain – one version translates the Old English as 'this she-wolf is a reward to my kinsman' – but the way the runemaster worked is clear enough. This man wanted his words separated. Punctuation practices evidently varied from the very beginning.

Interlude: Silent reading

In antiquity, to encounter someone reading silently was sufficiently unusual that it could elicit a comment. In Book 6 (Chapter 3) of his *Confessions*, St Augustine recalls how as a young man he wanted to ask questions of his mentor, St Ambrose, Bishop of Milan, but felt unable to do so when he visited him because of the way Ambrose was reading:

> When he read, his eyes scanned the page and his heart explored the meaning, but his voice was silent and his tongue was still ... when we came to see him, we found him reading like this in silence, for he never read aloud. We would sit there quietly, for no one had the heart to disturb him ...

Augustine puzzles over why Ambrose was doing this – not even using the muffled voice that someone would typically use when alone:

> Perhaps he was afraid that, if he read aloud, some obscure passage in the author he was reading might raise a question in the mind of an attentive listener, and he would have to explain the meaning or even discuss some of the more difficult points. If he spent time in this way, he would not manage to read as much as he wished. Perhaps a more likely reason why he read to himself was that he needed to spare his voice, which quite easily became hoarse. But whatever his reason, we may be sure it was a good one.

Translation by R S Pine-Coffin from *Saint Augustine: Confessions* (Penguin Classics, 1961).

... was diversity

Diverse punctuation practice is inevitable when there are several ways of marking the same thing. Inserting spaces is one way of separating words, but there are others. Here's a selection:

thisisnotanexampleofwordseparation

this is an example of word separation

this.is.an.example.of.word.separation

this+is+an+example+of+word+separation

thiSiSaNexamplEoFworDseparatioN

ThisIsAnExampleOfWordSeparation

this-is-an-example-of-word-separation

The last two are ways around the domain-name problem mentioned at the end of the previous chapter. If we can't use spaces to make it easier to read the words in an Internet address, then we can use hyphens or the curiously but aptly named 'camel case' (as in the two examples showing a mix of upper-case and lower-case letters).

In Anglo-Saxon times, we see a similar diversity, reflecting an earlier variability that was present among the writers of ancient Rome. People experimented with word division.

Some inscriptions have the words separated by a circle (as with the Undley bracteate) or a raised dot. Some use small crosses. Gradually we see spaces coming in, but often in a very irregular way, with some words spaced and others not – what is sometimes called an 'aerated' script. Even in the eleventh century, less than half the inscriptions in England had all the words separated.

The slow arrival of word division in inscriptions isn't so surprising when we consider their character. The texts that identify jewels, boxes, statues, buildings, swords, and so on are typically short and often predictable. If people know their church is called 'St Ambrose', then they will read its name (if they are able to read) regardless of how it is spaced. Nobody would interpret STAMBROSE as STAM + BROSE. Also, the physical environment makes punctuation unnecessary. If the aim of a full stop is to tell readers that a sentence has come to an end, then the boundary of a physical object will do that just as well. It's no different today. We don't need a full stop at the end of a sign saying WAY OUT. The right-hand edge of the sign is enough to show us that the message is finished.

If they are able to read ... In Anglo-Saxon times, most people couldn't. Only a tiny elite of monks, scribes, and other professionals knew how to write; so there was no popular expectation that inscriptions should be easy to read. Nor was there any peer-group pressure among inscribers. In a monastery, there would be a scribal tradition to be followed and a strict hierarchy, with junior scribes copying the manuscript practices of their seniors. By contrast, the sculptor or goldsmith producing an inscription would be someone working alone, with no guidance other than his own sense of tradition and aesthetic taste. Divergent punctuation practices were an inevitable result.

We see a similar diversity when we read the earliest

surviving Anglo-Saxon manuscripts – the meagre collection of glossaries, charters, wills, name-lists, poems, riddles, and religious texts from the seventh and eighth centuries that give us our first real sense of what Old English was like. Manuscripts, of course, are very different from inscriptions, as they contain sentences of varying complexity extending over several pages. They can also be revised and corrected, either by the original scribe or by later readers. But these early texts have one thing in common: unlike the inscriptions, they all display word-spaces.

By the seventh century in England, word-spacing had become standard practice, reflecting a radical change that had taken place in reading habits. Silent reading was now the norm. Written texts were being seen not as aids to reading aloud, but as self-contained entities, to be used as a separate source of information and reflection from whatever could be gained from listening and speaking. It is the beginning of a view of language, widely recognized today, in which writing and speech are seen as distinct mediums of expression, with different communicative aims and using different processes of composition. And this view is apparent in the efforts scribes made to make the task of reading easier, with the role of spacing and other methods of punctuation becoming increasingly appreciated.

In some cases, the nature of the genre made word-spacing inevitable. The earliest English manuscripts are alphabetical glossaries containing lists of Latin words with their English equivalents – essential aids for the many monks who were having to learn Latin as a foreign language. But imagine a glossary with no word-spaces! The different entries would run into each other and the whole thing would become unusable. Bilingual glossaries – as modern bilingual dictionaries – need good layout for readers to find their way about.

Word-spaces are inevitable, also, when glossing a continuous text. There's a copy of the Book of Psalms dating from around 825, known as the Vespasian Psalter. It's in Latin, with the words spaced, but someone has added word-by-word English translations – over 30,000 of them – above the Latin words in the space between the lines. Each gloss is easily visible, at a distance from its neighbours. Once again, the layout dictates the spacing.

What happens in genres where the text is a series of sentences, rather than a series of isolated words? Here too we see word-spacing, but the situation is more complex. Very often, some spaces are larger than others, probably reflecting a scribe's sense of the way words relate in meaning to each other. A major sense-break might have a larger space. Words that belong closely together might have a small one. It's difficult to show this in modern print, where word-spaces tend to be the same width, but scribes often seemed to think like this:

> we bought   a cup of tea   in the cafe

The 'little' words, such as prepositions, pronouns, and the definite article, are felt to 'belong' to the following content words. Indeed, so close is this sense of binding that many scribes echo earlier practice and show them with no separation at all. Here's a transcription of two lines from one of Ælfric's sermons, dated around 990.

> þærwæronðagesewene twegenenglas onhwitumgẏrelū;
> þær wæron ða gesewene twegen englas on hwitum gẏrelū;

> 'there were then seen two angels in white garments'

> Eacswilc onhisacennednẏsse wæronenglasgesewene'.
> Eacswilc on his acennednẏsse wæron englas gesewene'.

> 'similarly at his birth were angels seen'

Lines from the manuscript of Ælfric's sermon 'In ascensione domini',
British Library, Royal MS 7 C.xii, f.105r. The handwriting
is Anglo-Saxon minuscule in its square phase, c.990.

The word-strings, separated by spaces, reflect the grammatical structure and units of sense within the sentence. And a
careful examination of the original text shows an even more
subtle feature. Normally the letter *e* is written much as we
do today, as in the first two *e*'s in *acennednysse*; but when the
e appears before the space, its middle stroke is elongated,
acting as a bridge between the two word-strings. It's an early
kind of letter-joining, or *ligature*.

   The Ælfric sermon is quite late, for an Anglo-Saxon text,
but its use of word-strings and variable word-spaces is typical
of the time, and the practice continues until the very end
of the Old English period. The extract also shows the presence of other forms of punctuation (which I'll discuss in the
next chapter). Taken together, even in just two lines of text
it's possible to sense that there has been a major change in
orthographic behaviour compared with the unspaced, punctuationless writing seen in the English inscriptions and in
traditional Latin.

   The origins of the change are not simply to do with the
development of new habits of reading. They are bound up
with the emergence of Christianity in the West, and the influential views of writers such as St Augustine. Book 3 of his
(Latin) work *On Christian Doctrine*, published at the end of the
fourth century AD, is entitled: 'On interpretation required
by the ambiguity of signs', and in its second chapter we are

given a 'rule for removing ambiguity by attending to punctuation'. Augustine gives a series of Latin examples where the placing of a punctuation mark in an unpunctuated text makes all the difference between two meanings. The examples are of the kind used today when people want to draw attention to the importance of punctuation, as in the now infamous example of the panda who *eats, shoots and leaves* vs *eats shoots and leaves*. But for Augustine, this is no joke, as the location of a mark can distinguish important points of theological interpretation, and in the worst case can make all the difference between orthodoxy and heresy.

A sacred text has a hugely privileged position within a society. Great care needs to be taken to protect its identity, to ensure that it is transmitted accurately from generation to generation. At the same time, all sacred texts need to be interpreted and edited, so that their meaning will come across clearly and effectively to readers. The intervention takes a variety of forms. The impulse to make the work beautiful leads to decoration, with sometimes whole pages devoted to a single word or letter, as in the magnificently illuminated Lindisfarne Gospels. The impulse to teach leads to the addition of notes and commentary. And the impulse to clarify leads to the highlighting of individual words, names, or sentences, the marking of chapters and verses – and the insertion of punctuation marks.

Augustine argues that punctuation has a critical role to play in enabling readers to arrive at a correct interpretation of scripture, and he proposes two rules of thumb. The first and most important rule is to allow what we know about the world (the world of Christian faith, in his case) to influence our decision about where to place a punctuation mark. The second is to carefully examine the context in which a particular sentence is used, as this can clarify its meaning and suggest how a punctuation mark might help. But he is aware that these principles don't solve all problems of ambiguity in writing. He concludes:

> Where, however, the ambiguity cannot be cleared up, either by the rule of faith or by the context, there is nothing to hinder us to point the sentence according to any method we choose of those that suggest themselves.

Any method we choose. This personal decision-making lies at the very heart of punctuation, and becomes a recurrent theme over the next 1600 years.

3
To point, or not to point?

Word-spacing is an important first step in making a text easier to read, but it doesn't take us very far, once sentences become long and complex, and a written discourse starts to grow. Readers then need help. But the earliest texts from antiquity gave precious little guidance about how they were to be read.

Manuscripts did usually show the major divisions of a work, such as chapters or paragraphs. The beginning of a new section might be identified by a large (sometimes coloured or decorated) letter, or by indenting the first line, or by outdenting it – having it start in the left-hand margin. A mark in the shape of an ivy-leaf (or *hedera*) might indicate the beginning of a piece of commentary, distinguishing it from the preceding main text. Quite a lot of use was made of a special > mark in the margin to mark a quotation or a paragraph opening – it was called a *diple*, from the Greek word for 'double', referring to the two lines in the character. Apart from marks showing these major structural locations, blocks of writing were unpunctuated. There might be the occasional pause shown within a paragraph. Nothing more.

Punctuation, in short, was as much the job of the reader as the writer. An impulse to punctuate comes when readers encounter a piece of writing that is ambiguous or unclear, or where the provided punctuation is insufficient for their needs. If the writers haven't done enough, then readers feel they have to do something about it. Old manuscripts often show readers adding marks to a text to help their understanding. Sometimes readers have disagreed about what to do, and we see marks crossed out or replaced.

It's no different today. Even with the highly punctuated texts of modern print, we often find ourselves needing to add extra marks. People look at a text they need to speak aloud, such as a lecture, speech, or script, and mark places to pause, or underline words they want to emphasize. Actors might add arrows to show the voice rising and falling, or other features resembling musical notation. Newsreaders mark places where they need to be careful of a particular pronunciation, such as not adding an *r* in the phrase *law and order*. When people have to engage seriously with a text, as when studying or preparing for a business meeting, they underline, put marks in the margin, or highlight passages in bright colours to identify the bits they think are important.

Over the centuries, writers gradually came to realize that, if they wanted their meaning to come across clearly, they couldn't leave the task to their readers. And this was aided by the change in reading habits I referred to in the previous chapter. It's difficult to see how punctuation could have developed in a graphic world where *scriptura continua* was the norm. If there are no word-spaces, there's no room to insert marks. Writers or readers might be able to insert the occasional dot or simple stroke, to show where the sense changed, but it would be impossible to develop a sophisticated system that would keep pace with the complex narratives and reflections being expressed in such domains as poetry, chronicles, and sermons. However, once word-spaces became the norm, new punctuational possibilities were available.

It nonetheless took a while for a punctuation system to develop in England. The first missionaries, copying word-spaced manuscripts in their monastery scriptoria, evidently didn't feel the need for it. Their Latin was good, they knew the texts well, and their focus was on spiritual practices, so they didn't need the extra help that punctuation might provide. In any case, many authors thought it was the job of readers to discover the meaning of scripture for themselves, not for writers to 'dictate' how it should be interpreted by adding marks to the page. Punctuation was never going to be a priority in such a climate.

But times changed. Later generations of monks often had a poor knowledge of Latin, and became increasingly dependent on glosses into English. Literacy ability varied greatly. Bede, in a letter to Eusebius, abbot at Jarrow, in 716, complains about how he has had to edit his commentary on St John's *Apocalypse* in a certain way to take account of 'indolence' in his readers. By the time of King Alfred the Great, at the end of the ninth century, the combined effect of political turmoil, Viking invasions, and general intellectual apathy had led to the virtual disappearance of sophisticated literacy. In one of his writings – the preface to the English translation of St Gregory's *Cura Pastoralis* ('Pastoral Care') – Alfred contrasts the early days of Christianity in England with his own time, and bemoans the way learning has been lost:

> So completely had it declined in England that there were very few people on this side of the Humber who could understand their service-books in English or translate even one written message from Latin into English, and I think there were not many beyond the Humber either. So few they were that I cannot think of even a single one south of the Thames when I came to the throne.

He resolves to do something about it, initiating a programme of translation into English, and encouraging the learning of Latin.

It's a crucial turning-point. Suddenly, longer and more varied works begin to be written down in English, and to reach more people. Different styles emerge, both within poetry and prose. In poetry, we encounter long heroic narratives such as *Beowulf* alongside spiritual reflections such as *The Dream of the Rood* – early texts surviving in late manuscripts. In prose, we find political and legal texts such as laws, charters, and wills; religious texts such as prayers, homilies, and Bible translations; scientific texts dealing with medicine, botany, and folklore; and historical texts such as town records, lists of rulers, and the *Anglo-Saxon Chronicle*. There is much more to read, and many more people who want to read it. We are still centuries away from a world of reference where daily engagement with multiple texts is routine, where rapid and easy reading is essential, and where there is pressure on writers to express themselves clearly and effectively – 'in plain English', as it is often put. But the linguistic factors that enable us to be fluent literacy multi-taskers today can be traced back to the decisions made by writers a millennium ago. A stable orthography is one of these factors, and punctuation is the backbone of orthography.

The punctuation marks we see in Old English manuscripts vary a great deal, depending on the handwriting style used, and they are often idiosyncratic; but certain general features can be observed. There was clearly a sense that words were important units of text. They are important not only in learning one's mother-tongue ('how many words do you know?') but in learning another language ('what's the word for ...?'). In a world where two languages work together with different functions – as Latin and English did in Anglo-Saxon times – the ability to identify and process words easily and quickly is paramount. Individual words come to the fore in inscriptions, glossaries, lists of names, year-dates, and many other contexts. And in longer texts we see word-spaces supplemented by new signs to help readers identify where a word starts or where it ends.

Sometimes simple pointing suffices, as if we were to write:

this·is·an·example·of·middle·dots

Such 'interpunct' dots varied in height, influenced by the shape of the previous letter, but were usually at mid-level. They sometimes separated phrases rather than words, and even syllables within words. Their use is sporadic, working along with word-spaces in ways that are often difficult to interpret. In one line, they might suggest a pause; in another they might not. For example, in a tenth-century manuscript translation of Bede, we find a description of a solar eclipse:

ÞA·ƿÆS·GE·WORDENYMB

syx hund ƿyntra·⁊feower⁊syxtig æft(er) drihtnes
menniscnesse· eclipsis solis·þæt is sunnan·aspru
ngennis·

then was happened about
six hundred winters · and sixty-four after the lord's
incarnation · (*in Latin*) eclipse of the sun · that is sun eclipse

Lines from the Old English version of Bede's Historia
Ecclesiastica, *III, Bodleian Library, Tanner MS 10,
54r. The handwriting is Anglo-Saxon minuscule.*

This extract illustrates several features of the emerging punctuation system.

- The first line is written in decorated coloured capitals, showing that it's a new section of the text; the first letter is much larger than the others, and in this text ingeniously drawn in the shape of a person climbing a pole.
- The first three words are separated by a middle dot, but so is the first syllable of *geworden*; however, there's no dot or space before the word *ymb*.
- In the next line, the first phrase is separated from the rest of the line by a middle dot, with its three words spaced; we might expect the 'sixty-four' to have a dot after it as well, but instead we get a wider space.
- In the third line, middle dots separate the phrases, with the constituent words spaced.
- Abbreviations are being used: there are two instances of ⁊, the Tironian symbol for 'and' – so called because it was part of a system of shorthand used in ancient Rome, supposedly invented by Tiro, a freedman of Cicero – and an example of an omitted word-ending (the *er* of *after*) shown by a mark over the *t*.
- The scribe could not fit the Old English word for 'eclipse' (*asprungennis*) into the line, so he simply continues it on the next line; there is no hyphen or other indication that a word is being split in this way.
- We might expect 'lord' (i.e. Jesus Christ), to have a capital letter, but there are no initial capitals used for proper names.

This mixture of conventions is typical of manuscripts of the time.

As one reads through the manuscripts of Old English – less than a thousand in all – the differences in the use of punctuation are striking. Apart from spaces and dots, other marks are used to show word identity. Some writers make the opening letter of a word larger; some the closing letter – an early move in the direction of capitalization, especially for proper names. If a word didn't fit at the end of a line, its incomplete state would be shown in various ways. Some scribes simply crammed the remaining syllables into the space above the line. Some shortened the word, marking the abbreviation with a stroke above the last letter. Some introduced a *J*-like mark looking like a large comma: it's called a *diastole* (pronounced die-<u>ass</u>-toe-lee), a convention taken over from ancient Greek. A letter might have a stroke extended to suggest a continuation: these 'suspended ligatures' were often picked up on the next line, where the first letter showed a continuation stroke. (This practice of 'double hyphenation' lasted a long time. We'll see it again in Jane Austen, p. 100.) Gradually a special linking mark became usual, though its character varied. It might be a single horizontal mark at the end of a line (like the modern hyphen), or a double horizontal (=), or an acute accent (´), or a semi-circle below the line. The variation wouldn't be sorted out until the arrival of printing.

There are clear indications of a more sophisticated system emerging. Influenced by the practices of Irish monks, some Anglo-Saxon scribes began to use multiple marks to show pauses – the more marks, the longer the pause and the more 'final' the intonation. Two dots, one on top of the other (like a modern colon), would show a moderate pause in the middle of a sentence. A cluster of three dots (∵ – often called a *trigon*) would show a major pause at the end. An oblique line could mark a pause, as could a double oblique. In some writers it was the position of the dots in relation to the preceding letter that showed pausal distinctions: a system of two or three dots – placed at different heights – would mark pauses of different lengths. An interesting development was a mark like an acute accent placed on top of a diastole, so that the result looked a bit like a modern semicolon.

Distinguishing between major and minor pauses is probably enough if you are reading silently and simply need some help to see where one unit of sense ends and another begins. But if you are reading aloud, you need more than this. And in the Anglo-Saxon period, reading aloud once again became a priority – at monastery meal-times, and in church.

4
No question: we need it

It's impossible to overestimate the importance of reading aloud in the liturgy of the church. In Catholic Christianity of the time, the 'liturgy of the Word' ranked alongside the 'liturgy of the Eucharist' – as indeed it still does. The role of the lector was vital. Passages from scripture were read aloud during Mass – and for virtually all of the congregation outside of the monastery it would be the only way in which they would ever encounter the message of the Bible, as they were unable to read it for themselves. Within the monastery, reading the daily office and listening to spiritual reading were routine. Chapter 38 of the Rule of St Benedict (written in the sixth century AD) makes this very clear:

> Reading must not be wanting at the table of the brethren when they are eating. ...

> Let the deepest silence be maintained that no whispering or voice be heard except that of the reader alone. ...

> The brethren will not read or sing in order, but only those who edify the hearers.

Only good readers, note. Make a mistake, and you were in trouble, as Benedict goes on to say in Chapter 45:

> If anyone whilst he reciteth a psalm, a responsory, an antiphon, or a lesson, maketh a mistake, and doth not

humble himself there before all by making satisfaction, let
him undergo a greater punishment, because he would not
correct by humility what he did amiss through negligence.

In such a climate, anything which would help your reading to
come across well would be highly valued.

Punctuation was seen to be one of these valuable aids. The
influential eighth-century monk–scholar Alcuin, working at
the court of Emperor Charlemagne, and writing in Latin, says
in one of his poems (No. 94) that scribes need to pay careful
attention to it when copying works to be used in the liturgy:

let them put those relevant marks of punctuation in their
proper order, so that the lector may neither read mistakenly,
nor by chance suddenly fall silent before the holy brothers
in church.

But what did 'read mistakenly' mean? It was not only a matter
of knowing where to breathe, pausing between sentences, or
emphasizing the right words. It was everything to do with a
powerful oral delivery, in which the reader would bring out
the meaning of a text, proclaiming it with emotional conviction (so that it might reach the hearts and minds of the listeners) and giving it an appropriate rhythm (so that elements
of it might be more easily remembered). This demanded the
use of more reliable and meaningful punctuation marks.

These new marks, increasingly seen from the end of the
eighth century, are often referred to by the Latin name *positurae*, 'positions'. The distinction between a middle and a final
pause was made in a more systematic way, and began to be
linked with the grammar of a sentence. Paleographers have
developed a terminology for talking about these.

- A *punctus versus*, or 'turned point', marked the end
  of a statement, signalling a major break and thus a

relatively long pause. It would be heard typically as a
falling intonation. It looked somewhat like a modern
semicolon, with its tail usually dangling below the line
of writing. An example is shown on p. 12, where it
ends the first line of the manuscript. Later, this would
be replaced by the point (or *full stop*, or *period*) as the
primary way of showing a statement end.

- A *punctus elevatus*, or 'elevated point', marked a place
  where the first part of a sentence was over, but the
  sentence had not come to an end. It would be heard
  typically as a rising intonation. It looked like an inverted
  semicolon, though the upper mark was often more like
  an elongated acute accent than a comma. An example is
  shown at the end of the second line of text on p. 12.

The contrast between these two kinds of punctuation can be
appreciated in a modern example. Read this passage aloud:

When you arrive, get a key from the porter. When you leave,
hand it in at reception.

The normal reading (regional accents do vary a bit) is to have
rising tones on *arrive* and *leave*, followed by brief pauses; and
to have falling tones on *porter* and *reception*, with a longer
pause after *porter*. In older terms, we would have a *punctus
elevatus* followed by a *punctus versus*, twice over.

The third of the *positurae* was a real breakthrough: the
arrival of the question mark.

- A *punctus interrogativus*, or 'interrogative point', signalling
  that the sentence was a question. It looked originally
  like a point with a ~ (tilde)-like mark moving off to
  the right above it. There are several examples in the
  Colloquy of Ælfric, dating from around 1000 AD. This is
  a dialogue between a teacher and his pupils, so there are

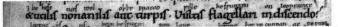

A line from the opening of Ælfric's Colloquy, *British Library, Cotton MS Tiberius A.iii, f. 60v. The handwriting is English Caroline minuscule.*

lots of questions. The English is in the form of a gloss over the Latin words, and it is there that we see this punctuation mark, as in this line where the teacher asks: 'Are you willing to be beaten while learning?' – *Uultis flagellari in discendo*

During the Middle English period, from the twelfth to the fifteenth centuries, a fourth mark was introduced:

- A *punctus admirativus* or *exclamativus*, a 'point of admiration' or 'exclamation', signalling that the sentence was to be spoken in an exclamatory way. It first appears in a few late fourteenth-century manuscripts, looking like a right-slanting colon with a longer accent mark moving off to the right above it. It would evolve into the exclamation mark of modern times.

This was also a period when there was considerable experimentation in the use of the marks inherited from Anglo-Saxon times. There was already great variation in the writing practices of the monks belonging to different religious orders and working in different monasteries. The variability became even more marked as manuscripts came to be produced outside monastery discipline. During the Middle Ages, we see notaries, clerks, commercial scribes, schoolteachers, and creative writers combining punctuation features from different systems and adding their individual preferences in an increasingly diverse range of texts.

We see new ways of marking the sections or paragraph

divisions of a text, such as the use of coloured initials or a distinctive mark – a letter C (for *capitulum*, 'little head') with a vertical line through it, still used today (in a modified form) as ¶. Originally called a *paraph*, the term as well as the symbol evolved into what printers call the *pilcrow* (derived from *paragraph*). We see marks being used to identify a parenthesis – at first angle brackets < > and later round brackets ( ). We see frequent use of what today we call forward slashes, //, indicating a major sentence division in a paragraph, and / for a short pause within a sentence. The short pauses are sometimes shown by an upright slash, |, or by a small semi-circular mark, the ancestor of the modern comma. And we see a mark evolve to meet a new need: to show a sentence division falling between the longer and shorter divisions already captured by existing marks. We know it now as the semicolon.

At the same time as writers were developing punctuation as a guide to oratory, an important development was taking place in the universities: the emergence of the *trivium*, the 'three ways' that provided a liberal arts foundation for higher education – grammar, logic, and rhetoric. Grammar had a broader meaning than it has today, encompassing aspects of the study of literature as well as the way language uses structure to convey meaning. But the result was a focus on the way discourses in general, and sentences in particular, were constructed, and the role of punctuation as part of this process. A grammatical approach to punctuation was the result.

The medieval period thus marks the beginning of the two perspectives for punctuation that lie behind so many of the usage issues of today: should punctuation be viewed from a phonetic or a grammatical point of view? I'll explore this in detail in later chapters, but the nature of the difference can be briefly illustrated through a modern example. Take the sentence:

Of particular importance in developing a new system is the need to provide a network of supporting agencies.

When this is read aloud, most people insert a short pause after the subject of the sentence – after *system*. To do otherwise makes the sentence sound rushed, and more difficult for listeners to assimilate. An approach to punctuation that reflects the sound of speech would therefore insert a short-pause mark here – a comma. But an approach based on grammar would ask a different question: do we need to mark the end-point of the subject of the sentence? Since the eighteenth century, the answer has been 'no'. The grammarians felt that the link between the subject and the rest of the sentence (the predicate) was so important that it should not be interfered with by the insertion of punctuation. And thus, anyone who wrote the following today would be considered to have made a mistake.

Of particular importance in developing a new system, is the need to provide a network of supporting agencies.

During the Middle Ages, we see increasing signs of punctuation marks being used within sentences, based on grammarians' views as to how the different parts of a sentence relate to each other. And because grammarians don't always agree about this, especially when it comes to evaluating the way meaning is distributed throughout a sentence, we see on the horizon another source of punctuational uncertainty.

The *positurae* were of great value in helping readers – especially inexperienced ones – to convey the meaning of a text accurately and effectively. They show two of the most important features of a punctuation system: the marks must be easy to see, and they must be sufficiently different from each other that there is no risk of visual confusion. But a third requirement of a punctuation system was missing: standard use. Writers of the same language should use marks in the same way, both in the way they are formed and in the linguistic functions they convey. As literacy grew significantly during the fourteenth century, a standardized system of punctuation was desperately needed, but for this to happen a cultural shift of considerable magnitude would need to take place. It came with the arrival of printing.

Interlude: Punctuation says it all

Chapter 9 of A A Milne's *Winnie-the-Pooh* (1926) deals with an emergency 'In which Piglet is entirely surrounded by water'. 'It rained and it rained and it rained.' Piglet is marooned in his tree-home, so Pooh and Christopher Robin have to work out a way to reach him. Christopher Robin can't think of anything; but Pooh suggests a novel kind of boat.

> Pooh said something so clever that Christopher Robin could only look at him with mouth open and eye staring, wondering if this was really the Bear of Very Little Brain whom he had known and loved so long.
>
> 'We might go in your umbrella,' said Pooh.
>
> '?'
>
> 'We might go in your umbrella,' said Pooh.
>
> '??'
>
> 'We might go in your umbrella,' said Pooh.
>
> '!!!!!!'
>
> For suddenly Christopher Robin saw that they might.

The ancients would never have believed that, one day, such little marks would be given such semantic responsibility.

5
The first printer

Imagine you are a printer in the Middle Ages in Europe. One of the first printers. You have manuscripts that need to be typeset. The spelling varies greatly between writers, and even within a writer. You will have to sort that. And the punctuation varies – from manuscripts that show hardly anything to those displaying a wildly idiosyncratic array of marks. You will have to sort that too. There are marks where the lines go at different angles and lengths, and groups of dots that go off in different directions. Spacing and layout is erratic, and there's a great deal of personal decoration on individual letters. Items of interest in a text are highlighted in all sorts of ways, such as by adding symbols and notes in the margins. The one comforting thing is that there seem to be far fewer punctuation marks to worry about than letters and spellings.

Although your new technology is offering all kinds of novel possibilities, and there are no precedents to guide you, you have to be realistic. Your readers are experienced readers of manuscripts. They are used to seeing handwritten punctuation marks; and despite the many idiosyncrasies among scribes, there does seem to be a fair amount of agreement in the form of certain symbols. So it will make sense to copy the scribal style as far as you can, and use marks that readers will recognize. But where there is a choice, you will need to make a decision. If a mark is sometimes written upright, and sometimes slanted to the left or right in various degrees, you will have to choose. In some cases having a choice will be useful, as the differences will help form the visual character of different fonts of type, such as 'roman' and 'italic'. In other cases, you will simply have to decide on one of the shapes and hope it will appeal.

In the case of William Caxton, who printed the first book in English, most of the typesetting decisions had already been made by earlier printers in northern Europe. He had previously been a merchant in the clothing industry in England, but moved to Bruges (in present-day Belgium), where he developed a business interest in (manuscript) bookselling. The printing industry had established itself in Germany and the Low Countries after Johannes Gutenberg's venture in Mainz around 1450. Caxton didn't get into the printing business until a decade later, by which time supplies of type were already available, manufactured by professional typecutters.

Caxton's first book, *The Recuyell of the Historyes of Troye* – 'a gathering together of the stories of Troy' – was printed around the end of 1473 in Bruges, in a typeface that would have been familiar to European readers. Three years later, he brought his new technology – and his printing assistants – over to England, and set up the first printing press in London in the precincts of Westminster Abbey.

The fonts of type included a few punctuation marks, and Caxton uses them – but sporadically, and not in a way that bears much relationship to present-day usage. If you read modern editions of his writing, what you will see is a repunctuated text for ease of reading, and this is some distance away from his original practice. Here's an illustration: the passage is from one of his prefaces (to a translation of Virgil's *Aeneid*). It tells a story about the way English vocabulary was developing at the time, with a northern word, *egges*, competing with a southern word, *eyren*, and thus presenting a publisher with the problem of which word his readership will be more likely to understand.

The first version is from Norman Blake's *Caxton's Own Prose* (1973, with some glosses by me):

> And that comyn [common] Englysshe that is spoken in one shyre varyeth from another. In so moche that in my dayes happened that certayn marchauntes were in a shippe in Tamyse [Thames] for to have sayled over the see into Zelande. And for lacke of wynde thei taryed atte forlond [Foreland] and wente to lande for to refreshe them. And one of theym named Sheffelde, a mercer, cam into an hows and axed [asked] for mete and specyally he axyd after eggys. And the goode wyf answerde that she coude speke no Frenshe. And the marchaunt was angry for he also coude speke no Frenshe, but wolde have hadde egges; and she understode hym not. And thenne at laste another sayd that he wolde have eyren; then the good wyf sayd that she understod hym wel. Loo! what sholde [should] a man in thyse dayes now wryte, 'egges' or 'eyren'? Certaynly it is harde to playse every man bycause of dyversite and chaunge of langage.

This is certainly much easier to read than the original; but it gives a completely wrong impression of Caxton's punctuation practices. What the manuscript actually shows is this:

> ne season/ and waneth & dycscreaseth another season/
>   And   1
> that comyn englysshe that is spoken in one shyre varyeth
> from a nother. In so moche that in my dayes happened that
> certayn marchaũtes were in a ship~ in tamyse for to haue
> sayled ouer the see into zelande/ and for lacke of wynde
>   thei   5
> taryed atte forlond.and wente to lande for to refreshe them

> ne season/ and waneth & dyscreaseth another season/ And
> that compyn englyshe that is spoken in one shyre varyeth
> from a nother. In so moche that in my dayes happened that
> certayn marchauntes were in a ship in tampse for to haue
> sayled ouer the see into zelande/and for lacke of wynde thei
> taryed atte forlond.and wente to lande for to refreshe them
> And one of theym named sheffelde a mercer cam in to an
> hows and axed for mete .and specyally he apyd after egges
> And the goode wyf answerde.that she coude speke no fren=
> she . And the marchaut was angry.for he also coude speke
> no frenshe. but wolde haue hadde egges/ and she vnderstode
> hym not/ And thenne at laste a nother sayd that he wolde
> haue eyren/then the good wyf sayd that she vnderstod hym
> wel/ Loo what sholde a man in thyse dayes now wryte. eg=
> ges or eyren/ certaynly it is harde to playse euery man/ by
> cause of dyuersite & chauge of langage . For in these dayes

Lines from William Caxton, The Recuyell of the Historyes
of Troye *(1471), British Library, G.9723.*

And one of theym named sheffelde a mercer cam in to an
hows and axed for mete .and specyally he axyd after eggys
And the goode wyf answerde.that she coude speke no fren=
she . And the marchaut was angry.for he also coude speke 10
no frenshe. but wolde haue hadde egges / and she vnderstode
hym not/ And thenne at laste a nother sayd that he wolde
haue eyren/ then the good wyf sayd that she vnderstod hym
wel/ Loo what sholde a man in thyse dayes now wryte. eg=
ges or eyren/ certaynly it is harde to playse euery man/ by 15
cause of dyuersite & chauge of langage. For in these dayes

The differences are fairly obvious, but it's important to look
carefully at them, as they show how far removed punctuation
still is from a well-developed system. It's often said that
printing standardized punctuation in English. So it did, for

the most part – but only eventually (and I'll discuss the cases where it didn't succeed in a later chapter). The first books do show a regularity in the shape of the actual marks, reflecting the use of identical pieces of type; but we are a long way from stability in the way they are used.

If we look in detail at the Caxton extract, and compare it with Blake's edition, several things stand out.

- The modern version sets the story out as a separate paragraph, but Caxton makes no such division, as the opening and closing lines illustrate.
- The story is told in an informal spoken narrative style, with several uses of *and*, so that it's often difficult to decide where a sentence boundary falls. This doesn't seem to bother Caxton, who simply uses a capital letter or a pause mark (either / or .) when he feels the need to help the reader follow the sense of the passage. But he does so in an inconsistent way. This short extract illustrates all four possibilities:
  - in line 1, a sentence begins with a capital letter and ends with a period, as it would today
  - in line 3, a sentence begins with a capital letter and has no period after *them* in line 6
  - in line 15, a sentence begins without a capital letter and ends with a period
  - in line 13, a sentence has neither an opening capital nor a concluding period.
  The modern version uses the first practice consistently.
- He also uses the period to show a short pause (as in line 6), where today we would use commas (as in the modern version lines 11 and 14) or no marks at all.
- He retains the forward slash as a mark of sense division, but gives it different values:
  - opening the new story in line 1

- marking minor sense breaks in lines 5 and 10, and before *by* in line 15
- marking sentence-like breaks elsewhere.

The modern version replaces all slashes by periods.

- Word-spaces are mostly as today (apart from *a nother* and *in to*), but spacing is erratic in relation to punctuation marks. The extract illustrates all four possibilities:
  - in lines 3, 5, 11, 14, and 16, there's no space before a period and a space after, as today; a space follows the slash in all cases except in line 11, where there's a space before and after
  - in line 8, there's a space before the period and none after
  - in lines 6, 9, and 10, there's no space on either side of the period
  - in lines 10 and 11, there's a space on either side of the period.

  The modern version regularizes spaces throughout.

- He uses a double stroke to show word division at the end of lines 9 and 14, but breaks the words in places that would not be acceptable today. The line-endings of the modern edition aren't shown above, but modern printing practice has enabled all the lines in this extract to be right-justified, so line-breaks are not needed.

There are several other points of difference. He doesn't use initial capital letters for proper names, as in lines 2 and 7. When words don't fit into the line, he uses abbreviations, as in lines 4 and 15. But the most noticeable feature of the modern version is the way it adds punctuation marks that are conspicuous by their absence in Caxton's day – the comma, exclamation mark, question mark, semicolon, and inverted commas. For these, we need to enter the sixteenth century.

A messy situation

We can get a sense of the relatively late development of punctuation awareness in English by looking at when the technical terms first come into the language. The word *punctuation* itself is not recorded in the *Oxford English Dictionary* until 1539. *Comma* in its sense as a punctuation mark, replacing the forward slash, is known from 1521. And during the second half of the century we encounter the first recorded uses (in their sense of marks) of *apostrophe* (1588), *colon* (1589), *full stop* (1596), and *point of interrogation* (1598 – the term *question mark* arrives surprisingly late, in 1905). The next two decades provide instances of *hyphen* (1603), *period* (1609), and *stop* (1616). *Semicolon* is much later (1644), as are the *note of exclamation* (1657), and *quotation quadrats* (1683 – what would in the nineteenth century be called *quotation marks*; a *quadrat* was a small metal block used for spacing). *Dash* and *bracket* are eighteenth century.

We should never read too much into 'first recorded uses', of course: they tell us only the first time lexicographers have (so far) discovered that someone has written a word down. Punctuation terms would have been in spoken usage, especially among printers, for some time before they first appeared in writing. Semicolons, for instance, began to be used in English books with some frequency in the 1580s, and isolated uses can be traced back to the 1530s. They were described in several other ways before the term *semicolon* became the norm, such as *comma colon*, *hemi-colon*, and *sub-colon*. But the dates do reinforce the main observation, which is that we have to look to the end of the sixteenth century, not the fifteenth, to find a system that is similar to what we use today.

During the 1500s, we see writer after writer trying to impose order on a very messy situation. Most agree that the three main marks reflect three degrees of pause. George Puttenham, in his *Art of English Poesie* (1589), advises his readers to follow Classical models, and recognize a comma (the 'shortest pause'), a colon ('twice as much time'), and a period (a 'full pause'). So that's the formula:

one period = two colons = four commas

When the semicolon arrived, making a four-degree system, its length was usually considered to be between that of the comma and the colon. A little earlier, John Hart, in his influential *An Orthographie* (1569), uses a musical analogy. If a comma is a crotchet then a colon is a minim. Children were actually taught to count one for a comma, two for a semi-colon, and so on (see my Interlude after Chapter 10).

The approach was frequently advocated until the nineteenth century, and is still encountered today in some recommendations for public speaking. If you try it, you'll quickly see that it's far too mechanical a system to cope with the complexities of English syntax. When followed pedantically, it produces the most bizarre and artificial rhythms. In the four-degree double-the-number system, a period is *eight* times the length of a comma!

But in Elizabethan England, many felt it was an ideal to be aimed at. It was an approach that, in the age of Shakespeare, especially appealed to actors wanting their scripts to give them as many clues as possible about how a speech should be read. However, it didn't appeal to publishers. They were not so concerned about phonetic values. To them, it didn't matter what length the marks represented as long as they made the sense clear. The role of punctuation, in their view, was to help readers, not speakers.

This is where we see the origins of virtually all the arguments over punctuation that have continued down the centuries and which are still with us today. Should a writer use punctuation as a guide to pronunciation (a 'phonetic' or 'elocutional' function) or as a way of making a text easy to read (a 'grammatical' or 'semantic' function)? How should a reader interpret someone else's use of punctuation: phonetically or semantically? And how should punctuation be taught and tested in schools? Indeed, *can* it be tested in the same way as we test maths or spelling, where there are clear rights and wrongs? A punctuation mark may be correctly placed from one point of view, but incorrect from another. Tests have to be extremely sophisticated in their phrasing to ensure that tester and testee are, as they say, both on the same playing field. And the sad truth is that tests usually aren't, so that students are penalized for using punctuation one way when the tester had expected another.

But this is to leap ahead (see Chapter 26). In the sixteenth century there were no punctuation or spelling tests like those of today because the orthography was still developing. Several of the marks were new to English printers and readers, who were unsure how to use or interpret them. We can see this in the way the marks appear in the work of different typesetters. One of the compositors of Shakespeare's First Folio clearly liked the semicolon, as he introduces it all over the place; another prefers the colon; another has a thing for commas. Messy indeed.

It's not at all easy trying to work out how to perform a

Shakespeare play when there is such variability. Some modern directors think the plays have too much. Peter Brook, for example, has this to say (in his *Diaries*, 21 August 1975):

> Shakespeare's text is always absurdly over punctuated: generations of scholars have tried to turn him into a good grammarian. Even the original printed texts are not much help – the first printers popped in some extra punctuation. When punctuation is just relaxed to the flow of the spoken word, the actor is liberated.

Others pay close attention to every little mark. When I was working with the company at Shakespeare's Globe for its 2005 production of *Troilus and Cressida*, where director Giles Block used the Folio text, there were many discussions between him and his cast over precisely how much value to attach to a comma. Here are two examples, from different plays, of the kind of issue that arises.

In *Julius Caesar* (3.1.86), Antony shakes hands with Caesar's murderers. There are no commas between the names and the pronouns – apart from after Casca:

> Let each man render me his bloody hand.
> First *Marcus Brutus* will I shake with you;
> Next *Caius Cassius* do I take your hand;
> Now *Decius Brutus* yours; now yours *Metellus*;
> Yours *Cinna*; and my valiant *Caska*, yours;
> Though last, not least in loue, yours good *Trebonius*.

Casca was the first to stab Caesar. Might we therefore imagine the actor playing Antony to take that comma seriously, delaying the onset of *yours*, and perhaps doing some business with Casca's hands at that point?

And here's an instance of a place where some would consider the original text to be overpunctuated, whereas others would not. It's at the beginning of *Henry IV Part 2* (1.1.131), when Morton has come in haste to the Earl of Northumberland, bringing news of defeat at the Battle of Shrewsbury. Modern editions tend to print it like this, as with the Arden text:

> The sum of all
> Is that the King hath won, and hath sent out
> A speedy power to encounter you, my lord ...

But in the First Folio, we see it printed like this:

> The summe of all,
> Is, that the King hath wonne : and hath sent out
> A speedy power, to encounter you my Lord,

Might not the commas reflect Morton's breathless state, and his nervousness in front of the Earl? Whether through accident or design, we have a text that can suggest an interesting reading or performance.

It's a complicated issue, because sometimes the printed text simply can't be trusted. Then, as now, printers made errors that weren't picked up in the proof-reading. And sometimes they ran out of type, so that they had to be inventive. The amount of type in a printer's distribution box was limited. There wasn't enough to print a whole book. Every few pages, the type that had been used to print those pages would be broken up and used again for the next few. And on occasion a printer could be caught short.

Take question marks. Printers were used to printing books of serious prose, where there's little need for question marks, so the number of pieces of question-mark type in their box would have been relatively small. But in plays, people are always asking questions – in *Hamlet*, most of all. So printers ran out, and we find them devising alternative ways of showing a question mark, such as by inverting a semicolon or by using a comma on top of a period. In the copy of the First Folio I use, when Hamlet harangues Laertes with the line 'Woo't weepe? Woo't fight? Woo't teare thy selfe?', the second and third questions end with a normal question mark, but the first has a period+comma. And in the column in which this line appears there are nine normal question marks and five abnormal ones. Nobody would notice – or, if they did, they would simply assume that these were simply alternative forms.

At times the language itself was no help. It's easy enough to punctuate a text if you can understand exactly what's being said. But what if a printer wasn't sure of the author's intentions? What to do, for example, with rhetorical questions? Even today there is uncertainty: how should we punctuate the response *How would I know* – ending with a question mark or an exclamation mark? (This was one of the motivations for the interrobang, which did both at once: see Chapter 20.) The speaker is using a question form but not really asking a question at all.

In the First Folio we see many examples where the compositors had no idea what was going on. We see utterances that are clearly questions being ended with exclamation marks, as when in *Coriolanus* (1.1.221) a Messenger arrives and speaks to Martius:

Mess. Where's *Caius Martius*?
Mar. Heere: what's the matter!

We see exclamatory utterances being ended with question marks, as when in *Julius Caesar* (3.4.39) Portia reflects on her situation:

Aye me! How weake a thing
The heart of woman is?

And we see hugely exclamatory utterances with non-exclamatory punctuation, as when in *Hamlet* (1.5.80) the Ghost cries out:

Oh horrible Oh horrible, most horrible:

Not quite the required dramatic effect, using a comma and a colon.

The uncertainty over the use of an exclamation mark is hardly surprising, as this became popular in English only during the 1590s, even though its existence had been recognized for decades. It's one of the marks listed in John Hart's book about the reforms he felt were needed in English orthography, *The opening of the unreasonable writing of our Inglish toung*, published in 1551. He called it 'the wonderer', and distinguished it from the question mark or 'asker'. In *An Orthographie*, he went further, suggesting that both of these marks should be used before as well as after a sentence, because the asking and wondering tunes are there from the sentence beginning. It was a nice idea, but it never caught on in English (though it did in Spanish, where a sentence-opening inverted ? and ! were introduced by the Spanish Academy in 1741). A nineteenth-century printer, George Smallfield, actually recommended using the Spanish inverted marks in English, but he was a lone voice.

Similar problems of consistency and interpretation affected the other punctuation marks that were being increasingly used at the end of the sixteenth century, such as the apostrophe, the semicolon, and quotation marks. I'll tell their stories individually in later chapters, but the general picture should be clear. Writers were ready to use the new array of punctuation marks, but were unsure about how to do so. Books on orthography were more interested in spelling reform than punctuation, and when they did give advice it was often partial and conflicting. Schoolteachers simply followed whatever book they had available. So, where should writers look for guidance to sort out the mess? Increasingly, they copied examples of what they felt was best practice, which was the punctuation as presented in widely read printed books. And because identical copies of a book were now available in large numbers, authors slowly but surely produced manuscripts that followed the same set of printing-house conventions.

Power to the printers. The compositors weren't sure how to use some of the new marks any more than their authors were, but they were in the more powerful position. There was no policy of sending proofs out to authors to check – that came a long time after. What a compositor typeset, people would read, whether it was what the author intended or not. And after a century of experience, printers were becoming more confident. During the 1580s we see evidence of them starting to replace punctuation marks in an author's copy. It's the beginning of a tradition of 'printers know best', which later evolved into 'publishers know best', and led to a new professionalism, in which editors and copy-editors took the primary responsibility to guarantee the production of texts that were clear and consistent, and reflected the identity of a publishing house. For the most part, authors didn't care. Unsure of their own practice, they were happy to leave such matters as spelling, layout, and punctuation to the professionals. But not all were happy – a new generation of writers on the English language least of all.

7

Breath, blood, and spirits

During the sixteenth century, two trends emerged that would change attitudes to punctuation. One was the interest in it shown by scholarly writers on orthography, especially those who were seriously involved in the task of spelling reform. The other was a recognition by playwrights that punctuation gave actors useful guidelines about how lines were to be said, as well as sometimes providing them with an intriguing plot device.

First, spelling reform. Although punctuation wasn't central to the task of standardizing spelling, it was seen as being affected by the same arguments that motivated the reformers – the need to develop a clear and uniform approach to the writing of English. Headteacher Richard Mulcaster, for example, devotes a whole section to punctuation in his educational guide called *The Elementarie* (1582). Foreigners do wonder at us, he says, 'both for the vncertaintie in our writing, and the inconstancie in our letters'. And in a section headed *Of distinction*, he describes thirteen marks (he calls them *characts*) which help 'the right and tunable vttering of our words and sentences'. In fact only seven of them are punctuation in its everyday sense, as he includes marks to show long and short vowel values, as well as a 'seuering note' (what we would now call a *dieresis*) separating the pronunciation of adjacent vowels.

It's interesting to see how Mulcaster handles punctuation, as his approach is typical of later writers. It's very much a phonetic perspective, all to do with breath and melody.

- *Comma*: a small croked point, which in writing followeth som small branch of the sentence, & in reading warneth vs to rest there, and to help our breth a litle.
- *Colon*: two round points one aboue another, which in writing followeth som full branch, or half the sentence.
- *Period*: a small round point, which in writing followeth a perfit [perfect] sentence, and in reading warneth vs to rest there, and to help our breth at full.
- *Parenthesis*: two half-circles, which in writing enclose som perfit branch, as not mere impertinent, so not fullie concident to the sentence, which it breaketh, and in reading warneth vs, that the words inclosed by them, ar to be pronounced with a lower & quikker voice, then the words either before or after them.
- *Interrogation*: two points one aboue another, wherof the vpper is somtimes croked which both in writing & reading teacheth vs, that a question is asked there, where it is set.

He also recognizes the two functions of the hyphen, marking them differently:

- *A uniting line*: a long stroke betwene two syllabs, whereby it is ment that those two syllabs ar parcells of one word.
- *The breaker*: two outright strokes one vnder another in the end of a line, and giueth vs to wit, that the word which it so breaketh is parted by full syllabs, whereof som be writen in the line before: som in that which followeth.

Clearly, punctuation for Mulcaster is primarily to do with reading aloud – what would later be called a *rhetorical* or *elocutionist* approach to the subject.

At the same time as the reformers were worrying about spelling, the dramatists were beginning to produce the works that would eventually make this period a golden age of play-writing. And in what people generally regard as the first comedy of that time, we actually see punctuation becoming part of the plot. This is Nicolas Udall's *Ralph Roister Doister*, written around 1550. In Act 3 Scene 4, the foolish braggart Ralph writes a love letter to a rich widow, Dame Custance. Matthew Merygreeke reads it aloud to her, but ignores the original punctuation, so that the sense is the reverse of what was intended, and Roister is rebuffed. Roister then blames the scrivener, who says it wasn't his fault: it was the reader not following the correct punctuation.

> ROYSTER: I say the letter thou madest me was not good.
> SCRIUENER: Then did ye wrong copy it of likelyhood.
> ROYSTER: Yes, out of thy copy worde for worde I wrote.
> SCRIUENER: Then was it as ye prayed to haue it I wote
> [am sure],
> But in reading and pointyng there was made some faulte.

There certainly was. Here are the two texts side by side. Note the length of the extract. Although there are earlier punctuation poems in English, nothing remotely resembles the scale of Udall's composition, which puts short pieces of wordplay (such as *Eats, Shoots & Leaves*) very much in the shade.

Scrivener's version

Sweete mistresse, where as I loue you,
　　nothing at all
Regarding your richesse and substance:
　　chiefe of all
For your personage, beautie, demeanour
　　and witte
I commende me vnto you: Neuer a whitte
Sory to heare reporte of your good welfare.
For (as I heare say) suche your conditions
　　are,
That ye be worthie fauour: Of no liuing man
To be abhorred: of euery honest man
To be taken for a woman enclined to vice
Nothing at all: to vertue giuing hir due price.
Wherfore concerning mariage, ye are
　　thought
Suche a fine Paragon, as nere honest man
　　bought.
And nowe by these presents I doe you
　　aduertise,
That I am minded to marrie you: In no wyse
For your goodes and substance: I can be
　　content
To take you as you are: yf ye will be my wife,
Ye shall be assured for the time of my life,

I wyll keepe you right well: from good
　　raiment and fare,
Ye shall not be kept: but in sorowe and care
Ye shall in no wyse lyue: at your owne
　　libertie,
Doe and say what ye lust: ye shall neuer
　　please me
But when ye are merrie: I will bee all sadde
When ye are sorie: I wyll be very gladde
When ye seeke your heartes ease: I will be
　　vnkinde
At no time: in me shall ye muche
　　gentlenesse finde.
But all things contrary to your will and
　　minde
Shall be done otherwise: I wyll not be
　　behynde
To speake: And as for all they that woulde do
　　you wrong,
(I wyll so helpe and maintayne ye) shall not
　　lyue long.

Merygreeke's version

Sweete mistresse where as I loue you
　　nothing at all,
Regarding your substance and richesse
　　chiefe of all,
For your personage, beautie, demeanour
　　and wit,
I commende me vnto you neuer a whit.
Sorie to heare report of your good welfare.
For (as I heare say) suche your conditions
　　are,
That ye be worthie fauour of no liuing man,
To be abhorred of euery honest man.
To be taken for a woman enclined to vice.
Nothing at all to Vertue gyuing hir due price.
Wherfore concerning mariage, ye are
　　thought
Suche a fine Paragon, as nere honest man
　　bought.
And nowe by these presentes I do you
　　aduertise
That I am minded to marrie you in no wise.
For your goodes and substance, I coulde bee
　　content
To take you as ye are. If ye mynde to bee
　　my wyfe,
Ye shall be assured for the tyme of my lyfe,
I will keepe ye ryght well, from good
　　rayment and fare,
Ye shall not be kepte but in sorowe and care.
Ye shall in no wyse lyue at your owne
　　libertie,
Doe and say what ye lust, ye shall neuer
　　please me,
But when ye are mery, I will be all sadde,
When ye are sory, I will be very gladde.
When ye seeke your heartes ease, I will be
　　vnkinde,
At no tyme, in me shall ye muche
　　gentlenesse finde.
But all things contrary to your will and
　　minde,
Shall be done: otherwise I wyll not be
　　behinde
To speake. And as for all them that woulde
　　do you wrong
I will so helpe and mainteyne, ye shall not
　　lyue long.

The ingenuity of this long passage impressed contemporary writers. Thomas Wilson, an influential writer on logic and rhetoric, uses it to illustrate ambiguity in the third edition of *The Rule of Reason* in 1553 – 'an example of soche doubtful writing, whiche by reason of poincting maie haue double sense, and contrarie meaning'.

It was a clever idea, and it was repeatedly employed. Shakespeare uses it during the play-scene in *A Midsummer Night's Dream* (5.1.108). Peter Quince addresses the assembled nobles with a prologue beginning:

Intended version	**Quince's version**
If we offend, it is with our good will	If we offend, it is with our good will.
That you should think we come, not to offend,	That you should think, we come not to offend,
But with good will to show our simple skill.	But with good will. To show our simple skill,
That is the true beginning of our end. ...	That is the true beginning of our end. ...

Theseus comments drily: 'This fellow doth not stand upon points.'

The device wasn't restricted to comedy. Towards the end of Christopher Marlowe's *Edward II* (line 2238ff), we see Young Mortimer plotting the death of the king. He knows he has to do it cunningly, so he leaves the punctuation out of a letter, allowing the text to be read in two ways. If he's accused, he plans to be able to say he had no part in it. The crucial unpunctuated line is: *Edwardum occidere nolite timere bonum est.* A word-by-word translation of the Latin is: 'Edward kill don't fear good is.' And Mortimer explains it in this way:

> *Edwardum occidere nolite timere, bonum est,*
> *Fear not to kill the king, 'tis good he die:*
> But read it thus, and that's another sense;
> *Edwardum occidere nolite, timere bonum est,*
> *Kill not the king, 'tis good to fear the worst.*

Unpointed as it is, thus shall it go.
That, being dead, if it chance to be found,
Matrevis and the rest may bear the blame,
And we be quit that caus'd it to be done.

(Spoiler alert.) His plan doesn't work out the way he hopes. The king dies, but so does he.

So, with both scholars of orthography and playwrights recognizing the role of punctuation, by the end of the sixteenth century the climate had altered, and this shows clearly in a new perspective: grammar. Grammarians had nothing to say about English punctuation in the fifteenth century for the simple reason that there were no English grammars. The first piece of writing that outlines the subject was written by a Sussex printer, William Bullokar, in 1586: a highly abbreviated treatment called *Pamphlet for Grammar*. It closely follows the standard Latin grammar of the time, by William Lily, with a focus on parts of speech, etymology, and spelling. Sentence construction and prosody are given very little space; and punctuation – which of course relates to these two areas – isn't mentioned at all.

We see the new orientation in a work that comes from an unexpected quarter: Ben Jonson's *English Grammar*, written sometime in the early 1600s. Who would have thought a dramatist would write an English grammar? But this was a special interest of Jonson's, who collected as many grammars of languages as he could find. In fact what has come down to us is an abbreviated version. The original full text was destroyed in a house fire in 1623.

At the end of his opening chapter Jonson vividly identifies the central role of punctuation in language:

Prosody, and orthography, are not parts of grammar, but diffused like the blood and spirits throughout the whole.

Orthography for him is 'right writing'. And after talking about syntax he develops the metaphor:

> All the parts of *Syntax* have already been declared. There resteth one general affection of the whole, dispersed thorough every member thereof, as the blood is thorough the body; and consisteth in the breathing, when we pronounce any *sentence*. For, whereas our breath is by nature so short, that we cannot continue without a stay to speak long together; it was thought necessary as well for the speaker's ease, as for the plainer deliverance of the things spoken, to invent this means, whereby men pausing a pretty while, the whole speech might never the worse be understood.

He goes on to describe the use of punctuation to mark these breathings: a comma ('a mean breathing'), a semicolon ('somewhat a longer breath'), a parenthesis (equivalent to a pair of commas), a colon ('two pricks', which he calls a *pause*), a period, an interrogation (?), and an admiration (!). An enthusiast for the new practices being used in Europe, he also devotes a separate chapter to the *apostrophus*, 'an affection of words coupled and joined together'.

Jonson is very concerned that people don't always get punctuation right, and he knows who to blame:

> *Apostrophus* is the rejecting of a vowel from the beginning or ending of a word. The note whereof, though it many times, through the negligence of writers and printers, is quite omitted, yet by right should, and of the learneder sort hath his sign and mark, which is such a semi-circle (') placed in the top.

Writers don't care about it; nor do the printers.

The 'negligence' of printers. I have some sympathy for the

poor compositors who had the responsibility of typesetting Jonson's works for the impressive 1616 Folio edition, which is heavily punctuated. He was always breathing down their necks, calling in at the printing-house most days and correcting as many errors as he could. 'Negligence' is actually quite mild compared with the falling-out Jonson had with a later printer when too ill to make routine calls to the printing-house. In a letter written in 1631 to the Earl of Newcastle, he calls John Beale a 'lewd printer' and an 'absolute knave', and observes: 'My printer and I shall afford subject enough for a tragicomedy, for with his delays and vexations I am almost become blind.'

Doubtless many of these vexations would have been because printers failed to respect Jonson's preference for heavy punctuation, reflecting the value he placed on it as a reader of scholarly texts as well as plays. He even inserted a colon between the two parts of his signature, *Ben:Jonson* – a practice common enough among scholars of the time when they abbreviated their first names. And in a short poem called 'To Groome Ideot', he tells someone off for reading his verse badly:

> For offring, with thy smiles, my wit to grace,
> Thy ignorance still laughs in the wrong place.
> And so my sharpnesse thou no lesse dis-ioynts,
> Than thou didst late my sense, loosing my points.

The last line: you obstructed the sense by not attending to the punctuation. Poor Groome, who not only reads Jonson's lines badly, but listens to it badly too, by laughing in the wrong place.

Jonson is unique in being both playwright and grammarian – and moreover one with a solid scholarly background, who knew about current humanist trends in mainland Europe as well as the role of punctuation in antiquity. He is the first in a series of seventeenth-century writers who took the subject very seriously, and saw it within the context of grammar. Not that the writers all agreed about how to punctuate. On the contrary. Jonson has an illuminating paragraph in his series of short observations (we would today call them blog posts) published in 1641 after his death under the heading *Timber: or Discoveries made upon Men and Matter*:

> What a sight it is to see writers committed together by the ears for ceremonies, syllables, points, colons, commas, hyphens, and the like? fighting as for their fires and their altars; and angry that now are frighted at their noises, and loud brayings under their asses skins.

Strong stuff. No wonder he fell out with his printers.

Printers would not have been used to such a combination of learning and temperament from a playwright. The printing industry was still quite small in the early 1600s. The book trade was concentrating on serious material, especially Bibles and other religious works. Plays were the least in the publishing kingdom. They were sporadic: less than a fifth of all plays were printed in the decades around 1600. They attracted small print runs, and made booksellers little profit. The playwright's world was also seen as a dangerous place, with theatres excluded from certain localities in London, and the content of plays viewed with suspicion on moral, religious, or political grounds. Thomas Bodley famously banned what he called 'riff-raff' books – including cheap quarto play editions – from his Oxford library. The number of presses and master printers was tightly controlled by the Stationers Company and by ordinances issued by the Star Chamber, and printers had to cope with far bigger issues than punctuation.

Accordingly, while printers took a great deal of care over

the way they typeset religious, legal, educational, historical, and other scholarly works, they were notoriously casual when dealing with plays, as they knew they would not be treated with the same level of attention. They must have been taken aback when they encountered a playwright who cared. But the new genres of spelling guide, dictionary (the first in 1604, Robert Cawdrey's *A Table Alphabeticall*), and grammar were a different matter. And during the seventeenth century we see a large increase in their numbers, with the authors looking in unprecedented detail at the way their writing was presented, and keeping an eye on punctuation as never before.

8

Grammar rules

The century after Jonson saw the publication of many ped-
agogical guides to punctuation, but there's no agreement
among them about how best to handle it. The messy situation
of the sixteenth century, outlined in Chapter 6, remained. Is
punctuation a guide to pronunciation or a way of making a
text easy to read? Is its purpose elocutional and rhetorical, or
is it to do with meaning and grammar?

As the teaching of grammar became routine in schools,
and as more treatments of English grammar became available,
we see the second approach becoming the norm. Grammar
offered the possibility of system and order where previously
there had been variation and idiosyncrasy. An approach
favouring actors and orators highlighted the problem: how
could half-a-dozen or so marks ever cope with the multifarious tones, tunes, and pauses of the speaking voice? Grammars, by contrast, recognized just eight parts of speech and
showed an apparently limited number of ways of combining these into sentences. If anything could bring punctuation
under control, it was going to be grammar.

That is why we begin to see such titles as Mark Lewis's
Plain and Short Rules for Pointing Periods Grammatically (published in about 1672). Not all grammarians were interested,
but during the seventeenth and eighteenth centuries about
60 per cent of the published grammars did deal with the
topic, even though we can sense at times a certain reluctance

to do so. For writers with a prescriptive temperament, looking to establish clear-cut grammatical rules of correct usage – the approach that became the norm by the second half of the eighteenth century – punctuation was something of a nuisance.

We can see these reservations in the most influential school grammar of the mid-eighteenth century: Bishop Lowth's *A Short Introduction to English Grammar* (1762), which ends with a chapter on punctuation. He draws a contrast between speech and writing: we have a variety of ways in speech to express the connections between sentences, he says, but in writing 'the whole number of Points, which we have to express this variety, amounts only to Four ... the Period, Colon, Semicolon, and Comma'. And he goes on:

> So the doctrine of Punctuation must needs be very imperfect: few precise rules can be given which will hold without exception in all cases; but much must be left to the judgement and taste of the writer. ... It remains, therefore, that we be content with the Rules of Punctuation, laid down with as much exactness as the nature of the subject will admit: such as may serve for a general direction, to be accommodated to different occasions; and to be supplied, where deficient, by the writer's judgement.

Lowth has often been described as the source of grammatical prescriptivism, but his grammar is much more nuanced in his descriptions, as these remarks illustrate.

This is the pattern followed by all the grammar-books that deal with punctuation. They start off confidently, list a series of rules, and conclude by warning readers that the rules don't always work. Books exclusively devoted to punctuation follow the same course. Joseph Robertson's *An Essay on Punctuation* (1785) illustrates the continuing emphasis on grammar. By contrast with writers such as Mulcaster and Jonson (Chapter 7), his opening definition doesn't even mention pronunciation at all:

> Punctuation is the art of dividing a discourse into periods, and those periods into their constituent parts: namely, a comma, a semicolon, a colon, &c.

He then lists forty rules governing the use of the comma in various parts of the sentence, and illustrates them in detail. Other marks are dealt with in less detail, and are similarly handled in terms of 'rules'.

But at the end of the book, Robertson has a prominent page headed 'Conclusion', where we read:

> These rules, I must confess, are liable to some exceptions, and are not sufficient to direct the learner in EVERY imaginable combination of words and phrases. It would indeed be impossible to frame such a system of rules, as should comprehend the whole extent of the language.

He just hopes that his approach will help the reader to

> divide his sentences, both in reading and writing, with greater accuracy and precision, than they are usually divided in the generality of books, wherein the punctuation is arbitrary and capricious, and founded on no general principles.

The problem is that, when we examine his rules in detail, we find they don't avoid the same criticisms. For instance, he's against inserting a comma between the subject and verb of a clause:

> The society of ladies, is a school of politeness.

This is 'improper', he says, and the comma should be omitted.

On the other hand, he sensibly recognizes that it may be necessary to pause after a lengthy construction:

> When the clauses are short, and closely connected, the point may be omitted. On the contrary, a simple sentence, when it is a long one, may admit of a pause.

And he illustrates this from another sentence:

> The good taste of the present age, has not allowed us to neglect the cultivation of the English language.

But if we compare the number of syllables in 'short' and 'long' examples, we find that they are the same – eight in each case. So why the comma in the second case and not the first? What counts as a 'long' sentence element? This is the kind of question the grammarians were unable to answer.

The year after Robertson published his *Essay*, David Steel wrote *Elements of Punctuation*, in which he goes through Robertson's rules one by one, adds his own commentary, and illustrates good practice from a variety of authors (notably Milton). He's in total agreement that grammar 'ought to be the basis of punctuation', but we quickly see the warnings appear. The use of periods poses few problems, he suggests, and the placement of commas can be decided with a good grammatical awareness of sentence construction, but when it comes to the distinction between colon and semicolon, he gives up:

> they are both chiefly useful in marking the degree of connexion between one sentence and another, and, in this, the connexion may be so variously felt, by different people, that two will seldom agree in the use of these points in the same passage.

He concludes:

> A nice acquaintance with punctuation is not, in my
> opinion, attainable by rules, as a knowledge of syntax may
> be acquired, but it must be procured by a kind of internal
> conviction, that the rules of grammar are never to be
> violated.

Where do we get this 'internal conviction' from? By reading
good authors: 'a reference to books would teach the minutiæ
better than any rules.' But as authors show diverse practices,
it all comes down, in the end, to personal preference. He
acknowledges that his own preference is to overpunctuate:

> Whenever I am doubtful if a sentence will admit a comma, I
> generally end my hesitation by inserting it, provided it does
> not militate against grammar; always preferring a rigid to a
> relaxed punctuation.

We see a similar subjectivity in the most influential of all
the eighteenth-century grammars, written by Lindley Murray.
His *English Grammar* (1795) sold over 20 million copies, and
was popular on both sides of the Atlantic, continuing to be
used throughout the nineteenth century and being repeatedly acknowledged. The essayist Thomas de Quincey, writing
in *Blackwood's Magazine* (April 1839), described the way it
'reigns despotically through the young ladies' schools, from
the Orkneys to the Cornish Scillys'. And in Chapter 29 of
The Old Curiosity Shop (1840–41), Charles Dickens describes
Mrs Jarley's efforts to attract a new class of audience to her
waxworks:

> And these audiences were of a very superior description,
> including a great many young ladies' boarding-schools,
> whose favour Mrs Jarley had been at great pains to
> conciliate, by altering the face and costume of Mr Grimaldi
> as clown to represent Mr Lindley Murray as he appeared

> when engaged in the composition of his English Grammar
> ...

Whenever the satirical magazine *Punch* wanted to draw attention to 'bad grammar', it would always refer to Murray, even in the closing decades of the nineteenth century.

When he comes to punctuation, Murray is well aware that he's dealing with something special. He treats it in a separate chapter, immediately adding a footnote:

> As punctuation is intended to aid both the sense and
> the pronunciation of a sentence, it could not have
> been exclusively discussed under the part of Syntax,
> or of Prosody. The nature of the subject, its extent and
> importance, and the grammatical knowledge which it
> presupposes, have induced me to make it a distinct and
> subsequent article.

He then follows Lowth and earlier writers by repeating the phonetic equation:

> The Comma represents the shortest pause; the Semicolon, a
> pause double that of the comma; the Colon, double that of
> the semicolon; and the Period, double that of the colon.

He accepts that the pauses can't be given an absolute value, as speech can be faster or slower; but he insists that 'the proportion between the pauses should be ever invariable'.

He then gives examples of the four main marks, devoting most space to the comma. Again following earlier writers – and often copying their examples – he identifies twenty rules relating commas to various types of syntactic construction. Some rules would later be contentious, such as his use of the 'serial comma' (see Chapter 26):

> The husband, wife, and children, suffered extremely.

David was a brave, wise, and pious man.

And some of his rules would now be seen as unnecessarily heavy, such as his recommendation that words like *so, hence,* and *first* should be set off by commas:

He feared want, hence, he over-valued riches.

But all of his rules would be followed, often slavishly, by several generations of grammarians and schoolteachers.

However, even Murray could see that there were factors present that couldn't be reduced to simple rules. His final paragraph on the comma reiterates Robertson's concern about length: 'In many of the foregoing rules and examples great regard must be paid to the length of the clauses, and the proportion which they bear to one another.' But note how he concludes: this will 'enable the student to adjust the proper pauses, and the places for inserting the commas'. In the end, it comes down, as Lowth had said, to 'the writer's judgement'.

An important point to note is that Murray clearly saw the two functions of punctuation: 'to aid both the sense and the pronunciation of a sentence'. This is a significant improvement on the views of people like Robertson, and it had already been identified by Steel, who saw how grammar and pronunciation could be connected:

Punctuation should lead to the sense; the sense will guide to modulation and emphasis.

This anticipates the important role given to semantics in the twentieth century (see Chapter 11).

Steel and Murray were writing towards the end of the eighteenth century, and had evidently been influenced by the new breed of elocutionists, who had been attacking any approach to punctuation that focused exclusively on grammar. The most influential of these elocutionists was Thomas Sheridan (1719–1788), the father of playwright Richard Brinsley Sheridan. His mid-century lectures on elocution were delivered to packed halls all over the country. A series could attract well over 1500 people, each paying a guinea to attend – which, translated into modern values, would be around £150,000. He also published his lectures as a course, selling at half-a-guinea a time. Elocution was big business, and people were prepared to pay for it in their desire to acquire a manner of speaking that would be elegant and acceptable in high society. There is, says Sheridan in his opening sentence, 'a general inability to read, or speak, with propriety and grace in public'. A correct understanding of punctuation, he thinks, is part of the solution.

He's in no doubt that punctuation is partly to blame for the malaise. Echoing Ben Jonson in the previous century, in his fifth lecture he points the finger at two familiar characters:

> There is no article in reading more difficult than that of observing a due proportion of stops, occasioned by the very erroneous and inaccurate manner, in which they are marked by printers and writers.

For Sheridan, concerned with effective reading aloud, the punctuation system is hopeless. He observes that it works inefficiently in both directions: there are many occasions when you need to pause in speech but there are no commas in the writing to guide you; and there are many occasions when there are commas in the writing but there should be no pause in speech. The grammarians are to blame, he thinks, because they have developed a model of punctuation that is of little relevance to the public speaker:

The truth is, the modern art of punctuation was not taken from the art of speaking, which was never studied by the moderns, but was in great measure regulated by the rules of grammar.

And there is a third villain in Sheridan's sights: teachers. In his opening lecture he talks of the way the schools have failed in providing students with a proper understanding of 'the visible marks of the pauses and rests of the voice':

the masters have not only been more negligent in perfecting pupils in the right use of these, but in their method of teaching, have laid down some false rules, under the influence of which, it is impossible that any one can read naturally.

False rules – the perennial and unavoidable criticism of spelling and punctuation manuals that has continued down to the present day.

It was perhaps a little unfair to blame the teachers, who for the most part were simply doing what the writers of the best-selling grammars were telling them to do. But Sheridan was right to single out the grammarians, whose focus had largely been on the syntactically intricate sentences of the written language, with little reference to speech other than the most basic recommendations about pausing. Anyone who tried to read a text aloud using the phonetic equations of Murray *et al.* would never hold an audience for long.

However, the elocutionists couldn't stop the grammatical steamroller. It's clear from the way authors wrote during the eighteenth century that they increasingly felt complex sentences needed a correspondingly explicit punctuation, with every syntactically important element identified to avoid uncertainty over how to read a discourse. The punctuation became heavier and heavier, as writers accepted the recommendations of the grammarians, and in cases of doubt added – like David Steel – extra marks.

The result can be illustrated by a sentence from the preface to Dr Johnson's *Dictionary* (1755):

> It will sometimes be found, that the accent is placed by the authour quoted, on a different syllable from that marked in the alphabetical series; it is then to be understood, that custom has varied, or that the authour has, in my opinion, pronounced wrong.

It's easy to see what has happened: a comma is used to identify the main chunks of syntax that make up the whole, and a semicolon links two sentences that are felt to be closely related in meaning. Some writers or printers would have gone even further than that, such as by separating the adverbs and writing 'It will, sometimes, be found' or 'it is, then, to be understood'. But a lightly punctuated version, such as the following, is something we don't see until the twentieth century:

> It will sometimes be found that the accent is placed by the authour quoted on a different syllable from that marked in the alphabetical series. It is then to be understood that custom has varied or that the authour has in my opinion pronounced wrong.

If you feel this is underpunctuated you may add commas to suit your taste; but few modern readers would insert as many as we see in Johnson.

Grammarians and elocutionists may have had their differences, but they were united on one point: opposition to the printers, whose 'negligence' had been remarked on by Jonson, Sheridan, and others. Both groups were concerned with establishing principles, and they didn't see much principle in the way the printers worked. It was time for a change. The printers had had their own way for too long.

Interlude: A punctuation heavyweight

" place, I am convinced that Mr. S— is in the right, and that
" the voice does not reſt in the ſame tone, even upon the ſame
" ſyllable; but goes on continually changing, not only upon
" different words and ſyllables, but upon the ſame ſyllable.
" And indeed I now begin to think, that to keep the voice in the
" ſame tone, even for the ſhorteſt time, or, in other words,
" to ſpeak in a perfect monotony, is a thing of art which nobody
" but a muſician can perform.   I am alſo convinced, that the
" voice does not only riſe or fall upon the ſame ſyllable (I mean
" in muſical modulation), but alſo that it ſometimes does both
" riſe and fall upon the ſame ſyllable, particularly upon ſuch
" ſyllables as make a word by themſelves, or are pronounced
" with any pathos; ſuch as the ſyllable *oh!* given as an inſtance
" by Mr. S—, who has obſerved, with great accuracy, that the
" voice riſes upon this monoſyllable twelve enharmonic intervals
" or quarter tones, but falls only ſeven.   Such ſyllables he very
" properly calls *circumflex*; and he has made a diſtinction of
" them, which no grammarian ever made, but which, for any
" thing I know, may be well founded in the uſe of the Engliſh
" language; into thoſe circumflexes which begin with riſing and
" end with falling; and thoſe which, *vice verſâ*, begin with
" falling and end with riſing.   And the obſervation he has
" made on the circumflex † of the monoſyllable *oh!* that it does
" not fall ſo much as it riſes by five quarter tones, is alſo an

Joshua Steele's *An essay towards establishing the melody and measure of speech* (1775) is a typical example of the heavy punctuation encountered in eighteenth-century texts. This is an extract from a letter, seen as a quotation, and thus marked by opening inverted commas at the beginning of each line – a normal convention of the time. Only one line lacks a punctuation mark; line 6 has four commas. Even the page number is set off by brackets.

9
The printer's dilemma

I imagine the state of mind of seventeenth- and eighteenth-century printers was similar to Caxton's, 300 years before: 'Lo! what should a man in these days now write?' They were in a difficult position, as they had two diametrically opposed kinds of author to deal with. One kind – let's call them Jonsonians – were scrupulous about punctuation, and insisted on checking every mark for printing accuracy, getting very annoyed if a printer dared to change anything. The other kind – let's call them Wordsworthians – couldn't have cared less, and were extremely grateful to get any help they could.

I single out Wordsworth because, by his own admission, he was hopeless at punctuation and abdicated all responsibility for it. As he was preparing the second edition of the *Lyrical Ballads*, he wrote to the chemist Humphry Davy (28 July 1800) and asked him to check the text for punctuation:

> You would greatly oblige me by looking over the enclosed poems, and correcting anything you find amiss in the punctuation, a business at which I am ashamed to say I am no adept.

He had never even met Davy! The suggestion had come from Coleridge. And not only does he ask this total stranger to correct his work, but later in the letter he asks Davy to send the corrected manuscript directly on to the printer, without referring back to him. Which bits of the end product's punctuation are due to Davy, the printer, or the author we shall never know.

A roll-call of literary authors between the seventeenth and nineteenth centuries would show them lining up under Jonson or Wordsworth. Among the Jonsonians is John Dryden, who in one of his letters (4 December 1697) complains to his publisher, Jacob Tonson, that 'the Printer is a beast, and understands nothing I can say to him of correcting the press', and in another insists that his work be printed 'exactly after my Amendments: for a fault of that nature will disoblige me Eternally'. Although relationships later improved, he was not at all happy with Mr Tonson, whom he pilloried in an epigram (published in *Faction Displayed*, 1705):

> With leering Looks, Bullfac'd, and Freckled fair,
> With two left Legs, and Judas-colour'd Hair,
> With Frowzy Pores, that taint the ambient Air.

Printers beware, when dealing with satirical poets! Or, as we shall see later, novelists like Mark Twain.

Keats also took a keen interest in the way his publisher dealt with his copy. In a letter of 27 February 1818 to John Taylor, he writes:

> Your alteration strikes me as being a great improvement—
> the page looks much better. And now I will attend to the
> Punctuations you speak of—the comma should be at *soberly*,
> and in the other passage the comma should follow *quiet*. I
> am extremely indebted to you for this attention and also for
> your after admonitions.

And Tennyson asked his publisher Edward Moxon (letter of 13 October 1832) to 'send me every proof twice over. I should like the text to be as correct as possible.'

Among the Wordsworthians is Thomas Gray, who in an

undated letter in 1768 gives over eight pages of instructions to Foulis Press about how to print his poems, but adds: 'please to observe, that I am entirely unversed in the doctrine of *stops*, whoever therefore shall deign to correct them, will do me a friendly office.' And Byron writes to John Murray (26 August 1813) to ask: 'Do you know any body who can *stop—I* mean *point—commas,* and so forth? for I am, I fear, a sad hand at your punctuation.' And in a P.S. to a later letter (15 November 1813) he adds: 'Do attend to the punctuation: I can't, for I don't know a comma – at least where to place one.'

Printers obviously had the final responsibility of making a work look attractive, so that people would buy it. They knew that browsers in a bookshop – then as now – pick up a book and flick through the pages to see if it is for them. And among the many factors which influence the decision to buy are the layout of the text and the clarity of the writing, in both of which punctuation plays an important part. So it's unsurprising that they paid especial attention to this aspect of the copy. It was not just a matter of adding the occasional comma. There were major ambiguities that had to be sorted, such as when an author failed to use quotation marks consistently, so that it was impossible to identify who was saying what in a conversation. Charlotte Brontë, in the persona of C Bell, writes (24 September 1847) to her publisher Smith, Elder & Co about the proofs of *Jane Eyre*:

> I have to thank you for punctuating the sheets before sending them to me as I found the task very puzzling – and besides I consider your mode of punctuation a great deal mo[re] correct and rational than my own.

The printers had to frequently correct her use of quotation marks and to insert colons, semicolons, and periods into what was a very lightly punctuated and difficult-to-read manuscript. She wasn't atypical. It wasn't until the late nineteenth century that it became routine for authors to submit clean copy on sheets of the same size, writing on just one side of the paper, and avoiding the heavy self-corrections that can make a manuscript illegible.

The major printing manuals of the period all address the issue. John Smith's *Printer's Grammar* (1755) is mainly about the work of the compositor, and deals with the different fonts, letter sizes, differences between large and small capitals, and other technical matters. When he addresses the topic of pointing, he distinguishes two kinds of writer:

> [some authors] point their Matter either very loosely or not at all: of which two evils, however, the last is the least; for in that case a Compositor has room left to point the Copy his own way; which, though it cannot be done without loss to him; yet it is not altogether of so much hinderance as being troubled with Copy which is pointed at random, and which stops the Compositor in the career of his business more than if not pointed at all.

Writers, Smith finds, are typically lax:

> most Authors expect the Printer to spell, point, and digest their Copy, that it may be intelligible and significant to the Reader.

He has no time for the grammarians, whom he accuses of artifice in the way they introduce rules (I imagine he is thinking of such things as the pause equations mentioned in Chapter 8) that have no basis in real life:

> When we compare the rules which very able Grammarians have laid down about Pointing, the difference is not very

material; and it appears, that it is only a maxim with humourous Pedants, to make a clamour about the quality of a Point; who would even make an Erratum of a Comma which they fancy to bear the pause of a Semicolon, were the Printer to give way to such pretended accuracies. Hence we find some of these high-pointing Gentlemen propose to increase the number of Points now in use.

And he adds that printers must take a firm stand when dealing with one of these high-pointing gentlemen.

Smith also draws attention to the increasingly important role of correctors – we would call them copy-editors today – whose role is to review manuscripts to avoid compositors having to make changes at proof stage. By the time Charles Stower wrote another *Printer's Grammar* (1808) – a much-used authority in the early nineteenth century – the balance of power had changed within the printing-house: the primary responsibility for accuracy of copy was now in the hands of the corrector, who 'should make it a rule never to trust a compositor in any matter of the slightest importance – they are the most *erring* set of men in the universe'. The corrector had considerable editorial power in those days. It is his responsibility, says Stower, to eliminate from a manuscript any anomalies 'of no real signification; such as far-fetched spellings of words, changing and thrusting in points, capitals, or any thing else that has nothing but fancy and humour for its authority and foundation'.

It was the same in the USA. By the end of the nineteenth century, the professionals employed by a publisher had grown to include proof-readers as well as copy-editors, and their role is highlighted by Thomas Mackellar in his influential *The American Printer: A Manual of Typography* (1866):

The world is little aware how greatly many authors are

indebted to a competent proof-reader for not only reforming their spelling and punctuation, but for valuable suggestions in regard to style, language, and grammar,—thus rectifying faults which would have rendered them fair game for the petulant critic.

Today, a single professional body combines both these editorial tasks: in the UK, it is the Society for Editors and Proofreaders.

None of this stopped petulant criticism being directed at publishers, when it came to punctuation. Henry Alford, Dean of Canterbury and author of *The Queen's English* (1864), has little to say about the subject, but when he does address it (in his section 124) he pulls no punches:

> I remember when I was young in printing, once correcting the punctuation of a proof-sheet, and complaining of the liberties which had been taken with my manuscript. The publisher quietly answered me, that *punctuation was always left to the compositors*. And a precious mess they make of it.

What sort of thing did they do? He goes on:

> The great enemies to understanding anything printed in our language are the *commas*. And these are inserted by the compositors, without the slightest compunction, on every possible occasion.

He is particularly angered by commas being used on either side of adverbs such as *too* or *also* (he is no supporter of Murray here) or separating adjectives in such phrases as *a nice young man*. He recalls a printer inserting a comma after the first word in *However true this may be*. And he blames printers for the excessive use of 'notes of admiration' (i.e. exclamation marks):

These *shrieks*, as they have been called, are scattered up and down the page by the compositors without mercy.

He recommends writers to use as few as possible.

However, on the whole during the nineteenth century there are signs of a growing rapprochement between grammarians and printers. We see the influence of printers in the content of some grammars; and we see printers taking more serious note of what grammarians have had to say.

Interlude: Strong language

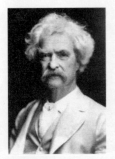

Mark Twain is famous for his long-running battle with printers and correctors.

In 1889:

Yesterday Mr. Hall wrote that the printer's proof-reader was improving my punctuation for me, & I telegraphed orders to have him shot without giving him time to pray.

In 1893:

> In the first place God made idiots. This was for practice. Then he made proof-readers.

And in 1898, in a letter to his publisher Chatto & Windus dated 25 July 1897:

> I give it up. These printers pay no attention to my punctuation. Nine-tenths of the labor & vexation put upon me by Messrs. Spottiswoode & Co consists in annihilating their ignorant & purposeless punctuation & <u>restoring</u> my own.
>
> This latest batch, beginning with page 145 & running to page 192 starts out like all that went before it – with my punctuation ignored & their insanities substituted for it. I have read two pages of it – I can't stand any more. If they will restore my punctuation themselves & <u>then</u> send the purified pages to me I will read it for errors of grammar & construction – that is enough to require of an author who writes as legible a hand as I do, & who knows more about punctuation in two minutes than any damned bastard of a proof-reader can learn in two centuries.

10

Passing the buck

The notion that printers should pay attention to scholars had been around a long time. We see it in the preface to the second volume of the meticulously detailed *Mechanick Exercises: Or, the Doctrine of Handy-works. Applied to the Compositors Trade* (1683). Joseph Moxon lays down the basic rule: 'a Compositor is strictly to follow his Copy', but immediately adds:

> the carelessness of some good Authors, and the ignorance of other Authors, has forc'd Printers to introduce a Custom, which among them is look'd upon as a task and duty incumbent on the Compositer, viz. to discern and amend the bad Spelling and Pointing of his Copy, if it be English.

How is the compositor to do this? Moxon recommends:

> it is necessary that a Compositer be a good English Schollar at least; and that he know the present traditional Spelling of all English Words, and that he have so much Sence and Reason, as to Point his Sentences properly: when to begin a Word with a Capital Letter ...

And when we get to the section where we might expect some detailed advice (p. 224), we see his total reliance on what the scholars have written:

> As he Sets on, he considers how to Point his Work, viz.

when to Set , where ; where : and where . where to make
( ) where [ ] ? ! and when a Break. But the rules for these
having been taught in many School-books, I need say
nothing to them here, but refer you to them.

It is an early example of buck-passing.

By the nineteenth century, printers were more explicit.
Here's the opening paragraph of a book written by the printer
George Smallfield in 1838, *The Principles of English Punctuation*:

> Punctuation is the art of dividing a written or printed
> composition into sentences, or into parts of sentences,
> by the use of points, or stops, for the purpose of marking
> the different pauses which the sense and an accurate
> pronunciation require. This definition of the word
> *punctuation* presupposes that the reader understands
> Grammar.

He then follows Murray scrupulously in his account of the
parts of speech, and carefully counts out the length of pauses
for commas, semicolons, colons, and periods. It's all very
derivative, but he has clearly read enough about grammar
to see that the situation isn't clear-cut. He knows that grammarians don't always agree. For example, he considers the
use of commas in this sentence:

> Climate soil, laws, customs, food, and other accidental
> differences, have produced an astonishing variety in the
> complexion, features, manners, and faculties, of the human
> race.

And he adds a note:

> Some Grammarians would omit the comma after certain
> words in most of the above examples, – after the nouns *food*
> and *differences*, *manners* and *faculties*.

Aware of the divided usage, he tries to justify his choice with a grammatical argument:

> If, however, the reader attentively considers the construction, he may be convinced, that *food* and *differences* are no more the nominative to the verb *have produced* than the preceding nouns are; and, that *manners* and *faculties* are no more the object of the verb, than *complexion* and *features*. By applying these observations to the other examples, the reader may possibly arrive at the conclusion, that in each sentence every one of the commas is necessary as a guide to the sense, and to an accurate pronunciation.

May possibly ... This may have convinced people in the nineteenth century, but it certainly didn't convince them in the twentieth. Neither of the commas after *differences* and *faculties* would be considered acceptable today.

We need to remember that this is not a grammarian writing, but a printer, trying to make the best of what the school-books say. And he's perceptive, able to see that what the school-books say is not always enough to solve the problems writers and printers face. Smallfield is confident enough to maintain the orthodox printer's position: if an author 'should not feel satisfied that he can point accurately, he would do well to leave this matter to the care and experience of his printer'. At the same time he notes: 'It may, however, occasionally happen, that his manuscript has been placed in the hands of an ignorant or a careless compositor.' He therefore ends his book with a list of proof-correcting marks – in effect, showing writers how to take the final responsibility for the appearance of their work.

In 1844, a Manchester printer, John Wilson, wrote a widely read treatise called *A Treatise on Grammatical Punctuation*. It is aimed at everyone, as his subtitle reflects:

designed for letter-writers, authors, printer, and correctors
of the press; and for the use of academies and schools.

Everyone is mentioned, because everyone is to blame. In a
long passage in his Introduction, he sums up the unsatisfac-
tory state of affairs. Punctuation, he says, has not received
the attention it deserves. While allowing a few exceptional
cases of competent usage, he fires at everyone (I break his
long paragraph into sections):

- The mental philosopher and the philologist seem to
  regard it as too trifling for attention, amid their grander
  researches into the internal operations of the mind, and
  its external workings by means of language.
- The grammarian passes it by altogether unheeded, or
  lays down a few general and abstract principles; leaving
  the difficulties of the art to be surmounted by the pupil
  as well as he may.
- The lawyer engrosses in a legible character, which,
  however, by its deficiency in sentential marks, often
  proves, like the laws of which he is the expounder,
  'gloriously uncertain' as to the meaning intended to be
  conveyed.
- The painter, the engraver, and the lithographer, appear to
  set all rules at defiance, by either omitting the points, or
  by misplacing them, wherever punctuation is required.
- The letter-writer, with his incessant and indiscriminate
  dashes, puts his friend, his beloved one, his agent, or
  his employer to a *little* more trouble, in conning over his
  epistle, than is absolutely necessary.
- Even the author – who of all writers, ought to be the
  most accurate – puts his manuscript into the printer's
  hands, either altogether destitute of grammatical pauses,
  or so badly pointed as to create an unnecessary loss of
  time to the compositor.

And as for the printer:

- It is a fact well known to those connected with the press, that compositors in general have a very deficient knowledge of punctuation.

His own book, he hopes, will result in progress. But, a century and a half on, much of what he says could apply just as appositely today.

Wilson puts all his money on the grammatical approach, and cites Lindley Murray as his main source. In his Introduction he asserts that 'the art of punctuation is founded more on a grammatical than on a rhetorical basis; that its chief aim is to unfold the meaning of sentences, with the least trouble to the reader; and that it aids the delivery, only in so far as it tends to bring out the sense of the writer to the best advantage'. At the same time, he recognizes that the grammatical treatises are 'deficient either in an explanation of exceptions and difficulties – in examples and exercises – or in rules and remarks, illustrative of the diversified functions …'.

Throughout the nineteenth century, we see a growing realization that the existing grammar-books weren't providing the answers that people wanted. How could they, when they persistently expressed their uncertainty over rules and introduce their personal preferences? But there was no alternative. The only kind of grammars that were available were those derived from Murray. Every decade in the century thus produced treatises on punctuation which could do no more than state that the problem still existed and reformulate the same tired answers. One final example, before we move on, from the most influential of all guidelines to appear in the 1900s: Horace Hart's *Rules for Compositors and Readers at the University Press Oxford*, first published in 1893 as a single sheet of guidance, and soon amplified into a small book (I quote from a 1950 edition). Hart was printer for Oxford University and controller of the university press for over thirty years.

This is a wide-ranging work, which at times goes well beyond what an author or grammarian would need to know, dealing with the typographical aesthetics of punctuation. For example, Hart recommends thin spaces to be used before apostrophes in such phrases as *that's* (= *that is*) in order to distinguish them from the ones used to mark possession. He allows no space between the initials in a name: *W.E. Gladstone*, not *W. E. Gladstone*. Indentation of the first lines of paragraphs is to be generally one em (the width of a letter *m*). No grammarian or author, not even Mark Twain, would be exercised about such things.

Hart maintains the traditional view about writers and punctuation, that they are 'almost without exception either too busy or too careless to regard it', and he accepts the responsibility of doing something about it. He knows that compositors are human too, and even quotes Alford's 'However' example to illustrate the way in which they have sometimes let authors down (p. 72). But where is the printer's knowledge of punctuation to come from?

> The compositor is recommended to study attentively a good treatise on the whole subject. He will find some knowledge of it to be indispensable if his work is to be done properly.

The advice isn't as sound as it seems. A good treatise is presumably one that would have provided Hart with answers to all the punctuation decisions that he had to make, as well as explaining the stylistic variation that existed. And the sad fact of the matter is: there was no such thing.

The grammarians let Hart and his earlier colleagues down in several ways. The treatises often failed to agree in their recommendations (such as whether to set off single adverbs by commas). Books written at different periods reflected changes in fashion (such as whether to punctuate abbreviations). Any late nineteenth-century printer following Lindley Murray would find that several of Murray's rules were no longer being observed by most writers (such as whether to put a comma between subject and predicate). And in place of principles that could be learned and applied, there would often be little guidance other than a general statement followed by examples, from which the reader was supposed to be able to generalize. Hart could do no other than adopt the same practice. For example, his section on the semicolon begins simply: 'Instances in which the semicolon is appropriate.' There's no further explanation of what is meant by 'appropriate', or what an inappropriate use of a semicolon might be.

Hart knows what the core problem is: there are two systems in use, one he calls 'close and stiff' (a heavy style), the other 'open or easy' (a light style). He doesn't think it's the job of the printer to tell an author which one should be used. But when he looks at the grammars, he finds that they say the same thing: where usage is divided, the ultimate decision about punctuation rests with the author. So studying attentively a 'good treatise' is not always going to help. When a manuscript displaying unusual punctuation arrives at the publishers, is the idiosyncrasy due to authorial ignorance or authorial deliberation? If one of Hart's staff makes a change, will the response be Wordsworthian delight or Twainian fury?

What the nineteenth century shows is that punctuation is a classic case of 'passing the buck'. When there is a confident writer, a competent printer, and a straightforward grammatical or rhetorical decision to be made, there's no problem. But where there is uncertainty over how to punctuate, disagreement among the professionals, or inconsistency in a

published work, we see circles of shifting blame and respon-
sibilities. Writers ask publishers to sort out their inadequa-
cies. The publishers do the best they can, but when things
go wrong they blame their correctors or compositors or cite
a lack of guidance from grammarians. The grammarians
do the best they can, but when their rules don't work they
explain it by referring to divided usage among – the writers.
The writers blame themselves or the way they were taught in
school. The schoolteachers explain that they are only doing
what they have been told to do by the grammars, or by the
dictats of a government-approved syllabus. And ministries of
education, concerned about standards of achievement, make
decisions based on what they think is the best practice – of
grammarians and writers.

The printers looked to the grammarians for help; and
the grammarians sometimes looked to the printers. A good
example is the way Lindley Murray adds a section of his
grammar devoted to 'other characters, which are frequently
made use of in composition'. He lists the apostrophe, caret,
circumflex accent, hyphen, acute accent (showing stress),
breve (to show vowel length), diæresis (Murray's spelling –
¨ to separate vowels), section mark (§), paragraph mark (¶),
quotation marks, crotchets (square brackets), index (the hand
☞), brace (}), asterisk, ellipsis (…), obelisk (†), and parallels
(||) – the last two showing sidenotes or footnotes. (Wilson
goes even further in his listing of special symbols, including
astronomical, mathematical, and medical signs.) Each item is
given a brief description and illustration of its use. Murray's
account is by no means complete – for example, he shows
the apostrophe being used only with singular nouns, as in
'a man's property' – but his explanations are accurate as far
as they go, and in some cases are quite detailed, as in his
description of the asterisk:

An Asterisk, or small star *, directs the reader to some note in the margin, or at the bottom of a page. Two or three asterisks generally denote the omission of some letters in a word, or of some bold or indelicate expression, or some defect in the manuscript.

None of this information comes from his thinking as a grammarian. It derives from his experience as a reader and from working with printers.

A century on from Horace Hart, nothing much seems to have changed with respect to punctuation. Grammars and style manuals keep saying rules have exceptions. Copy-editors regularly debate best practice. Rows between publishers and authors continue, as do rows between teachers and politicians. Children may have their homework corrected in different ways by different teachers in the same school. The average adult, left with a legacy of uncertainty, buys a self-help manual and then finds it doesn't solve the problem. Popular guides, such as Lynne Truss's *Eats, Shoots & Leaves*, do a grand job persuading people that punctuation matters, and that we need standards, but do not give a complete account of what those standards are, or provide an explanation of all the variation that exists. Matters then come to the boil, as they did in 2013, when teachers and parents find their children are having answers marked wrong in school punctuation tests solely because the examiners have discounted what is actually a widely accepted usage (see Chapter 26).

It seems as if the problem of punctuation is insoluble. But looking at it from the point of view of modern linguistics, this is only because people have been approaching the subject in an incomplete way, opting for partial accounts, and ignoring some critical factors. In particular, the kind of grammatical approach we've seen so far hasn't been as helpful as it needed to be. Although a great deal of what Lowth, Murray, and their disciples had to say was accurate enough, and would be echoed in any modern grammar, their accounts were short, selective, artificial in their prescriptions, and unbalanced in their coverage. The parts of speech were treated in some detail, but the description of sentence structure, and the way elements of the sentence interacted, was superficial. This is a deficit that would not be corrected until the emergence of descriptive grammars during the twentieth century; but it had immediate consequences for the way these authors presented punctuation.

To give just one illustration of what I mean: as we'll see in Chapter 13, there is a hierarchy of importance in punctuation, relating to the hierarchy that exists in grammar. All grammars agree that the sentence is the most important feature, and should be dealt with first. We would therefore expect the first mark to be treated in any account of punctuation to be the period, as this is the main way in which a sentence is identified. But traditional accounts all begin with the comma – even Wilson's, who totally accepted the need for a grammatical approach – and don't deal with periods until after they've worked their way through semicolons and colons. It's easy to see why. They are following the old system of pause length, beginning with the shortest pause and moving towards the largest. But how can we understand the role of the marks that occur within sentences if we have not first understood the marks that identify sentences as wholes? We need a more sophisticated sense of grammatical structure if we're going to make progress in developing a more satisfactory approach to punctuation.

We also need a more comprehensive frame of reference. History clearly shows us that a phonetic approach, focusing on the impact of punctuation on listening and speaking, is not the whole story. Nor is the whole story told through a grammatical approach, focusing on the way punctuation is used in reading and writing. Some sort of combined account is essential. But neither of these approaches can provide the whole solution to the problem because the factors that account for divided usage involve issues that fall outside of these domains. In particular, the subjectivity that seems to be inherent in punctuation – for every writer refers to it – has to be acknowledged. If we want a complete explanation of the way punctuation marks are used, we need to incorporate a further two perspectives that have received only passing mention in my historical account: semantics and pragmatics.

Interlude: The Good Child's Book of Stops

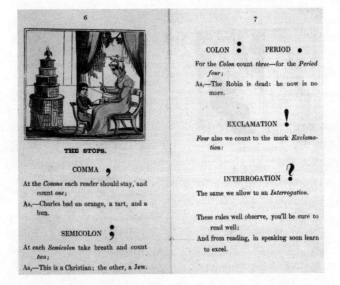

THE STOPS.

COMMA ,

At the *Comma* each reader should stay, and count *one*;

As,—Charles had an orange, a tart, and a bun.

SEMICOLON ;

At each *Semicolon* take breath and count *two*;

As,—This is a Christian; the other, a Jew.

COLON :   PERIOD •

For the *Colon* count *three*—for the *Period* *four*;

As,—The Robin is dead: he now is no more.

EXCLAMATION !

Four also we count to the mark *Exclamation:*

INTERROGATION ?

The same we allow to an *Interrogation.*

These rules well observe, you'll be sure to read well;

And from reading, in speaking soon learn to excel.

It didn't take long for nineteenth-century publishers to realize that punctuation presented children with difficulties similar to those encountered in spelling and grammar, and they began to publish colourful and playful accounts of the various marks. Leinstein Madame, as she is called on the title page of *The Good Child's Book of Stops*, which is undated, but appeared around 1825, is plainly an advocate of the phonetic approach. She recommends a steady increase in pause lengths as the child moves from comma to semicolon to colon to period. It's not as drastic an equation as the doubling method advocated by some earlier writers, which ended up with eight beats for a point; but it is still artificial, bearing no relation to what people actually do when reading aloud. Try reading any piece of prose aloud by counting in this way, and watch how quickly you lose your listeners.

11

The way forward: meanings and effects

One of the messages that comes across loud and clear over the centuries is that punctuation is all about meaning. That's the bottom line, whether we think of the written language as something to be read aloud or to be read in silence. It's the need to make the meaning of a written text clear that motivates our use of punctuation. Clarity. Making sense. Avoiding ambiguity. These are the words that turn up over and over in books and essays on punctuation. Authors continually stress the need to bear meaning or sense in mind when thinking about which mark to use. David Steel: 'Punctuation should lead to the sense.' John Wilson: 'The chief aim in pointing a discourse, and its several branches, is to develop, as clearly as possible, the *meaning* of the writer.' Meaning is the subject-matter of *semantics*, which is why a *semantic* approach to punctuation is important. Grammar plays a critical role in making sense, but other aspects of language contribute too, such as vocabulary and the way we talk about our tones of voice (*he said briskly*). When we are thinking of how to express something in writing, or working out what a piece of writing means, we take all these semantic cues into account.

But semantics alone is not enough to account for the way we use language. Often we're faced with a *choice* when we want to express a particular meaning – a choice that conveys different intentions or effects. In grammar, for example, we have the choice of writing *I will* or *I'll*: the meaning is the same, but the effect is different – the second usage is more informal than the first. Similarly, in punctuation we are sometimes offered a choice of forms, such as whether to use a comma or not, or whether to use single or double inverted commas, and we need to know what the consequences are of using one rather than the other. Authors continually stress the need for punctuation to be effective – to help orators or writers elicit a desired response in their listeners or readers – and this is a matter of choosing the right marks. Authors also find it important that a page should 'look' right, and this too is a matter of choosing the right marks. Making choices is at the heart of *pragmatics*, which is why a *pragmatic* approach to punctuation is important. It's here that we will explore many of the loose ends that we've seen bedevilling earlier accounts, such as references to a writer's 'judgement' or 'taste'.

We need to use both perspectives, semantic and pragmatic, when evaluating punctuation. If you find it difficult to understand what someone has written because of the way punctuation has been used, then you're reacting semantically. But if you don't like the look of what someone has written – saying, for example, that a page is 'cluttered' – then you're reacting pragmatically. Pragmatics is a particularly important perspective because it focuses on *explaining* rather than simply describing usage. Why did we use a particular punctuation mark? Why didn't we use some other mark instead? What was the intention of the writer? What was the effect upon the reader? The answers take us into a world well beyond linguistics, as they are to do with the writer's social background, cognitive skills, occupation, education, and aesthetic sensibility. No account of punctuation will ever succeed if it doesn't consider all these factors. And no-one will ever learn to punctuate well – or teach punctuation well – if they remain unaware of these factors, and how they interact.

The semantic approach is the one we see represented throughout the history of punctuation. As we saw earlier, it was the chief concern of many writers in antiquity, such as St Augustine, worrying over the ambiguity of signs, and it provides a continuous theme in later writing. During the eighteenth century especially, we find innumerable teaching exercises in which the student has to add marks to an unpunctuated piece of text in order to show its meaning. There are many ingenious examples. One of my favourites is the sentence used by the anonymous author of *The Expert Orthographist* (1704):

Christ saith St Peter died for us.

The author invites us to consider what would happen if we put a comma after *saith*, as opposed to two commas, after *Christ* and *Peter*. It's an early instance of *Eats, Shoots & Leaves*. In all such cases, punctuation resolves the difference between two (or more) meanings. This is semantics.

Teachers in the nineteenth century used to play semantic punctuation games, to make their students aware of the importance of the subject. This verse was very well known:

Every lady in this land
Hath twenty nails upon each hand;
Five and twenty on hands and feet:
And this is true, without deceit.

The student has to work out what has gone wrong, and present a correctly punctuated alternative:

Every lady in this land
Hath twenty nails; upon each hand
Five; and twenty on hands and feet:
And this is true, without deceit.

Percival Leigh does similar things in a short chapter on punctuation in his *Comic English Grammar* (1840). He recommends that a student consider 'the different effects which a piece of poetry, for instance, which he has been accustomed to regard as sublime or beautiful, will have, when liberties are taken with it in that respect'. And he takes liberties with Shakespeare to illustrate his approach, such as Macbeth's exclamation to his frightened servant:

Where get'st thou that goose look?

which he rewrites as:

Where get'st thou that goose? Look!

Teachers do the same sort of thing today.

The pragmatic approach can be illustrated from one of the main trends that affected punctuation during the twentieth century. In the early 1900s, people were showing their addresses in correspondence like this:

Mr. J. B. Smith,
144, Central Ave.,
London, S.W.1.

By the late 1900s, it was like this:

Mr J B Smith
144 Central Ave
London SW1

There's no difference in meaning between these two examples; but there is a major difference in fashion. A heavily punctuated style was normal at the beginning of the twentieth century; a punctuation minimalism at the end. This is pragmatics.

The pragmatic approach is not so often encountered in early writing on punctuation, though it's there in antiquity when writers discuss how to punctuate a text so that orators can be more effective in getting their message across. But pragmatic judgements about the use of punctuation increased as writing became stylistically more diverse. By the eighteenth century, legal, religious, journalistic, and historical writing had each developed its individual style of punctuation. As a result, to judge the punctuation in a piece of writing it became necessary not only to ask 'Is it clear?', but also 'Is it appropriate?' And a punctuation style that would be judged acceptable in one set of circumstances might well be judged unacceptable in another.

We need both semantic and pragmatic perspectives if we're to develop the kind of combined approach to punctuation I recommended at the end of the previous chapter. Successful communication, whether through speaking or writing, requires that we express ourselves clearly, and present our language in a way that allows our intention to be effectively conveyed to our addressee(s). And with each written communicative act, we need to make a decision as to whether we need punctuation – and if so, what kind – to enable this to happen.

Our choice of punctuation is going to be chiefly guided by semantic or pragmatic considerations. Normally, it will be semantics: we will aim to make our meaning clear to the reader. But there are occasions when pragmatic factors take precedence: we can decide to use a mark, or not use a mark, because it looks beautiful/ugly, because it's easier/more difficult to write/type/text, because it's available/unavailable in a chosen font, because it takes up more/less space on a page, or simply because we were taught that way (without necessarily knowing why). In particular, the 'look' of the page can become a priority in guiding our choices of which punctuation marks to use. This turns out to be a major factor in literary writing.

An aesthetic reason is clearly at the forefront of novelist Cormac McCarthy's mind. In an interview with Oprah Winfrey in 2008, he comments: 'There's no reason to blot the page up with weird little marks.' And in his most famous novel, *The Road* (2006), we see the result of this view (the extract is from p. 247):

> They hurried down the beach against the light. What if the boat washes away? the boy said.
>
> It wont wash away.
>
> It could.
>
> No it wont. Come on. Are you hungry?
>
> Yes.
>
> We're going to eat well tonight. But we need to get a move on.
>
> I'm hurrying, Papa.
>
> And it may rain.
>
> How can you tell?
>
> I can smell it.

Although the reason given for this sparse style is pragmatic – achieving an uncluttered look to the page – it's important to note that the choice is also partly semantic. The style gives an impression of bareness and simplicity, which works well with stories that have primitive, unsophisticated, or apocalyptic themes – and *The Road* is nothing if not apocalyptic.

Authors aren't always the best judges of their own writing when it comes to punctuation. McCarthy says: 'if you write properly you shouldn't have to punctuate ... I believe in periods, in capitals, in the occasional comma, and that's it.' But actually, that isn't it. Even in this short extract we see question marks, line indention, and some use of apostrophes – and in his interview he admits that colons are important, as when introducing a list. Writers do tend to underestimate the extent to which they rely on punctuation, even if they are minimalists.

We also need to note that choices in punctuation have consequences for other areas of language. A minimalist approach has an immediate effect on style. If you choose not to have quotation marks, you have to write in such a way that it's absolutely clear who is speaking. McCarthy knows this, and remarks about those writers who want to follow his style: 'you really have to be aware that there are no quotation marks to guide people and write in such a way that it's not confusing about who's speaking.' He himself puts in clues, as we see above with 'the boy said' and 'Papa'. The extract also illustrates how the conversational turns between partici-pants need to be short, so that the reader doesn't lose track. McCarthy acknowledges: 'It's important to punctuate so that it makes it easy for people to read.' But to do without marks such as semicolons, sentences also have to be short and structurally simple – as they are in McCarthy's style. As soon as they become complex, with many subordinate clauses, the pressure to add punctuation can't be ignored.

McCarthy admired James Joyce. 'James Joyce is a good model for punctuation. He keeps it to an absolute minimum.' When people say this, they're usually thinking of examples such as the final sequence in *Ulysses*, where Molly Bloom has a stream-of-consciousness soliloquy that goes on for over forty pages, and is punctuationless apart from occasional para-graph indention. Here Joyce is more daring than McCarthy, in that he makes no use at all of the apostrophe (he has *Im* for *I'm* as well as such forms as *couldnt* for *couldn't*). A new paragraph begins:

that was a relief wherever you be let your wind go free who knows if that pork chop I took with my cup of tea after was quite good with the heat I couldnt smell anything off it Im sure that queerlooking man in the porkbutchers is a great rogue I hope that lamp is not smoking fill my nose up with smuts better than having him leaving the gas on all night ...

But note the consequences for Joyce's sentence construction. In stream-of-consciousness, the sense-units being connected (sentences, clauses, phrases) are short and self-contained, enabling us to process it (or, as actors, to read it aloud) chunk by chunk. As soon as Joyce wants to go in for a multi-person dialogue or to develop an idea in a more complex way, this technique no longer works, and punctuation comes back in.

Most of *Ulysses* is punctuated. There are no quotation marks, but a long dash introduces a new speaker. As well as periods and commas, we find question marks, exclamation marks, apostrophes, colons, semicolons, and ellipsis dots. Even in Molly's soliloquy there are initial capitals for names, a few names in italics, forward slashes (as in *1/4*, and in abbreviations such as *6/-*), and an instance of letter substitution (*a--e* for *arse*). The impression of punctuation-lessness comes chiefly from the absence of quotation marks – a technique increasingly used by present-day writers, such as McCarthy, NoViolet Bulawayo (illustrated below), and Cynan Jones in *The Dig* (2014).

These examples illustrate the way creative writers can manipulate punctuation marks for semantic and pragmatic effect. But the success of their writing depends on their awareness of the consequences of these manipulations, otherwise readers won't be able to follow what is going on. If a writer deviates too far from the conventional use of punctuation, the result can be ambiguity or unintelligibility (from a semantic point of view) or inappropriateness or unacceptability (from a pragmatic point of view). A poet might get away with a lot of rule-breaking – as we will see in the case of E E Cummings (or e e cummings, as later writers, delighting in his penchant for typographical innovation, described him) – but most writing circumstances don't allow a great deal of deviance.

At least, when you're alive, you can make your own case to the publisher about preserving your desired punctuation. But what happens after you're dead? A different character now joins the company of punctuation-deciders listed in Chapter 10: the literary editor, ready to make fresh semantic and pragmatic decisions.

Interlude: Punctuation minimalism

The impression of unsophisticated innocence in NoViolet Bulawayo's story *We Need New Names* (2013) is well conveyed by the absence of quotation marks. The child narrator, from Africa but now living in America, describes how she met a woman at a wedding (the extract is from Chapter 12):

Can you just say something in your language? she says. I laugh a small laugh, because what do you say to that? But the woman is fixing me with this expectant stare, which means she is not playing, so I say:

I don't know, what do you want me to say?

Well, anything, really.

I let out an inward sigh because this is so stupid, but I remember to keep my face smiling. I say one word, *sa-li-bo-na-ni*, and I say it slowly so she doesn't ask me to repeat it. She doesn't.

Isn't that beautiful, she says. Now she's looking at me like I'm a wonder, like I just made magic happen.

What language is that? she says. I tell her, and she tells me it's beautiful, again, and I tell her thank you. Then she asks me what country I'm from and I tell her.

It's beautiful over there, isn't it? she says. I nod even though I don't know why I'm nodding. I just do. To this lady, maybe everything is beautiful.

12

Interfering with Jane Austen

This is the opening sentence of Jane Austen's *Persuasion* (1818):

> Sir Walter Elliot, of Kellynch Hall, in Somersetshire, was a man who, for his own amusement, never took up any book but the Baronetage; there he found occupation for an idle hour, and consolation in a distressed one; there his faculties were roused into admiration and respect, by contemplating the limited remnant of the earliest patents; there any unwelcome sensations, arising from domestic affairs changed naturally into pity and contempt as he turned over the almost endless creations of the last century; and there, if every other leaf were powerless, he could read his own history with an interest which never failed.

Readers have long admired the balanced and elegant character of this sentence, with its three *there*-constructions building up a rhetorical peak, subtly linked by semicolons. But the punctuation is almost certainly spurious. That's not how she wrote at all.

We know this thanks to a splendid project, led by Professor Kathryn Sutherland of the University of Oxford, which has collated all the extant handwritten fiction manuscripts of Jane Austen in digital form. You can see them online at the appropriately named <www.janeausten.ac.uk>. There isn't very much, as all the original manuscripts of the novels were

the joke exceedingly. Anne thought his
triumph over Stephen rather too long.
At last however, he was able to in-
vite her upstairs, & stepping before her
said — "I will just go up with
you myself & shew you in — I cannot
stay, because I must go to the P. Office,
but if you will only sit down for
5 minutes I am sure Sophy will
come — and you will find nobody
to disturb you — there is nobody but
Frederick here —" opening the door as
he spoke. — Such a person to be passed
over as a Nobody to her! After being
allowed to feel quite secure — indifferent
— at her ease, to have it burst on her
that she was to be the next moment
in the same room with him!
No time for recollection! — for planning behaviour, or regulating man-
ners! There was time only to turn
pale, before she had passed through the
door, & met the astonished eyes of
Captain Wentworth who was sitting in the
fire, pretending to read & prepared for
no greater surprise than the Admiral's
hasty return. — Equally unexpected
was the meeting on each side. There
was nothing to be done however but
to stifle feelings & be quietly polite;
and the Admiral was too much on the

Page 4 of the rejected Chapter 10 of Persuasion. *It is written in brown iron-gall ink – a medium used by most English writers from the Middle Ages until the twentieth century. The quoted extract begins at line 3.*

destroyed after the books were printed – routine practice in an age long before author's holographs came to be valued in the way they are today. But what survives gives us a remarkable insight into her way of writing. And it is a goldmine for punctuation enthusiasts.

Here's a short extract from *Persuasion*, from one of two chapters (page 4 of Chapter 10) which are the only surviving examples in Austen's handwriting of a novel that was completed for publication. If you know the book well, you won't recognize the text because these chapters were replaced in the published version. She changed the ending – and fortunately the unrevised text was never destroyed.

> At last however, he was able to in:
> :vite her upstairs, & stepping before her
> said — "I ~~shall~~ will just go up with
> you myself & shew you in — I cannot
> stay, because I must go to the P. office,   5
> but if you will only sit down for
> 5 minutes I am sure Sophy will
> come. —— and you will find nobody
> to disturb you — there is nobody but
> Frederick here —" opening the door as   10
> he spoke. — Such a person to be paſsed
> over as a Nobody to <u>her</u>! — After being
> allowed to feel quite secure — indifferent
> —at her ease, to have it burst on her
> that she was to be the next moment   15
> in the same room with him! —
> No time for recollection! — for plan:
> :ning behaviour, or regulating man:
> :ners! — There was time only to turn
> pale, ...

I've chosen an extract where there is hardly any crossing-out, so that the style can be more easily seen. There are several interesting punctuation features. Word-breaks at the end of a line aren't signalled by hyphens, but by two colons – one at the end of the first line and the other at the beginning of the next (a throwback to the ancient tradition described in Chapter 3). Frequent exclamation marks convey the character's excitement. And above all, there are the dashes – a notable characteristic of Austen's style.

Handwriting does many things that print cannot do. The spatial relation of lines to each other can alter dramatically. Letter-sizes can vary enormously in a way that the contrast between upper-case and lower-case cannot capture. And if a dash is there to represent a pause, then the length of the dash tells us something that is lost when all dashes are reduced to a single piece of type in print. Look at the long dash in line 8, for example. Why such length? Read on in the novel. It anticipates 'opening the door as he spoke'.

You won't see many dashes in the published book. We'd expect a publisher to do a certain amount of polishing, such as removing handwritten abbreviations (*&* vs *and*), correcting spelling mistakes (*recieve*), and ensuring house-style consistency (*judgment* vs *judgement*); but what Austen's editor did was far more radical. As Sutherland points out in *Jane Austen's Textual Lives* (2005), the manuscripts were normalized either by an editor at her publisher's (John Murray) or by a corrector in the printing-house. New paragraphing is introduced. Sentence construction is changed to follow prescriptive norms. Gone are her rhetorical dashes and her use of initial capitals on common nouns. And there is a huge amount of repunctuation, as seen in Sutherland's comparison of a section of manuscript in Austen's hand and the final text as it was printed.

M^rs^. Clay's affections had overpowered her Interest, & she had sacrificed for the Young Man's sake, the possibility of scheming longer for Sir Walter;--she has Abilities however as well as Affections, and it is now a doubtful point whether his cunning or hers may finally carry the day, whether, after preventing her from being the wife of Sir Walter, he may not be wheedled & caressed at last into making her the wife of Sir William.---

Mrs. Clay's affections had overpowered her interest, and she had sacrificed, for the young man's sake, the possibility of scheming longer for Sir Walter. She has abilities, however, as well as affections; and it is now a doubtful point whether his cunning, or hers, may finally carry the day; whether, after preventing her from being the wife of Sir Walter, he may not be wheedled and caressed at last into making her the wife of Sir William.

Whoever corrected this is clearly under the influence of the heavy punctuational style recommended by the nine-teenth-century grammarians I described in Chapter 8. And, as Sutherland points out, the process continued into the twentieth century, with subsequent editions reflecting later prescriptive preferences. For example, R W Chapman, whose five-volume edition appeared in 1923, considered the novels 'under-punctuated'. Sutherland reports an instance when Chapman asked the *Oxford English Dictionary* editor Henry Bradley for advice about how to punctuate the phrase 'a quick looking girl' (describing Susan Price in *Mansfield Park*). Should he use a comma or a hyphen? Bradley's response (a letter of 14 February 1922) is illuminating: do neither.

> Your alternatives of comma and hyphen imply different constructions, and I am not quite sure which is right, or whether the author may not have felt the collocation as

> something between the two ... is it not possible that if we
> demand that it *must* be either comma or hyphen, we shall
> be insisting on a precision of grammatical analysis which
> punctuation has rendered instructive to readers of today,
> but which *c*1800 only a grammarian would be capable of?

Chapman let Austen's version stand in this instance; but in many other cases he implemented a policy, following the tradition going back to Lindley Murray, that punctuation exists to foster grammatical precision. And Sutherland concludes:

> he prepared a text which actively and misguidedly promoted
> Austen's twentieth-century reputation as a conformant and
> prim stylistician.

The issues now go well beyond the linguistic, and raise fundamental questions about the role of editorial intervention in literature, and what exactly we are studying when we analyse the linguistic choices encountered in a text. Austen is not an isolated case. Many other authors have had their punctuation emended in a similar way.

In the case of Daniel Defoe's *Robinson Crusoe*, we have an even more complex situation, as several printers were involved, and there is no surviving author's manuscript. Defoe's publisher, William Taylor, farmed the manuscript out to a printer, Henry Parker, and the first edition appeared on 25 April 1719. Demand was so great that a second edition was required, and this was set in a hurry by three different printers, appearing two weeks later. A month later, there were two further editions set by the same three printers, and two more in August set by Parker alone. The textual variations introduced by the printers are an editorial nightmare for anyone trying to establish a version that comes closest to what Defoe intended. And variations in punctuation, according to Evan

R Davies, the editor of the Broadview 2010 edition, are most frequent of all. He writes:

> To a reader accustomed to twenty-first grammatical conventions, the first edition of Robinson Crusoe can seem hopelessly mispunctuated, replete with fragmented clauses, run-on sentences, capricious commas.

He illustrates with a short comparison:

1st edition	6th edition
I consulted several Things in my Situation which I found would be proper for me, 1st. Health, and fresh Water I just now mention'd, 2dly. Shelter from the Heat of the Sun, 3dly. Security from ravenous Creatures, whether Men or Beasts, …	I consulted several Things in my Situation which I found would be proper for me, 1st. Health, and fresh Water I just now mention'd. 2ndly, Shelter from the Heat of the Sun. 3dly, Security from ravenous Creatures, whether Man or Beast. …

Apart from the lexical changes (such as *Men* to *Man*), we see a grammatical punctuation replacing the rhetorical style. However, there is nothing 'capricious' about it. Both versions are systematic, but the later edition shows the clear influence of a printer wishing to make a text conform to the rules as laid down in the grammars of the time.

Those who have edited the few surviving manuscripts in Defoe's hand have noted a highly individual style, with idiosyncratic abbreviations and little punctuation. Davies generally keeps the punctuation of the first edition except where 'the meaning of the prose is seriously undermined', in which case he uses the punctuation of later editions. And, crucially, he gives a list of these changes – an eminently desirable practice that ought to be followed universally. For example, on p. 51, we read:

> in an ill Hour, God knows, on the first of *September* 1651 I
> went on Board a Ship bound for *London;*

We learn that the first edition has a period after 'knows'.
Nobody would disagree with the decision in this case. But
the few instances where there is clearly an error are far out-
numbered by the hundreds of instances where any emendation would be a matter of stylistic choice.

Modern editions have continued to make the punctuation
conform to modern standards, as with Austen, so that the
present-day reader encounters a text that is orthographically
familiar. But ease of reading is gained at the expense of a
distancing from Defoe's style – and in this case, from the
character of the narrator, Crusoe. As Davies concludes:

> Whether by accident or by art, Defoe created a text that
> matches its protagonist: neither Strunk nor White, but
> sprawling, rambling, and discursive.

William Strunk Jr and E B White are the authors of a good-
usage manual, originally published in 1919 – the equivalent,
to American readers, of Fowler in Britain.

Novelists who use as little punctuation as possible do so
in an interesting way. They omit the features that were later
arriving in the history of English orthography, as described in
Chapter 6, such as quotation marks, semicolons, and apostrophes. They don't usually (James Joyce is an exception)
mess about with the oldest features, such as periods and
paragraphs. The same applies to poets whose punctuation
is highly idiosyncratic: there may be variation in the use of
one kind of feature (such as the use of dashes), but there is
respect for others, such as stanza separation and the identity
of the poetic line. All of this suggests that writers manipulate
some features of orthography more readily than others.

This is indeed the case. As in any system, some features of punctuation have a critical role: the system would collapse if they were not there. Other features are less important: if they were missing, the written language would survive. We see this selectivity in practice in writers like Cormac McCarthy, as well as in the distinctive markings observed in the oldest English manuscripts. And from it we reach a conclusion of major significance for anyone involved in teaching or learning about punctuation: some marks are more important than others. The system, in a word, is hierarchical.

Interlude: Another case: Emily Dickinson

 In the case of Emily Dickinson, we do have manuscripts, also written in a distinctively punctuated personal style, and this has caused not a little anxiety among some editors. For example, in the Random House 2000 edition of her *Selected Poems*, there is a Note on the Text as follows:

> Dickinson wrote her poems in an eccentric longhand which featured the capitalization of substantive nouns and the use of the dash as a form of all-purpose punctuation. ... In order to make the poems more accessible to the eye of the modern reader, the oddities of punctuation and capitalization have been regularized in this edition.

The result can be illustrated by comparing two poems:

No. 113 in *Emily Dickinson: The Complete Poems* (Faber and Faber, 1970)

Our share of night to bear –
Our share of morning –
Our blank in bliss to fill
Our blank in scorning –
Here a star, and there a star,
Some lose their way!
Here a mist, and there a
   mist,
Afterwards – Day!

No. 2 in *The Selected Poems of Emily Dickinson* (Random House, 2000)

Our share of night to bear,
Our share of morning,
Our blank in bliss to fill,
Our blank in scorning.
Here a star, and there a star,
Some lose their way.
Here a mist, and there a
   mist,
Afterwards – day!

Is the regularized version really 'more accessible'? And are we really reading Emily Dickinson in the 2000 edition? Not to my mind.

Is there a punctuation system?

Some punctuation marks are more important than others, either because they mark a major pause or because they show a major grammatical break. This means that punctuation is a hierarchy, in which some visual features identify the largest units of writing and others identify smaller ones. And it's a hierarchy that exists regardless of whether you see punctuation as primarily a representation of speech or of grammar.

It seems an obvious point, yet this principle is not apparent in the way the grammarians, printers, and editors of earlier centuries introduced the subject. We would expect the most important orthographic features to have been dealt with first, in their expositions. That's certainly how present-day teachers work, when teaching young children to write. They want them to 'write in sentences', and that means, first and foremost, learning to use full stops, or periods. Here's an illustration, from a four-book series called *Punctuation*, by F W Ledgard, published in 1977, aimed at students from age eleven upwards. The opening chapter of Book 1 is called 'Full Stop', and it begins:

> Reading is like driving a car or riding a bicycle. For some
> of the time you go smoothly along but every now and then
> you have to stop. When you are driving or cycling, you have
> a STOP sign or red traffic light to make sure you stop at
> the end of a road and don't have an accident. These are the
> most important of all road signs.

> In reading you have a stop sign as well. It is called the
> FULL STOP (.) and there must be one at the end of every
> sentence. Of all punctuation marks it is the most important.
> Whenever you see one, you must stop. If you take no notice
> of the full stop and go straight on, you will have an accident
> with your reading just as you would with a car or a bicycle.

The advice isn't perfect, as full stops are not the only punctuation marks used at the ends of sentences, but the emphasis is correct. Full stops are crucial for coherent reading and writing. They are 'the most important'.

It is an emphasis we don't find in the early writers. As I mentioned at the end of Chapter 10, everyone began their accounts with the comma, then went on to the semicolon and colon, and ended with the full stop. I have found no exceptions. The authors seem to have been instinctively following the long-standing tradition I described earlier of moving from the shortest pause to the longest, reinforced by the feeling that, because there were more problems to be dealt with relating to the use of the comma, these should be handled first. We see the back-to-front presentation even in the simplest accounts, such as *The Good Child's Book of Stops* (p. 86), where the period isn't even given a separate section, but lumped together with the colon for poetic reasons. Nobody was ever going to get a good sense of punctuation as a system of marks that way.

System is the operative word here, as it always is in linguistic description. In pronunciation, we talk about the 'vowel system' or the 'intonation system'; in grammar we talk about the 'tense system' or the 'pronoun system'. What does this mean? It means there is a choice to be made. Within a system, the language provides us with a set of options from which we choose whenever we say or write something. If I decide to use a personal pronoun at the beginning of my sentence, I have a seven-way choice: *I, you, he, she, it, we, they*. I could start the following sentence with any of them:

--- fell down.

Notice that we use only one member of the system at a time, at any one place in the discourse. We say *I fell down, You fell down*, and so on. If I opt for *he*, I immediately 'tell' my listener that I'm not talking about *I, you, she, it, we, they*. If I opt for *they*, I exclude all the other possibilities. And the same point applies even if I join two pronouns together: *You and I* contrasts with *You and he* or *He and she*.

Some systems, such as pronouns, have several members. Some have just two. Consider modern English nouns, which operate with a number system. We have a choice between just two members: singular and plural – *horse* vs *horses*. The meaning is 'one' vs 'more than one'. The two meanings define each other. Just as with pronouns, to choose one of the members excludes the other. This is a crucial principle, when we start thinking about punctuation, because – despite its apparently chaotic character – this is a system too.

When we talk about punctuation as a system, we mean that, at any one place in a written discourse, a choice has to be made from the set of options the language makes available. As with grammar, the marks define each other. And as with grammar, choosing one of the members excludes the others. So the important thing – the really important thing – is to be aware of what the options are, at any place in the discourse as we read or write. What options are available to us at the top level in the punctuation hierarchy? What options are available at lower levels?

This way of looking at punctuation isn't just abstract reasoning. It reflects everyday practice. Faced with the task of writing a sentence, the decision has to be made: how shall

I punctuate it? At the end of the sentence, what options are available to me? At the beginning, what options are available to me? In the middle, what options are available to me? And what options are available, faced with a blank page, on paper or screen, before I start writing anything at all?

The blank page. This is the real starting point. And it's something that was ignored by the early grammarians. The manuscript writers of antiquity recognized its importance, as we saw earlier, but – presumably because it was so obvious – it was taken for granted in the age of print. And yet this is the first thing to be decided. It is the topmost level of the hierarchy. If I am writing, where do I start on the page, and what are my options, as I put pen to paper or finger to keyboard? If I am reading, where do I look first, and what options has the writer used to guide me through the text?

14

Starting at the top

Within a continuous piece of writing, or *text* – whether it be a book, a chapter, an essay, a newspaper report, a letter, a signpost, an email, a blog … – two things immediately stand out: the individual words, and the blocks of writing into which the text is organized. Space is the defining factor that gives each its identity. Words, identified by the spaces that surround them, are at the bottom of the punctuation hierarchy, and I'll discuss issues to do with their identification later. At the top of the hierarchy are the linguistic units that stand out because of the way they've been placed against the white space of the page or screen. These raise issues of punctuation that go above and beyond the level of the individual sentence.

What are these units? They are the elements that convey the semantic organization of a text, such as title, subtitle, chapter heading, subheading, headline, running head, footnote, caption, page number, address, signature, and of course the body copy of the text. From a pragmatic point of view, they convey the writer's opinion as to the importance and relevance of the element in the text as a whole. In some texts, such as a school essay, the organization may be minimal, displaying little more than a heading and body copy, along with its paragraphing. In others, such as a retail website, there may be a complex visual organization in which multiple elements compete for attention. At this point we enter the domain of graphic design, which deals with issues (such as

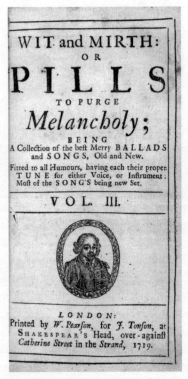

The title page of Wit and Mirth, *British Library, G.18343–8.*

layout, choice of font, and the use of colour) that go well beyond the subject of this book.

But in all cases, the question has to be addressed: to punctuate or not to punctuate? If a writer wishes to draw the attention of a reader to a particular part of a text, how is this to be done? Is punctuation to be used, or will other features perform the same role? Fashions change, in this respect. In earlier printed texts, title pages were often heavily punctuated, as we see with *Wit and Mirth* (1719).

Masthead of the Oxford Gazette, *British Library 97.h.1*

The title on the front page of the first English newspaper (1665) is also end-pointed. And running heads in books (such as the one at the top of this page) were routinely ended with a period until the twentieth century. These are all seen as archaic practices today, where the stylistic fashion is to have elements of this kind look as uncluttered as possible. We rarely (never?) see a period in a title or heading today.

But the issue of whether to punctuate remains a live option. For example, in 2014, an author and a copy-editor had an exchange over whether to use a colon in chapter headings that were all of the following kind:

From *mint* to *dosh*: words for money

This is how the heading appears in the Contents. But in the chapter itself, there is a new layout and typography which made the colon redundant:

From *mint* to *dosh*
WORDS FOR MONEY

The author (me, in this case) accepted the design decision, though he continued to feel that the semantic dependence of the two parts of the heading would have been reinforced by the use of the colon.

We are so used to reading the punctuational conventions of our own time that it's easy to forget that these are just that – conventions – and that they have to be learned. Children have to learn them when they first engage with literacy. When writing, they have to decide on the location of their written language on the page (leaving margins at the head, foot, and sides), and whether to punctuate it. In reading, they have to evaluate the significance of what other writers have done. They will tend to copy what they've seen in their reading books, but a common early practice is to add marks all over the place. Having noticed punctuation – or having had their attention drawn to it by a parent or teacher – they use it ubiquitously, until the overuse is pointed out. I recall one youngster (age about seven) who put a full stop at the end of every line of his story, regardless of sense. Another who put one between each word of the story title. Yet another had a fascination with semicolons. When I asked her why she used them so much, she replied that she liked the size and that they were pretty. And when I suggested that a full stop was the normal way of ending a sentence, she looked very dubious, and observed that if you wanted to show something had come to an end, then surely the bigger the better?

A historical perspective is always useful when it comes to understanding a present-day punctuation practice. Virtually all the issues (the obvious exception is the Internet) have been identified and debated in earlier times, and it's well worth reflecting on the strengths and weaknesses of the decisions made by these writers in order to see why some conventions were dropped and why others have continued in use. Although general issues to do with the overall semantic and pragmatic organization of a text were rarely explicitly discussed by writers on punctuation coming from the elocution or grammatical traditions, they were very much in the mind of writers in antiquity.

As we saw in Chapter 3, in the discussion of old manuscripts, there were several ways of marking a new section in a piece of writing. The first letter of the opening word might be enlarged, coloured, or decorated. A special mark might be placed in the margin, such as an ivy-leaf or diple (>). In later manuscripts, we see a specific paragraph mark, or paraph, ¶, and this was taken over by printers as the *pilcrow*. Anyone who reads the sixteenth-century *Book of Common Prayer* will see it used to mark significant changes in the discourse, such as:

¶ *Then shall the Priest saye.*

Present-day liturgical texts often continue the practice, such as identifying a change of speaker in a dialogue exchange:

¶ *Minister.* Lord hear our prayers.
¶ *Answer.* And let our cry come unto thee.

We also see the pilcrow in documents with sequentially numbered paragraphs, such as often appear in legal and academic texts. And it has entered the electronic age. The pilcrow doesn't have a presence on keyboards (though it can be found in any list of Special Symbols), reflecting the way it has gone out of general use. But it's still there in Microsoft Word and some other text management systems as a hidden symbol showing a carriage return.

The pilcrow may not be in everyday use, but the linguistic feature it represented is still as important a feature of written language as it ever was: the semantic division of a text into sections. It's important to note that – notwithstanding the word's etymology – we are here talking about sections, not paragraphs. A section might be a single paragraph, but more often it includes a series. In *The Book of Common Prayer*, the pilcrowed headings are often followed by several paragraphs. In a modern novel, a section can include an indefinite number of paragraphs running over several pages.

Section-breaks show the way writers have organized their text into semantic units. We often see them within the chapters of a book, representing a thematic shift that's greater than the one that motivates a new paragraph, but not so great that it motivates a new chapter. It can mark a scene-change, a new character, an alternative time frame, or any general shift of narrative perspective. Here's an example from the opening lines of a novel (Hilary Crystal's *The Memors*, 2013):

> On Saturday the twelfth of June, three things happened to Mikey, aged four years and two months. Two good things and one bad thing.
>
> The two good things. He put his wellington boots on all by himself, on the right feet, for the first time. He went to the park with his Mum and his sister, and learned how to make a swing go all by himself.
>
> And the bad thing? Something frightened him, and he didn't know what it was. But the really bad bit was afterwards, when he was scared because he couldn't remember, and couldn't remember why he was scared.
>
> He wasn't the only one.
>
> ***
>
> Bob Holpweed tucked the local newspaper under his arm and went to the park. ...

Here the section-break introduces a new character and a new series of events. If it were not there, it would seem as if Bob

Holpweed was part of the first topic, and was scared like Mikey, which is certainly not the case.

Because section-breaks are important semantically, they need to be clearly identified. So, if we decide to use them, what punctuational options are available to us? The simplest way is to introduce a larger amount of white space than would normally be used between paragraphs. It would be possible to print the above example as follows:

... because he couldn't remember, and couldn't remember why he was scared.

He wasn't the only one.

Bob Holpweed tucked the local newspaper under his arm and went to the park. ...

The problem with extra white space, though, is that it's invisible in certain locations. If a section happened to end at the bottom of a page, the contrast between section-break and paragraph-ending would disappear. Spacing is also of less value when paragraphs have no indention and are separated by a line of white space, as in the following kind of setting. With two degrees of white space, the contrast is not so easy to see.

On Saturday the twelfth of June, three things happened to Mikey, aged four years and two months. Two good things and one bad thing.

The two good things. He put his wellington boots on all by himself, on the right feet, for the first time. He went to the park with his Mum and his sister, and learned how to make a swing go all by himself.

And the bad thing? Something frightened him, and he didn't know what it was. But the really bad bit was afterwards, when he was scared because he couldn't remember, and couldn't remember why he was scared.

He wasn't the only one.

Bob Holpweed tucked the local newspaper under his arm and went to the park. ...

This is an unusual setting for novels, but it's commonplace these days in letters, business reports, web pages, and many kinds of official document.

The problem of white-space ambiguity is solved by the introduction of a punctuation mark of some kind. *The Memors* uses triple asterisks (called a *dinkus*), with extra space above and below. In other texts we may see single asterisks, longer sequences of asterisks, three asterisks placed in a triangle (⁂, called an *asterism* – there's an example on p. 131), a sequence of dots or dashes, a horizontal rule, or some ornamental symbol such as a stylized form of a leaf (such as ❧, the hedera of old manuscripts, now called a *fleuron*). A wide range of characters can provide a section-spacing function, easily visible online under the heading of *dingbats* – a term whose origin is obscure, but which has similarities to words invented to describe entities that have no obvious name (like *dingus*, *doobery*, *thingummy*). They include geometrical shapes with variable ornamentation, such as stars, crosses, diamonds, squares, and circles. Choosing a dingbat may involve pragmatic considerations, as some of the symbols (such as a cross) can convey a cultural meaning that the writer may not intend.

Ornamental marks of this kind raise more general pragmatic issues. They are evidently felt to be appropriate for artistic texts, for we see many such symbols in novels, short stories, and poems. We also see them in nonfiction works intended for a general readership. But they are conspicuous by their absence in academic and technical writing, business reports, legal documents, and other texts of a formal or official kind. In such contexts, sections tend to be numbered or have their numbers preceded by a formal section mark (§), which allows succinct and convenient cross-reference. The section-mark also allows a number contrast: '§3', '§§3–5'.

The benefit of numerical punctuation is that it allows unlimited extension, though the longer the sequence, the more difficult it will be to remember and the more likely there will be errors in cross-referencing. A complex hierarchical system, though, requires a correspondingly complex sectioning, as with the conceptual divisions in the paper edition of *The Historical Thesaurus of the Oxford English Dictionary*, where we see numerical sections extending to many subdivisions:

03.10.13.15.05.01.04 (*n.*) *Channel Islands coins*
double 1862 · Jersey penny 1862– (*now History*)

Following the numbers back through the hierarchy, we are taken to:

03.10.13.15.05.01 *Coins collectively*
03.10.13.15.05 *Currency*
03.10.13.15 *Money*
03.10.13 *Trade and commerce*
03.10 *Occupation/work*
03 *Society*

What is notable about such cases is the way other typographical conventions help to keep the entries legible, such as the use of bold, italic, and roman fonts, and indention for the lexical examples. White space also separates the entries, to avoid the page appearing too dense:

03.10.13.15.05.01.03 (*n.*) *Irish coins*
harp 1542–1606 · harp-groat 1543 · harped groat 1547
· rose-pence 1556 · smulkin 1571; 1617 · harp-shilling
1591; a1592 · harper 1598–1839 · patrick 1673/4 · thirteen
c1720–1830 · fourpence-halfpenny 1722–1872 · thirteener
1762–1836 · tenpenny 1822–1825 · thirteen-penny 1828 ·
sun-groat 1861 · twenty-pence piece 1990–

03.10.13.15.05.01.04 (*n.*) *Channel Islands coins*
double 1862 · Jersey penny 1862– (*now History*)

03.10.13.15.05.01.05 (*n.*) *Foreign coins*
pening OE · pund OE · shilling<scilling OE-1776 · crown …

There is an immediate reduction in legibility if the white
space is removed:

03.10.13.15.05.01.03 (*n.*) *Irish coins*
harp 1542–1606 · harp-groat 1543 · harped groat 1547
· rose-pence 1556 · smulkin 1571; 1617 · harp-shilling
1591; a1592 · harper 1598–1839 · patrick 1673/4 · thirteen
c1720–1830 · fourpence-halfpenny 1722–1872 · thirteener
1762–1836 · tenpenny 1822–1825 · thirteen-penny 1828 ·
sun-groat 1861 · twenty-pence piece 1990–
03.10.13.15.05.01.04 (*n.*) *Channel Islands coins*
double 1862 · Jersey penny 1862– (*now History*)
03.10.13.15.05.01.05 (*n.*) *Foreign coins*
pening OE · pund OE · shilling<scilling OE-1776 · crown …

Imagine a whole page like that. The Plain English Campaign
in the UK makes no bones about it: 'Use white space' is one
of the basic recommendations in their online 'Guide to design
and layout'. And they explain:

Many people work hard on their writing style yet pay little
attention to how their words appear on the page. They

don't realise, for example, that pages dense with body text are very off-putting.

It's a recommendation for everyone, even young learners. Children sense the value of the white space surrounding the pictures and text in their first reading books, and we often see their recognition of its value in their first attempts at continuous writing, in the way they locate their name and date at the top of a story, or lay out their words. And if a child has failed to appreciate the importance of spacing, this is the very first thing a parent or teacher needs to draw their attention to.

There's quite a lot to be learned, as being in control over white space involves several considerations. David Mackay and Joseph Simo identified six variables in their best-selling *Help Your Child to Read and Write, and More* (1976):

- you have to leave appropriate margins on each side of your lines
- your lines should be horizontal between these margins
- your letters should have spaces between them (until you learn 'joined up')
- your words should have consistent word spaces between them
- your sentences have to have consistent sentence spaces between them
- your lines of writing should have consistent line spaces between them.

And they observe:

Children do not easily manage to control all these until they have had considerable practice in writing their own texts. They will take longer to do so if left to find them out for themselves. Discussion of the physical aspects of a book, including the lay-out of the pages, will help them to understand what they themselves must do as writers.

For punctuation, this perspective is essential, because the contrast between the use of space and the use of marks underlies the entire orthographic system. Punctuation is all about making divisions to aid understanding in writing, and these divisions can be shown either by a physical mark or by manipulating the extent of the white space. Adapting what I said above: to mark, or not to mark, that is the question. Do I let space do the job, or do I rely on special marks to do it, or do I use a combination of the two? This is the first set of options that we all have to decide about when we start our journey along the punctuation road.

Interlude: Learning about layout

April 18th
I am going to a
party. Andrew will go
to the swimming-bath
with someone I know
he is called philip. I
have not done. the
invitation. yes said
my daddy to me you
have not done the
invitation. I am going
to do it when I
get home

This example of a handwritten story from a six-year-old boy
(reproduced in David Mackay and Joseph Simo's *Help Your
Child to Read and Write, and More*) shows that a great deal of
learning about the function of white space has already taken
place. There are two thematic elements – the date and the
story – clearly demarcated by their location. The page boundaries are not visible in this scan, but there are good left-hand
and right-hand margins, and the lines are quite well justified
on the left. Spaces between lines are erratic, but he has not
done badly considering there were no rules on the page to
guide him. Word-spaces are fairly regular, as are the spaces
between sentences.

A traditional view of punctuation would home in on the
erratic use of full stops and the lack of inverted commas
around the direct speech. But these have to be weighed
against the many positive features of layout, as well as the
signs of more specific progress (the capitalized *I*, the hyphen
in *swimming-bath*). Any marking of this story that highlighted

only the errors would be doing this child a disservice. As Mackay and Simo point out:

> This little boy has a clear idea of what a page should look like. He has mastered almost all the problems and has only to refine what he already knows about handwriting.

But how often is such progress recognized in the kind of testing that young children are subjected to these days?

15

Paragraph preferences

In preparing to write something, our first decision – after we've chosen where to place our text on the page or screen – is whether to present it as a single block of writing or to divide it into sections. That's the top level in the punctuation hierarchy. The next decision is whether what we have to say is thematically so varied that we need to use paragraphs.

Organizing our writing into paragraphs has been a standard part of an English-teaching syllabus for generations. Traditional stylistic recommendations included the need for semantic coherence (the 'unity' of the paragraph) and semantic focus (if the paragraph has several sentences, one of them must be 'in control' – what is usually called the *topic sentence*). Older style guides insisted on more than one sentence per paragraph, usually at least three; but novelists, journalists, and now websites have shown that it's perfectly possible to write rhetorically effective single-sentence paragraphs. Some publishing guides recommended an upper limit (such as six sentences) to avoid paragraphs becoming visually difficult to assimilate – a helpful suggestion, as paragraphs that take up most or all of a page are certainly difficult to follow, and in non-literary writing raise questions about the writer's ability to focus. The style guides also generally insisted on the topic sentence appearing at the beginning of a paragraph – again, a helpful recommendation, but one that good writing has shown to be artificial if it's interpreted too rigidly.

For most writers, the punctuation decision in relation to a paragraph is so obvious that it hardly needs to be thought about: one indents the first line. The procedure is called *indention* or *indentation* – the choice reflects different publisher preferences – the former being more widely used, probably because it shows a closer relation with the verb (to *indent*, not to *indentate*). But even this apparently simple procedure reflects choices from a set of options. We can choose to indent, to 'outdent', or to do neither of these things.

If we take the last course, then we need some alternative way of showing that a paragraph has come to an end, and this is done by the use of extra white space, as we saw in the previous chapter. It's a style that works well enough for short texts, such as typed letters and emails, but it fails in longer texts, for the same sort of reason that white space between sections fails: at the bottom of a page, if the last line of the paragraph happens to reach the right-hand margin, it's immediately ambiguous whether the paragraph has come to an end or not.

In texts such as letters, the choice between an indented or an unindented ('full-block') style is a pragmatic one, reflecting what is fashionable at a particular time. (The semantic content will be the same whichever method is used.) In English, the current fashion is for the full-block style. One advisory website (Lynn Gaertner-Johnston's *Business Writing*) describes this style, where nothing is indented (including the date, address (of the recipient), salutation, closure, and signature), as 'modern and sleek'. She contrasts this with a 'modified block style', in which the letter-openings and -closings are centred – a style she describes as 'less modern and sleek'. This in turn is contrasted with a 'modified-block style with indented paragraphs', which she describes as 'fussy and dated looking'. And she concludes:

If your organization wants to come across as up to date and elegant, choose the full-block style. If you want to appear up to date yet a bit traditional, consider the modified-block style. If you want to appear traditional and old-fashioned, the modified-block style with indented paragraphs might work, but remember that it doesn't look elegant.

Notions such as 'traditional' and 'elegance' may be subjective, but they are significant, and are involved at every level of the punctuation hierarchy. At the end of the day, getting the pragmatics right is perceived to be more important than any other kind of reasoning, as it can condition whether a recipient is going to be bothered to read a text at all – or, in the case of a book, whether to buy it. In the case of children learning to read, pragmatic decisions of this kind can be influential in determining whether the literacy task is made easier or more difficult.

Note that pragmatic considerations relate especially to the genre in which we are writing. I have never seen an indented email, for example. The technology motivates each paragraph of the text to start at the left-hand edge of the screen. A carriage-return automatically locates the cursor at the beginning of the line, and it would take an effort of will to introduce an indent. In writing for a blog or a website, similarly, the default software produces full-block text, and we would have to specify an indention to avoid it (and this is not always easy, or even possible with some systems). For children who have never known anything other than an Internet world, with the screen central to their communicative lives, this poses an extra difficulty that teachers need to anticipate. If indented writing is the desired style in the classroom, there is a cognitive distance between this and what is perceived to be 'cool'. Accordingly, some discussion in class of the pragmatic nature of the difference is bound to be helpful in fostering literacy motivation.

In typing, with margins set by the system, what I called 'outdenting' is not something writers would ever have to consider; but it is of course possible if the system is programmed to allow it, and in handwriting it's always there as an option, so we do need to take it into account in any comprehensive view of punctuation. The style is technically called *reverse indention* or *hanging indention*, and is routinely used when information is being presented as a list, such as items in dictionaries and encyclopedias or the entries in indexes. The effect is the opposite of conventional indention, where the first line of a paragraph is indented and the other lines are ranged to the left-hand margin. With reverse indention, the first line of the paragraph is ranged to the left-hand margin, and the rest of the paragraph is indented. The *OED Thesaurus* entry at the end of the previous chapter provides an illustration, as does the index at the end of this book.

Some children seem to go in for reverse indention when they are learning to write: the first line of their stories is ranged left, and everything else is indented. The practice has probably been influenced by the layout of early readers, where pieces of text can appear against their associated illustrations in virtually any part of the page, and where an opening line may be followed by lines with varying degrees of indention. Looking through the story-books my children read when they were young, I see dozens of examples, such as this paragraph from Virginia Lee Burton's *Mike Mulligan and His Steam Shovel* (1939, but I have the Puffin Books edition of 1977). A colourful illustration takes up two-thirds of the page, and the text on the right is laid out as follows, following the curve of the picture:

It was Mike Mulligan
and Mary Anne
and some others
who smoothed out
the ground and filled
in the holes

When children see this kind of design alongside conventional setting, it isn't surprising to see them transfer this aspect of their reading experience into their early writing. It's one of the things that teachers soon correct.

The visual effect of reverse indention can be achieved even within an indented paragraph, if the writer wants to include a quotation or a list, as the items are usually set as indented rectangular blocks, often in a smaller point-size. The present book is an illustration. For a single quotation, indention with surrounding white space is sufficient to identify the item as semantically distinct from the surrounding text, as in the business-letter example. Quotation marks aren't used in such circumstances, nor is there further indention of the first line of the quote (though this was a practice in older books). For a list, legibility is assisted by pointing each indented item with a punctuation mark in the form of a bullet, as in the summary from Mackay and Simo at the end of the previous chapter. A range of dingbats (p. 118) is available for this purpose, with handwritten texts often showing a great deal of personal variation, using dashes, arrows, and all kinds of idiosyncratic squiggles. In academic texts, the items may be numbered, especially if the writer wants to draw attention to a semantic progression or to refer to one of the items later in the discourse.

When preparing material that will be printed, whether on paper or screen, writers leave most of the design decisions to the publisher and typesetter. They don't need to be bothered about the amount of space to leave between paragraphs, which must be noticeable but not too much (otherwise the paragraphs will seem disconnected), as this will be decided by the printer. Similarly, the printer decides the width of the first-line indent, which again must not be too small (or it won't be seen) or too large (or the opening line will seem disassociated from the surrounding text). There's no absolute measure with such matters (though people often think in terms of 'an inch'). The width of an indent will depend partly on the point-size of the type being used, and partly on the length of a line. A wide indent on a short line would look absurd.

However, these decisions are not just made by printers. They are made by all of us when we use handwriting, and are thus of importance in the early stages of teaching young children to write. The width of the page, and the length of the lines, will affect the overall acceptability of a child's indention. Special circumstances warrant special rules – such as the rule requiring the first letter of the first word of the first line of a letter to be located immediately under the comma at the end of the salutation:

Dear Hilary,
              Many thanks for your letter …

A different practice insists on having the first word of the first line underneath the first letter of the addressee's name:

Dear Hilary,
    Many thanks for your letter ...

Teachers pass their preferences on to their pupils, and once learned, indention habits stay with us for ever – at least, among those adults who still do use handwriting – and are rarely varied.

Any account of indention, finally, must allow for cases where the options differ because a special convention is being used. Look at the beginning of any chapter in this book: no indention for the opening line. Nor, in books where chapters contain subheadings, will there be indention for the opening line after the subheading. The same convention affects the first lines of magazines and newspaper articles. It was not always this way: a century ago, we routinely see indention for opening lines, as in this example from *Punch* (4 February 1914):

CHARIVARIA.

THE statement, made at the inquiry into the Dublin strike riots, that 245 policemen were injured during the disturbances has, we hear, done much to allay the prevailing discontent among the belabouring classes.

In addition, the fact that the reader is encountering an opening line may be reinforced by other punctuational conventions. The first letter may be larger than the rest (a *drop capital*), often very much larger, as we saw in the *Oxford Gazette* (p. 113) – a practice that has its origins in early manuscripts. If the first letter isn't larger, the first word or two of the text may be printed entirely in capitals, so that we read:

> A MEETING of European ministers
> being held in Brussels is likely to end
> with little agreement, despite the late

A combination of semantic (attention-drawing) and pragmatic (house-style) factors underlies such practices, which are enormously varied, reflecting the concern of individual institutions and publications to maintain a distinctive visual identity.

Variation is also the dominant impression as we extend our reading experience across genres, and across texts within genres. The relative prominence of sentences within a paragraph can be made explicit by typography, such as bold type, italics, or underlining – a much-used strategy in an era when large amounts of text and small amounts of time combine to motivate rapid reading. Whole paragraphs may be highlighted in this way. In particular, the paragraph theme can be made to stand out by being inserted in a contrasting style at the beginning of the first line:

> **Future meetings** It is proposed to hold meetings at
> intervals of three weeks during the first part of the year ...

It's a style especially used when there are already several other headings in the document, and the writer doesn't want to give such prominence to an item of relatively minor importance.

This last example shows how paragraphing, the second level of the punctuation hierarchy, interacts with the levels on either side of it. If the writer decides nonetheless to treat the information as sections, it would appear like this:

Future meetings
It is proposed to hold meetings at intervals of three weeks during the first part of the year ...

Here the interaction is with the level above: the choice is between sectioning or paragraphing. And there is also a possible interaction with the level below, for it might have been written like this:

> **Future meetings.** It is proposed to hold meetings at
> intervals of three weeks during the first part of the year ...

This kind of additional pointing is a feature of older or conservative writing styles. We see a colon following the paragraph opener in, for example, Hansard reports of debates in the House of Lords:

> **Lord Quirk:** My Lords, in this interesting debate ...

Why the extra mark when the typography would do the job just as well? To answer this, we must turn to the third level in the punctuation hierarchy: the period.

256   PUNCH, OR THE LONDON CHARIVARI.   [December 17, 1870.

A FULL STOP.

Elder Sister. "Now, when you See a little Round Dot like that at the End of a Sentence, it means you're to Stop."
Harry. "I will—and go and Play."

16

Periods, period.

You would have thought that the oldest of all punctuation marks would have had its name settled by now. But this one still has alternatives: is it a *stop*, a *full stop*, a *point*, a *full point*, a *period*? Ben Jonson called it a *prick*. I have some sympathy.

There are regional differences. British English traditionally prefers *full stop*; American English prefers *period*. In both cases, the term has entered the spoken language. In the days when people read telegrams aloud, the constituent sentences would be separated by the word 'stop'. Americans frequently say that 'something is the case – period.' Printers prefer *point*, continuing the Latinate tradition in describing punctuation, where the term was *punctus*, and this term was often used in earlier centuries, as we've seen. But we also need to talk about *pointing*, referring to the whole system of marks, so this can be confusing. The US usage of *period* has spread further than any of the others. It's the term found in the appendix on punctuation by the authors of the (UK-published) *A Comprehensive Grammar of the English Language* (1985), which I use as my primary reference for all things grammatical. So I'll follow that practice in this book from now on.

The chief function of the period is to mark separation. Writers in antiquity recognized this when they used a dot to separate words and larger units (the interpunct). In modern English, we see it operating both towards the top and at the bottom of the punctuation hierarchy, and it has a subtle presence in most of the other separating marks – we see it within the form of the question mark, exclamation, semicolon, and colon. Even the comma can be thought of as a period with a tail.

In modern typesetting, other methods are also available to perform a separating function. A change of typeface from roman to bold or italic will do the job just as well. This is the issue raised at the end of the previous chapter. It's semantically tautologous to use both boldface and a period to separate the heading from the following text in this example:

Future meetings. It is proposed to hold meetings at intervals of three weeks during the first part of the year ...

The modern principle is to avoid graphic tautology: don't use two conventions when one would do. Use the fewest possible marks to make your meaning clear. However, publishers and writers of a conservative temperament – such as one imagines would be influential in the House of Lords – will incline towards the heavy punctuation of an earlier era, where graphic tautology was often extreme, as in the multiple use of quotation marks illustrated on p. 66. When asked to justify such a usage, both pragmatic and semantic arguments will be heard. A pragmatic argument might focus on aesthetics ('it looks nicer') or heritage ('it's always been that way'). A semantic argument will very likely focus on legibility ('easier to read') or clarity ('reinforces the link between the heading and what follows'). I found myself torn in exactly this way during the copy-editing argument I described on p. 113, though in the end I let pragmatics overrule semantics.

At the bottom of the hierarchy, we see the separating force of the period operating when we need to express the semantic unity of a sequence of numerals, as in times, dates, ages, money units, section numbers, decimals, act/scene/line divisions, and so on. The period allows us to distinguish between numerals with different values (such as hours vs minutes, or days vs months vs years):

6.40 pm
1.1.15 (1st January 2015)
1.6 years
£3.50
§1.3
3.007
IV.i.326

In electronic addresses, this separating use of the period (now renamed as 'dot') has extended to include the different elements making up a URL:

www.davidcrystal.com

I'll discuss this further in a later chapter.

It's important to note that the only function of the period in these cases is to separate, and as such it is sometimes replaced by any of the other marks that have a separating function. So we also see times written as 6:40 pm, section numbers as §1:3, ages as 1;6 years, and (in some countries) decimals as 3,007. English-speaking countries use the period to separate decimals, but it's worth noting that there are some partial exceptions. Both period and comma are used in Canada, where English and French are official languages. And South Africa also adopted the comma as a decimal separator, though the period is widely used.

What's interesting about this use of the period is that its separating function is unlike the one it has further up the hierarchy, where it separates sentences. At word and phrase level, it also acts to preserve the unity of the items it separates – that is, it has a linking function. We need *all* the separated elements to arrive at the correct semantic point: *1.1.15* refers to a particular day; *§1.3* to a particular section. In this respect, the same function could be performed by the hyphen, and in informal writing we do sometimes see this. I've often seen dates scribbled out as 1-1-15, for example.

This ability of the period to simultaneously function as separator and linker is no longer present in its other low-level role – as a marker of abbreviation. Formerly, a period was an obligatory element in abbreviated words, so we find *A.D.*, *p.m.*, the *B.B.C.*, and so on. Today, such pointing would rarely be seen: *AD*, *BBC*, and (as above) *pm*. It is another example of a pragmatic shift: rejecting what is perceived to be unnecessary graphic clutter – a general reflection of the 'fussiness' that modern business letter-writers are advised to avoid.

This is often said to be a late-twentieth-century trend, but in fact its roots go back much earlier, to a century before. In 1844, the printer John Wilson notes that some punctuators omit the period after abbreviations that retain the last letter, such as *Mr* and *Mts*. He comments: 'Analogy, however, and reputable usage in a vast majority of cases, are alike opposed to the omission of this mark.' But by 1880 reputable usage had changed. In 1880, Mark Twain wrote a piece for The Contributors' Club, the final section of Volume 45 of *The Atlantic Monthly*. This is the famous essay in which he adumbrated the maxim that has since often been quoted: 'Language was made for man, not man for language', and in it he reflects on ' the suppression of the period signifying abbreviation':

> *Per cent* is now common, and such forms as *Mr*, *Dr*, and *Rev* are receiving the sanction of use by writers who cannot be accused of either ignorance or carelessness.
>
> A poet may safely, even creditably, call a gentleman a 'gentle.' 'Gent.' is a satisfactory term for genealogical

purposes; why may we not go a step further, and omit the period?

A century on, and the omission of the period in all abbreviations is well on the way to becoming the norm, especially on the Internet, but there are still several variations in practice worldwide, and certain types of abbreviation are more likely to retain it (such as *a.s.a.p.*). Here, pragmatics rules: publishing houses and style guides opt for a solution, in the interests of aesthetics and consistency, and expect their users to follow it. But it is not easy predicting publishing preferences, and I have given up trying to do so. In a recent book I wrote for one publisher, periods were required for such abbreviations as *eds* (editors) and *vols* (volumes); in another, for a different publisher, they weren't. Teachers of punctuation need to be aware of the huge diversity of practice, alert their charges to the variation that exists, and establish pragmatic guidelines of their own (especially, the importance of being consistent in a single piece of writing, and to watch out for cases where there may be potential ambiguity, such as *No.* vs *no*). The criteria used by examiners – whether sensible or not – will also be an influential pragmatic factor.

Higher up the punctuation hierarchy, the situation is much clearer. The period no longer has a role as a linker: its sole use is to separate sentences. This is its basic function, acknowledged in every punctuation manual I have read. Phrasing varies, but in all cases the period is said to be required at the end of a sentence to mark the completion of what the writer considers to be a unit of sense. Some traditional grammars would talk about a period marking a 'complete thought', but as one's 'thought' (whatever that is) is often incomplete at the end of a sentence, or may extend over several sentences (as in the case of a paragraph), this fuzzy notion is generally avoided in modern treatments. It is taking me seven sentences to 'complete' the thought that motivated the present paragraph, for example. And if I were to rewrite my second sentence replacing the colon by a period, the amount of 'thought' in the paragraph would be the same, even though the number of sentences would have increased by one.

There is no fixed grammatical rule which tells us what a unit of sense is. Traditional grammars were desperate to find one, and would insist on such 'rules' as 'a sentence must have a verb' or 'a sentence must have a subject and a predicate'. In certain kinds of writing – in formal monologues in particular – these rules are realistic and useful, as they draw writers' attention to the need to make their thoughts explicit, in the absence of simultaneous feedback from a listener. But they are by no means universal. Pick up virtually any example of what is considered to be 'best writing' – novels, plays, poems ... – and we see that units of sense ended by periods may contain any grammatical construction, whether including a verb or not.

Here's the opening of a well-known novel: Charles Dickens's *Bleak House*. The units of sense are absolutely clear, regardless of the grammar they contain:

London. Michaelmas Term lately over, and the Lord
Chancellor sitting in Lincoln's Inn Hall. Implacable
November weather.

The same thing happens in poetry. Here are the opening lines of Ted Hughes's poem 'Moonwalk':

A glare chunk of moon.
The hill no colour
Under the polarized light.

Like a day pushed inside out. Everything
In negative.

And, as a third example: some lines from a play – Samuel
Beckett's *Waiting for Godot*. Estragon asks Vladimir if he can
remember what they asked Godot for:

VLADIMIR: Oh … nothing very definite.
ESTRAGON: A kind of prayer.
VLADIMIR: Precisely.
ESTRAGON: A vague supplication.
VLADIMIR: Exactly.

Again, the units of sense are clear, thanks to the use of the
period, even though the grammatical structures are various
and (in the last example) Vladimir's responses are gram-
matically autonomous, unconnected to any 'fuller' previous
sentence.

It's important to appreciate that these examples are not
'exceptions'. They are normal, and have been in the language
since it began. Here's another instance, in modern spelling:

I'm a hunter.
Whose?
The king's.

This is an exchange from Ælfric's *Colloquy* (see p. 11), a rare
example of an Old English conversation, written around 1000
AD. We would find similar instances throughout the history
of English literature, increasing in number as writers try to
reflect more realistically the patterns and rhythms of everyday conversation. They all illustrate the perspective that is
essential for understanding the use of the period: we do not
think in the carefully articulated sentences recommended by
traditional grammars. We think in units of sense, which are

sometimes expressed through subjects and verbs, but just as often are not. Sentences are the way grammar enables us to express all these units of sense, whatever their structural constituency. And a period is the chief way of showing that we have reached the end of one of our units of sense.

The chief way, but not the only way. Using the systems approach I advocated in Chapter 13, if we want to understand the semantic and pragmatic functions of the period, we need to see how it operates as one of a set of options available to us when we reach the end of a unit of sense. If we don't do this, we will end up making false generalizations about the period, such as the one I quoted at the beginning of that chapter: 'there must be one at the end of every sentence.' This is plainly not the case, as the following set of sentences illustrates. There are six options:

It's time you went home.
It's time you went home?
It's time you went home!
It's time you went home –
It's time you went home …
It's time you went home

Actually, there are more than six if we include at this point repeated instances such as

It's time you went home!!!
It's time you went home!?

But I'll deal with those later.

The traditional classification of sentences as statements, questions, commands, and exclamations is important, but when used in relation to punctuation it clearly isn't the whole story, for all these examples are grammatical statements, and yet they are punctuated differently. When would we use one and not the others? A complete semantic specification of all the contexts would take a book in itself, but an indication of the essential differences is as follows:

- *It's time you went home.* Traditionally the default option, in which the statement is neutral with respect to the other options, conveying none of the emotional tones we find there – a simple 'statement of fact'. But times are changing, as we'll see.
- *It's time you went home?* The addition of a questioning tone, with all the semantic consequences that this brings, which can include genuine enquiry, abrupt instruction, and uncertain suggestion. We interpret such a sentence in the light of the context in which it is used, and relate it to the tone of voice it would have if it were spoken.
- *It's time you went home!* The addition of an exclamatory tone, again with all the semantic consequences that this brings, ranging from command to disbelief.

These are the three familiar options, corresponding to the grammatical alternatives available in English, where a statement can be syntactically changed into a question (*Is it time you went home*), a command (*Go home*), and an exclamation (*What a home*). Because the syntax conveys the meaning in these examples, we don't actually need punctuation to express the difference between them, though of course modern convention does require it. Yet even here there are exceptions, which I'll discuss in the next chapter.

The remaining three options are not usually mentioned in traditional accounts of punctuation, but they mustn't be ignored, especially because they have become increasingly noticeable in Internet orthography:

- *It's time you went home* – The addition of an abrupt tone, with a wide range of semantic consequences.

- *It's time you went home* … The addition of an ambiguous tone, also with a wide range of semantic consequences.
- *It's time you went home* No final punctuation mark, leaving the semantic interpretation apparently wide open.

This last one, in particular, is likely to raise an eyebrow, for it seems to have no punctuation at all and thus to go against a thousand years of orthographic evolution. But even nothing has a value, in language, as we shall see.

17

Devilish dashes –

It's time you went home –

I can't prove it, but if a count could be made of all the punctuation marks used in handwriting from Anglo-Saxon times, I suspect the dash would be top of the list. It is the easiest of marks to separate units of sense, whether sentences or parts of sentences, and as a result it has had a long history of antipathy from teachers and stylists who have been concerned that, if writers rely on the dash as a mark-of-all-trades, they will never master the more discriminating uses of punctuation. Some, savouring the alliteration, called it an invention of the devil! On the other hand, as we saw in earlier chapters, it was the punctuation mark of choice for Jane Austen and Emily Dickinson, among many others, and some writers (such as Edgar Allan Poe) were keen to defend it.

The nineteenth-century radical writer William Cobbett provides an early example of antagonism. His *Grammar of the English Language* (1829) is written as a series of letters to his son, and in Letter 14 he cautions the young man against the dash:

> Those who have thought proper, like Mr. Lindley Murray,
> to place *the dash* amongst the *grammatical points*, ought
> to give us some rule relative to its different longitudinal
> dimensions in different cases. The *inch*, the *three quarter-inch*,
> the *half-inch*, the *quarter-inch*: these would be something

determinate; but, *'the dash,'* without measure, must be a most perilous thing for a young grammarian to handle. In short, *'the dash'* is a cover for ignorance as to the use of points, and it can answer no other purpose.

But even Cobbett allows that there are occasions when the dash can be useful. He grudgingly accepts it after a period 'in crowded print, in order to save the room that would be lost by the breaks of distinct paragraphs', adding: 'This is another matter.'

Judging by his remarks, Cobbett seems to have been obsessed with the physical form of the dash, rather than its function. And indeed, printers have had to deal with this point, in order to avoid confusion with the dash-like hyphen. During the nineteenth century, the terminology of *en* and *em* became established as ways of measuring the amount of printed matter in a line of type. An en was a block of metal type that was the width of the letter *N*; an em was the width of the letter *M*. Printers would talk of an 'en space' or an 'em rule', and describe a desired space on a page as having the width of 'three ems', and so on.

When used for the dash, it motivated two lengths that came to have different linguistic functions. The en dash developed three main uses.

- It marks specific ranges in dates, times, distances, and numbers: *January–March*, *3–5 pm*, *London–Holyhead*, *Chapters 16–18*. It is also used for open-ended ranges, as in the age-span of a not-yet-dead personality (*1963–*). Mnemonic: the dash can be read as *to* (or *through* in US English). (But teachers who use this mnemonic must point out that it's important not to mix conventions by writing *I was there from 3–5 pm*, as this can miscue the reader into thinking that a continuation is intended: *from 3–5 pm until 8–9 pm.*)

- It marks a coordination: *a father–son relationship, the Smith–Jones series, the Sykes–Picot Agreement, the North America–Eurasia tectonic plate.* Mnemonic: the dash can be read as *and*.
- It marks a contrasting position: *3–1 to Liverpool, the England–France match, the Ali–Frazier fight.* Mnemonic: the dash can be read as *versus* or *as opposed to*.

In informal writing, the fixed length of the en dash is replaced by a dash of indeterminate length, often making no distinction with a hyphen. In print, however, it was soon noticed that problems of legibility and ambiguity lurked behind this apparently simple mark. There's a legibility problem if the writer wants to join hyphenated words:

the primary-school-secondary-school distinction
the primary-school–secondary-school distinction

And there's an ambiguity problem in such cases as these:

the discovery was made by Campbell-Jones in 1962 – one person
the discovery was made by Campbell–Jones in 1962 – two people

a Conservative-Liberal argument – it has views from both parties
a Conservative–Liberal argument – it is between the two parties

It was argued that any disregard for the en dash could lead to an ambiguity. If we did not know the participants, how would we ever know if *Sykes* and *Picot* were one person or two, or even *Ali* and *Frazier*? A hyphen/en-dash distinction was soon being rigidly enforced in style guides, despite the fact that context resolved most ambiguities. The rules were being formed during a strongly prescriptive climate where any hint of ambiguity, no matter how slight, was something to be avoided at all costs.

Things then got out of hand, and the rules became increasingly complex and artificial. It wasn't long before wholly imaginary ambiguities were being cited to justify the distinction, such as the insistence on using an en dash after a prefix before a hyphenated word, as in *non–English-speaking peoples*. Most of these recommendations now seem to be generally disregarded, but some style guides do still include them, and there is a great deal of variation in what counts as 'correct practice'.

The en dash retained its position throughout the era of typewriting, when typists were taught to show it with a double hyphen (and a triple hyphen for em dashes), and this option has continued into modern keyboards, where there are no separate keys for en or em dashes (though the distinctions are of course encodable, as in HTML's – and —). Other specific options have been devised to distinguish such entities as a minus sign or the kind of dash that links the parts of a telephone number. But on the whole the trend has been towards simplification. Double and triple hyphens are hardly ever seen today (an exception is in the mock-handwritten exchanges in some comic strips). And the use of the em dash has come to be widely replaced by the cleaner-looking space-en-space (as in this book):

an example—short though it is—of an em-dash

an example – short though it is – of a space-en-space dash

There have also been a few specialized semantic developments in the dash world – notably, the *swung dash* (or *tilde*), used from the mid-twentieth century in several academic disciplines (such as mathematics and linguistics) in a range of technical senses. In dictionaries it stands for a headword (or part of a headword):

frenzied *adj* marked by frenzy (*the dog's ~ barking*)

It can also mean 'approximately' (*~50 emails*) and, in a tabular list, 'the same as above' (as an alternative to a double inverted comma). Among the pragmatic options is its use as a visual alternative to a bullet or a straight dash in front of the items in a list. A few people have used it as an ornate alternative to a straight dash, but this usage isn't (yet) widespread.

Whether printed solid or spaced, the em dash has received its due share of recognition by grammarians, as it's one of the main ways of showing an included unit in a sentence. When the inclusion is medial and short, it takes its place alongside other *correlative* uses of punctuation – marks that have to be used twice. The basic options are threefold:

The editor, David Jones, said that he would make a decision soon.

The editor (David Jones) said that he would make a decision soon.

The editor – David Jones – said that he would make a decision soon.

The comma option gives the two elements the same degree of semantic importance. It is also the least obtrusive, and would be the default usage when the included text is short. But if the inclusion gets longer, and contains an increasing amount of information, the semantic imbalance makes the sentence increasingly difficult to assimilate. We begin to lose a sense of its structure, especially if there are multiple commas:

The editor, who was appointed by the board in January,
with the specific role of introducing the policy to a younger,
online readership, said that he would make a decision soon.

The problem here is that the comma is being made to do
several different jobs at the same time. It separates items in
a list (*younger, online*), and it separates two clauses (*January,
with*), as well as showing the inclusion of everything between
editor and *said*. Inserting dashes or round brackets immediately
makes the structure more transparent:

The editor – who was appointed by the board in January,
with the specific role of introducing the policy to a younger,
online readership – said that he would make a decision
soon.

If the included element is an entire sentence, then the
comma is immediately ruled out, and we are left with the
other two options:

The editor – he was appointed by the board in January –
said that he would make a decision soon.

The editor (he was appointed by the board in January) said
that he would make a decision soon.

What is the semantic difference between dashes and
round brackets? I'll look at the role of the latter in more detail
in Chapter 30, but the essential contrast is between formal
planning and informal spontaneity. In the above examples,
brackets tell the reader that both points are to be noted, but
the editor is the primary point. Dashes suggest to the reader
that the editor's name is of less significance to the writer.
They convey an informal impression, as if the addition were
an impromptu remark. They capture a dynamic movement
that is missing with round brackets. As such, they are much

more likely to be found, for example, in modern play scripts, as in this double instance from Tom Stoppard's *Rosencrantz and Guildenstern Are Dead*:

> I had an actor once who was condemned to hang for stealing a sheep – or a lamb, I forget which – so I got permission to have him hanged in the middle of a play – had to change the plot a bit but I thought it would be effective, you know – and you wouldn't believe it, he just *wasn't* convincing!

Replacing the dashes by round brackets not only alters the rhythm but presents us with a curiously inconsistent tone, with the colloquial syntax clashing with the more stately punctuation.

> I had an actor once who was condemned to hang for stealing a sheep (or a lamb, I forget which) so I got permission to have him hanged in the middle of a play (had to change the plot a bit but I thought it would be effective, you know) and you wouldn't believe it, he just *wasn't* convincing!

Dashes are the modern way. In early ages, round brackets were used for both these functions (as I'll illustrate later).

The association of round brackets with a well-planned text suggests that the content of the included item is closely related in meaning to what appears in the surrounding text. Conversely, if the included item is an unexpected digression, it is more likely to be found within dashes.

> The editor – am I allowed to reveal this? – said that he would make a decision soon.

Dashes are thus the mark of choice when someone wants to convey a disjointed or chaotic series of thoughts. In this

connection, probably the best dash user in English literature
is Laurence Sterne, in *The Life and Opinions of Tristram Shandy,
Gentleman*. Here's an example in Chapter 21 of Book I:

> Pray what was that man's name,---for I write in such a
> hurry, I have no time to recollect or look for it, —— who first
> made the observation, 'That there was great inconstancy in
> our air and climate?'

It's perfectly normal in Sterne to read paragraphs containing
a dozen dashes, and moreover of different specific lengths,
with strings of up to five hyphens being used. Here's a short
example of this style:

> My brother does it, quoth my uncle *Toby*, out of *principle*—In
> a family-way, I suppose, quoth Dr. *Slop*.—Pshaw!—said my
> father,—'tis not worth talking of.

This is in fact the whole of Chapter 13 of Book 2, showing
the way Sterne delights in playing with literary conventions.

The example also illustrates how the long dash (often
longer than a single em) can be used to incorporate dialogue within a paragraph. Sterne uses it at the beginning of
a paragraph too, anticipating the later use of the long dash
instead of quotation marks to introduce a quotation or a new
speaker, as I mentioned earlier (p. 94) in relation to James
Joyce's *Ulysses*:

> —Well, good health, says Ned.
> —Good health, Ned, says J.J.
> —There he is again, says Joe.
> —Where? says Alf.

As a further illustration of the stylistic difference between
dashes and parentheses, note what happens if the included
item is left to the end of a sentence. Here it makes more sense

to talk of the element being an afterthought rather than an inclusion, but the semantic function is exactly the same. It conveys an impression of spontaneous amplification. There's an example earlier in this chapter:

> When the inclusion is medial and short, it takes its place alongside other *correlative* uses of punctuation – marks that have to be used twice.

Why did I write it in this way? Because I don't know whether my reader will be familiar with the technical use of *correlative*. If I don't gloss it, I may leave some readers in the dark:

> When the inclusion is medial and short, it takes its place alongside other *correlative* uses of punctuation.

But if I build it into the sentence, readers who are familiar with the term might think I'm talking down to them:

> When the inclusion is medial and short, it takes its place alongside other *correlative* uses of punctuation, which are marks that have to be used twice.

I can imagine a reader thinking with irritation: 'I know what *correlative* means, Crystal, you don't have to tell me!' The dash allows me to express a 'take it or leave it' effect. If you know what *correlative* means, ignore what follows. If you don't, pay attention to it.

Edgar Allan Poe made a similar point. In a Marginalia column for *Graham's Magazine* (February 1848), he made a vigorous defence of the dash, inveighing against the way printers replaced dashes by a semicolon or comma – a reaction, he felt, to the excessive use of the dash by writers a few decades before. The dash, he said (defining and illustrating at the same time), 'represents a *second thought – an emendation*'. And he goes on:

The dash gives the reader a choice between two, or among three or more expressions, one of which may be more forcible than another, but all of which help out the idea. It stands, in general, for these words – 'or, *to make my meaning more distinct.*' This force *it has* – and this force no other point can have; since all other points have well-understood uses quite different from this. Therefore, the dash *cannot* be dispensed with.

Finally, we should note the use of the em dash to show that there's been an interruption in a dialogue. This convention is very old. We see it in Shakespeare's First Folio, when Hal and Poins persistently interrupt the tavern-waiter Francis (*Henry IV Part 1*, 2.4.40):

> *Prin.* How long haſt thou to ſerue, Francis?
> *Fran.* Forſooth fiue yeares, and as much as to——
> *Poin.* Francis.
> *Fran.* Anon, anon ſir.
> *Prin.* Fiue yeares : Berlady a long Leaſe for the clinking of Pewter. But Francis, dareſt thou be ſo valiant, as to play the coward with thy Indenture, & ſhew it a faire paire of heeles, and run from it?
> *Fran.* O Lord ſir, Ile be ſworne vpon all the Books in England, I could finde in my heart.
> *Poin.* Francis.
> *Fran.* Anon, anon ſir.
> *Prin.* How old art thou, *Francis* ?
> *Fran.* Let me ſee, about Michaelmas next I ſhalbe——
> *Poin.* Francis.
> *Fran.* Anon ſir, pray you ſtay a little, my Lord.
> *Prin.* Nay but harke you Francis, for the Sugar thou gaueſt me,'twas a penyworth, was't not ?
> *Fran.* O Lord ſir, I would it had bene two.
> *Prin.* I will giue thee for it a thouſand pound : Aske me when thou wilt, and thou ſhalt haue it.
> *Poin.* Francis.

There's no standard width. The typesetter simply extends the dash to fill the rest of the line.

So, in the light of these various uses of the em dash, why

would someone end a sentence with a dash, as in *It's time you went home* –? This isn't an interruption. The speaker has decided to come to a sudden stop. Why would speakers do this? It's a favourite novelist's device, when characters suddenly realize that they are unwilling or unable to carry on. Perhaps they have said too much, or are too upset to continue. There are several possible interpretations, which a novelist often glosses:

> 'It's time you went home –'
> Martha stopped abruptly, remembering that the police were watching the house.

The effect has a long history. Classical rhetoricians called it *aposiopesis*, from a Greek verb meaning 'to keep silent'.

An interlude about the D—

During the eighteenth century, a long dash came to be used as a mark of supposed anonymity in newspapers, novels, letters, cartoon captions, and some public announcements. It was used for places and people where the writer wished to avoid writing a name out in full. In a novel, it might be because the actual location or person is unimportant. In a letter, the identity would be known to the reader, so the writer would be sharing some sort of joke or perhaps hinting at a sensitive issue – as when Jane Austen writes to Cassandra (8 January 1799) about 'W— W—'s Mama' (probably a reference to a neighbour). In newspapers, it was used as a tabloid trick to avoid a legal comeback, enabling someone to be mentioned without actually saying who they were.

Punch, the arch-enemy of hypocrisy in the nineteenth century, was quick to attack the practice. In issue No. 23 in 1845, we see a reporter (a 'penny-a-liner' – a journalist paid by the line) apparently having an attack of conscience at the way a magistrate (a Mr Gibbs) dealt with a case:

USE AND ABUSE OF THE " ——."

THE penny-a-liner is sometimes touched with strange tenderness towards the scoundrel of respectability, for assuredly there is such an animal, and a wicked pest he is. This "conscience and tender heart" was a day or two since strongly developed by the reporter of a case heard at the Mansion House. A young woman was charged before the unaccountable GIBBS with robbery :

"It appeared from the reluctant statement made by the young woman, that CAPTAIN P—— had been paying attention to her in Norwich, and had promised to marry her, but that, finding his intentions were not honourable, she had left the town and come to London to avoid his importunities ; that the Captain followed her to town, and perceiving that she was determined to shun him, charged her with having robbed him of his trunk, just as she was getting into an omnibus."

Now, if Private POTTS or PRINGLE had been guilty of such infamy, he would not have been treated with the tenderness of a "——." No ; POTTS or PRINGLE would have been written full, every letter taking its proper share of the iniquity. But then, "what in the Captain's but a choleric word," in the aforesaid private would have been very abominable indeed. The way in which the case was disposed of is no less edifying—no less encouraging to scoundrel captains, wherever they may be.

> "The Captain *sent a certificate* to the Mansion House stating that *he had no intention to appear against the young woman, and the* LORD MAYOR *discharged her.*"
>
> And so, at the Captain's wish, the LORD MAYOR thinks no more of the case than if it were part and parcel of the accounts of Walbrook! Either the Captain compromises a felony, and is abetted therein by a magistrate, or he has committed a gross rascality. In such case, why was his name suppressed? Why was it not gibbetted in the paper, that its owner might meet the contempt of every honest man—the scorn of every virtuous woman? But no; it would seem that the "——" was expressly invented for the rascal of respectability.

Punch repeatedly satirized the practice. In an 'Imaginary Conversation' published in No. 27 (1854), the dialogue is introduced by a list of the anonymous characters:

IMAGINARY CONVERSATION.

An Apartment at Osborne. HER M——Y *is graciously pleased to be hearing* HER R——L H——S THE P——S L——A C——E A——A *read to her out of Punch.* The EARL OF A——N *and* LORD J——N R——L *are announced, and* HER M——Y's *smile at the graceful satire in which Mr. Punch enwraps his profound wisdom, is utterly and entirely misconceived by the two Ministers into an expression of pleasure at their arrival.*

Readers of the time would have needed no gloss. For modern readers: Princess Louisa Caroline Alberta (sixth child of Queen Victoria), the Earl of Aberdeen (First Lord of the Treasury), Lord John Russell (President of the Council).

18

Ellipsis dots or ...

It's time you went home ...

An unspaced sequence of three periods is usually called an *ellipsis* – more fully, *ellipsis dots* or *suspension dots*. *Ellipsis* means that something has been left out. In grammar, it refers to the omission of part of a preceding sentence, as in the sequence *Where are you going? Home.* (= *I am going home.*) In punctuation, along with the dash, it's the main way of expressing semantic incompleteness.

We see it in traditional formal writing when a piece of information is deliberately omitted, as when we choose to exclude part of a quotation:

> The important point ... is that the article will be published.

Here the omitted words might be 'I must emphasize'. There's no rule governing the amount of text that is covered by ellipsis dots, but it would be unusual for the separated units not to be close to each other in the original text.

A related use shows that a quotation could have continued, but has been arbitrarily ended, as in my examples from *The Memors* in Chapter 14:

> Bob Holpweed tucked the local newspaper under his arm and went to the park. ...

And we also see it expressing continuation when we wish

to convey the notion of 'something that it is unnecessary to specify further':

> Imagine a sequence of numbers: 5, 10, 15, 20 …
> To be or not to be …
> When in Rome, you know …

There are several examples of ellipses at the ends of sentences or quotations in the present book. See, for example, its use in the title to Chapter 1, taken up as *continuation dots* in the title to Chapter 2. Or the various quotations in Chapter 12.

This use of ellipses can be manipulative, and isn't always ethical. Imagine a play review in the *Daily Blah* that begins like this:

> The production is less the brilliant, perceptive
> interpretation and electrifying performance claimed in
> its publicity, than a bathetic pandering to the London
> audience's most basic instincts.

Then later, you read:

> Brilliant, perceptive … electrifying. (*Daily Blah*)

With any form of advertising, it always pays to check what's been omitted.

A third type of ellipsis can be illustrated by the way I used it at the very beginning of Chapter 14:

> a continuous piece of writing, or *text* – whether it be a book,
> a chapter, an essay, a newspaper report, a letter, a signpost,
> an email, a blog …

This is a further example of 'something that it is unnecessary to specify further', but here the meaning is vaguer. I am assuming the reader will be able to add to this list, but there is no guarantee that each reader will add to the list in the same way. Writers have to be careful when using ellipsis like this. They need to ensure that the reader will be able to see the semantic connection between the items in the list. If the unifying factor isn't immediately obvious, the writer needs to make it clear in the context, to avoid a charge of lazy writing.

Ellipsis dots have not always had a good press, for this reason, and some stylists recommend avoiding them. But this is going too far. When used carefully, the vagueness they convey can be dramatically valuable. In dialogue it can mark a silence, with all that this entails – uncertainty, threat, embarrassment, melancholy, something unspoken ... Harold Pinter was the literary master of this kind of rhetorical ambiguity. In *The Caretaker*, the aggressive Mick tells the homeless arrival Davies about his brother Aston:

> MICK. He's supposed to be doing a little job for me ... I keep him here to do a little job ... but I don't know ... I'm coming to the conclusion he's a slow worker.
> *Pause.*
> What would your advice be?
> DAVIES. Well ... he's a funny bloke, your brother.
> MICK. What?

It's up to the director and actors to interpret these ellipses, and there are several possibilities, most of them uncomfortable. Menace is never far away during a Pinteresque pause. Silences are ominous, not golden.

Ellipses dominate the graphic character of *The Caretaker*. I've never seen anything to match the elliptical nature of its final lines:

> ASTON: You make too much noise.
> DAVIES: But ... but ... look ... listen ... listen here ... I mean ...

> *ASTON turns back to the window.*
> What am I going to do?
> *Pause.*
> What shall I do?
> *Pause.*
> Where am I going to go?
> *Pause.*
> If you want me to go ... I'll go. You just say the word.
> *Pause.*
> I'll tell you what though ... them shoes ... them shoes you
> give me ... they're working out all right ... they're all right.
> Maybe I could ... get down ...
> *ASTON remains still, his back to him, at the window.*
> Listen ... if I ... got down ... if I was to ... get my papers ...
> would you ... would you let ... would you ... if I got down
> ... and got my ...
> *Long silence.*
> *Curtain.*

This kind of writing works because it's possible for us to relate the speech patterns to our everyday experience of pausing and tone of voice. We do often speak in this way. For example, if we were to write down the following spoken exchange, ellipsis dots provide the most appropriate means of conveying the unspoken part of the message:

A: Where's the er ...
B: First on the right upstairs.

Any spoken evasion of a tricky or awkward subject can be represented in writing in the same way:

A: I think you should ... you know ...
B: Tell him, you mean?

No other punctuation mark conveys tentativeness like this, suggesting a voice trailing off into an uncertain silence.

Certain types of novel and short story also rely on ellipsis dots at critical points in the narrative. Detective stories depend on them when the characters withhold information, either deliberately or because they die before they can reveal what happened:

> 'Who did it? Who did it?'
> 'It was ... it was ...'

Here the incompleteness is a critical plot device, for if the victim had been able to finish his sentence, the story would have been over. Any interrogation scene is likely to use ellipsis dots, with interrogators posing leading and unfinished questions and interrogatees responding – either deliberately or through exhaustion – with evasive and partial answers. Investigators who are puzzled rely on them too:

> Was the weapon here, somewhere, in this house? Was that why Joe Burch was uneasy and conciliatory?
>
> Poirot did not know. He did not really think so. But he was not absolutely sure ...

This is the end of the chapter. The ellipsis as cliffhanger – a favourite device of Agatha Christie (Chapter 5 of *Mrs. McGinty's Dead*, 1952).

Ellipsis dots have gained a new lease of life in electronic communication, where they perform a variety of functions. This isn't the place to go into the various technical uses they have in programming languages, but everyone who works or plays online will have had to understand the following uses of ellipses:

- A request for further information, following a command.

An example is the contrast between *Save* and *Save As...*
In the first case, a page will be saved without any further
action on the part of the user. In the second, the user
needs to provide a filename.

- An indication that there are options available:
  Preferences... Zoom...
- A report on the status of an operation: *Updating...*
  Downloading...
- In contexts such as chatrooms or instant messaging, a
  signal to a recipient that the sender is about to send a
  further message:

Dave says: I think I have that info...
Dave says: It's on Friday

- An indication that a link does not fit in the space
  available – something that happens often in short-
  message formats such as Twitter. In this example,
  the full address of the link has been automatically
  abbreviated to respect the limit of 140 characters:

A comment on the latest horror story to come out of
the KS2 grammar tests in the UK: http://david-crystal.
blogspot.co.uk/2013/09/on-not...

Visually, the graphic form of ellipsis dots seems very
straightforward, but there are some subtleties of usage, both
in manuscript and in print. If we decide to use them in handwriting, such as in an informal letter, they are often errat-
ically written, with different amounts of space on either side,
and with varying spaces between the dots. The number of
dots may also vary, in what is called *extended ellipsis*. Writers
add as many dots as they want, reflecting a personal style or
just a playful whim. We also sometimes see varying numbers
of dots in print, such as in comic strips, especially when

characters continue a conversation across the panels. And varying numbers of dots are common these days on screen. In informal Internet exchanges, we may see long sequences, as multiple repetition is a simple matter of holding down the period key.

So .... are you going to come over?

Doubtless some of these sequences have a semantic purpose, reflecting the length of the intonation pattern the writer has in mind, or conveying degrees of attitude or implication. Just as likely, the number of dots in a string has no semantic point, merely reflecting an idiosyncrasy on the part of the sender.

Although printers have the option of varying the width of spaces when typesetting a page, there is no such option available to the general user. Whether using an old-style typewriter or the latest keyboard, pressing the space-bar introduces a space of fixed width. Thus the only matter that is under the control of the writer is whether to introduce a space or not, either within the ellipsis itself (... vs . . .) or at its boundaries, where there are four possible options:

(a) The important point ... is that nobody is excluded.
(b) The important point...is that nobody is excluded.
(c) The important point... is that nobody is excluded.
(d) The important point ...is that nobody is excluded.

Most publishers go for (a), using a specific ellipsis character that keeps the dots together and includes a moderate degree of space between them, and this is available if you are desktop publishing. The unspaced version, (b), though formerly common, is now generally avoided on the grounds that it results in a dense-looking text, with decreased legibility – but it will nonetheless still be encountered.

Are there any grounds for asymmetrical spacing, as in (c)

and (d)? In the above examples, where the ellipsis simply means 'material omitted', it would be considered bad practice. But in certain circumstances the exact location of the ellipsis can have a linguistically contrastive force. Imagine you want to omit a piece of the following discourse.

> Is there any shred of evidence that Smith travelled by train to London with Jane Williams? Is there any evidence that Brown travelled to Manchester? Is there any evidence that Jones travelled to Glasgow?

You have three options, each of which is signalled by a different placement of the dots:

- *Option 1: something has been removed from between the two sentences*

  Is there any shred of evidence that Smith travelled by train to London with Jane Williams? … Is there any evidence that Jones travelled to Glasgow?

- *Option 2: something has been removed at the end of the first sentence, but nothing has been removed at the beginning of the second*

  Is there any shred of evidence that Smith travelled by train to London…? Is there any evidence that Brown travelled to Manchester?

- *Option 3: something has been removed from the beginning of the second sentence, but nothing has been removed from the end of the first*

  Is there any shred of evidence that Smith travelled by train to London with Jane Williams? …that Brown travelled to Manchester? …that Jones travelled to Glasgow?

In Options 2 and 3, as shown here, the ellipsis is often placed solid against the adjacent text, reinforcing its role as part of its mother sentence. Solid setting is the norm in Internet commands, such as *Save As…*

These are illustrations of the way the linguistic system operates, not rules of usage. Practice varies enormously among individuals and among the style manuals, and defies easy summary. In the days of heavy punctuation, we would even see ellipses within square brackets, reinforcing the point that the dots are added by the author and are not part of the original text:

The important point […] is that nobody is excluded.

And one usage issue in particular is worth noting: practice is divided over whether there should be a fourth period if the ellipsis occurs at the end of a statement and there is another sentence following. Compare:

Imagine a sequence of numbers: 5, 10, 15, 20 …
Imagine a sequence of numbers: 5, 10, 15, 20 ….

The four-point option is much more common in American English than in British English printing. A fourth dot may seem unnecessary, but it can be justified if we think of it indicating a semantic contrast with other marks:

Imagine a sequence of numbers: 5, 10, 15, 20 ….
Imagine a sequence of numbers: 5, 10, 15, 20 …?

In most cases, though, the typographical variations relating to the presentation of ellipsis dots have little or no semantic content. The choices are made solely on aesthetic, house-style, or other pragmatic grounds.

After this typographical excursus, we can now return to

It's time you went home ... This is quite unlike the first examples in this chapter, where we know exactly what the ellipsis represents – a specific chunk of quoted text or a specific series of numerals. It's more like Pinter or Christie, where we need to know about the relationship between the participants before we can decide what this sentence means, and how it would have been said aloud. All we can say with certainty is that it lacks the tone of finality we associate with the period, the interrogative tone of the question mark, or the confrontational tone of the exclamation. But what nonfinal means in this context is open to question. We can play a game adding imaginary continuations:

> *It's time you went home* ... *you've had too much to drink.*
> *It's time you went home* ... *as I've been telling you for the past half-hour.*
> *It's time you went home* ... *but I do hope you'll stay the night.*

The place where ellipsis dots have proliferated is in informal Internet exchanges, where they are a convenient – some people would say a lazy – way of avoiding conventional punctuation. There's more to it than laziness, though. For on the Internet, something unexpected has happened to the period.

19

The value of nothing

It's time you went home

Ellipsis dots are a relatively modern convention. In older books their function is expressed by a long dash, which is how Lindley Murray, for example, illustrates ellipsis in his grammar. And in nineteenth-century novels and magazines, the dash is the norm. Now that both options are available, there's a potential semantic contrast of attitude, as the two previous chapters have illustrated. But what possible reason could there be for using no punctuation mark at all at the end of a sentence?

When we look at punctuation as a system, we can see an answer. Zero punctuation is a way of avoiding *any* of the meanings conveyed by other sentence-ending marks. If we don't want to suggest a finality (.), a question (?), an exclamation (!), a tentative continuation (...), or an abrupt ending (–), we can use nothing at all. But what sort of contexts would motivate a writer to do such a thing? There are two main circumstances: poetry, and the Internet.

Here's the beginning of Roger McGough's poem 'The Care Less Cat', from his collection *That Awkward Age* (2009):

> You win at the races
> You lose your keys
> The cat couldn't care less
> Trip over your laces

> And scrape your knees
> The cat just couldn't care less

And so it goes on, each line a separate sentence, and four-teen stanzas in all, without a single period until the very last line. When McGough reads this poem aloud, he told me (in February 2014), 'the line-break acts as a beat and the end of a stanza as a pause'. This makes sense. Because the graphic cues are there in the spacing, it isn't necessary for him to add further marks. On the other hand, he felt that 'Mr Sappho' (also in the collection), 'which is denser and features two voices, demanded the return to a more traditional style of punctuation':

> *'I'm off to Lesbos with the girls.'*
> *'Yes, boss, shall I warm your pearls?'*
> We josh, as she goes upstairs to pack.
> Not so much a holiday as the chance to get away
> From those humdrum domestic chores.
> And to be honest, to get away from me.

That makes sense as well. The longer the line, the stanza, and the poem, the more likely you are to punctuate, if you want your writing to be grammatically and semantically clear.

But there are also pragmatic as well as semantic reasons for punctuationless poetry. McGough comments on 'The Care Less Cat', and also on the next poem in the collection, 'Mr Nightingale', which adopts the same style:

> My poems are usually short and I like a clean page. All too often, punctuation squiggles seem to gather like dust.

This is exactly the attitude we've seen expressed by novel-ists such as Cormac McCarthy (Chapter 11). And other poets who adopt the same strategy would doubtless agree. There are no sentence-ending marks in T S Eliot's 'Eyes that last I saw in tears'. There are none in Lawrence Ferlinghetti's 'The world is a beautiful place'. Many other examples can be found in twentieth-century literature.

What is going on here? The lack of periods promotes a sense of continuity of the thought, similar to the stream-of-consciousness I've already remarked upon in James Joyce. If you want your lines and stanzas to be separate and thematically distinct from each other, yet flowing and semantically unified, this is one way you can do it. And avoiding sentence-ending marks also affects the pace of the thought – and thus the speed with which particular lines are spoken. A good example is the third stanza of Dylan Thomas's 'The hunchback in the park', which begins with a series of unstopped sentences:

> Like the park birds he came early
> Like the water he sat down
> And Mister they called Hey mister
> The truant boys from the town
> Running when he had heard them clearly
> On out of sound

The increased energy in the third line would be entirely lacking if the boys' sentences had been conventionally punctuated:

> And 'Mister', they called, 'Hey, mister.'

Note also what happens if end punctuation is added to the opening lines:

> Like the park birds he came early.
> Like the water he sat down.

What the poet now presents to us is two separate events,

rather than an experience in which birds, water, arrival, and sitting are integrated into a single moment of memory. That's the annoying thing about language, from a poet's point of view: its sequential character forces you to describe a scene by starting at point A, then moving to point B, and then C. That's a plus in a conventional narrative, but if you want to present a scene holistically, it's a serious minus. So anything that can help convey the simultaneous character of your perception is going to be valuable, and not using punctuation is one of the best techniques to achieve this.

If the only instances of periodless sentences were to be found in poetry, there would be no clear explanation of the sentence *It's time you went home*, which would then simply be dismissed as an error. But sentences without end-periods are everywhere – in book-titles, newspaper headlines, road-signs, posters, product labels, advertisements, and many other locations where the period is unnecessary because the completion of the sentence is indicated by the proximity of a physical boundary. It is a modern, specifically late twentieth-century trend. In the eighteenth century, even the advertising headings in a newspaper column would be punctuated:

> To be SOLD.
> Advertisements.

During the nineteenth century, we see the emergence of a mixed style. One advertisement for a tooth-powder, published in about 1830, repeats the product name twice: the first time it is end-stopped:

> NEWTON'S
> RESTORATIVE
> TOOTH POWDER.

The second time it isn't. And during the twentieth century

ads became increasingly punctuationless, with type, layout, and colour handling any required semantic contrastivity.

It's therefore not surprising to see the development of a punctuationless style in Internet settings where the physical – in this case, the electronic – boundaries suffice to mark sentence-ending. Users sense this, so that even those who would routinely use a period in other writing find themselves dropping it when engaged in a written exchange where there are pressures of space (as in texting and tweeting) or time (as in the quickfire interactions of instant messaging). Studies are few, but the general impression is that between 40 and 50 per cent of statements in short messages have no final period. The line-break has taken over the function of the period. We don't need both.

This isn't because Internet users are ignorant about punctuation, as some media pundits have suggested. On the contrary. When short messages contain more than one sentence, the first one is almost always separated from the second by some sort of mark – often by more than one, as we'll see in the next chapter. And users are stylistically aware of what they are doing. I recently had the chance to go through a corpus of text-messages produced by students in the upper years of a British secondary school (around sixteen years of age). There were hardly any sentence periods. But a corpus of essays from the same students showed a perfectly regular use of punctuation. Clearly these students were well aware of the stylistic differences between text-message and essay – and they were very ready to talk about the way punctuation varied between the two.

It isn't just a young person's thing, nor is it especially recent. An instant-message chat between my wife and my daughter in 2007 contained 123 turns, and there was only a single use of the period (after an unusually long sentence in the conversation). There were a few exclamation marks and question marks, but otherwise the interaction looked like this:

H: i'd better do a bit of work, i suppose
H: our visitor didn't come in the end
L: me too
H: not well
L: see you later
H: great – yes in all evening
H: have a good day
L: ok, will try video

Neither party used periods, notwithstanding the age difference between them (and putting this as tactfully as I can: neither were under thirty). I have similar examples going back to the 1990s.

What I wasn't expecting, in my encounter with the young students – though, thinking about it now, I shouldn't really have been surprised – was to see a shift in the semantic values attached to the period. In a style where the default punctuation is zero, any positive marks are bound to take on new values. In traditional contexts, as we saw earlier, the period is the 'neutral' mark, conveying the least amount of emotion. If zero becomes the neutral mark, then the role of the period will change. As Ben Crair put it, in an online report for *New Republic* (25 November 2013):

The Period Is Pissed: When did our plainest punctuation mark become so aggressive?

(For UK readers: he means 'angry', not 'drunk'.) The writer was reflecting his sense of what was happening in US usage, and I've encountered exactly the same thing in Britain. If a writer uses a line-break to mark the sentence end of a short message, then using a period must convey to the reader that something semantically extra has been added. And this 'extra' is some indication of seriousness or finality, which can be interpreted in a variety of ways. Here's one of Crair's examples:

> Say you find yourself limping to the finish of a wearing workday. You text your girlfriend: 'I know we made a reservation for your bday tonight but wouldn't it be more romantic if we ate in instead?' If she replies:
> we could do that
> Then you can ring up Papa John's and order something special. But if she replies,
> we could do that.
> Then you're either going out or you're eating Papa John's alone.

Crair sums it up:

> people use the period not simply to conclude a sentence, but to announce 'I am not happy about the sentence I just concluded.'

Crair thinks 'This is an unlikely heel turn in linguistics', but actually it's perfectly predictable, given the systemic nature of punctuation. Change one value, and the others change too. The British students gave me several examples, such as:

> A: what time do we meet
> B: seven oclock [= neutral]
> B: seven oclock. [= I've told you already. You should know, stupid!]

Naomi Baron and Rich Ling saw the same sort of thing going on in a 2011 study of American student text-messages. This next comment from Natalie illustrates. If you're having an argument, she says, and the other person puts a period at the end of their sentence

> It'll be like really abrupt. And you'll be like oh that sounded like they are mad.

Almost all the comments about punctuation recorded by Baron and Ling were from girls. The boys had little to say about it, other than complaining about the way girls used too many exclamation marks and emoticons. But both groups showed through their comments that they were well aware of what was going on.

Looking back over my own family instant-message exchanges, I see we do similar things. Starting a chat is easy enough. Ending it is much trickier, as we never know whether our interlocutor is going to add an extra message. The period is a useful way of saying 'I'm finished' or 'I'm winding up'. I've seen several conversations where there are no periods at all until the participants are about to end, as in the final exchange of this conversation between my wife and my son:

> B: 11–12 tomo is a v good time to call.
> H: excellent.

The zero phenomenon seems universal. Following a webinar I gave for the International Association of Teachers of English as a Foreign Language (IATEFL) in May 2013, the chatbox received 110 reactions from teachers of English from around the world. All except three were statements, mostly one-liners adding some sort of appreciative comment, saying thank you or goodbye, or expressing agreement with what someone else had said. Over half (57) had zero punctuation, and only 7 used a final period (including one instance of > – a symbol that appears above a period on some keyboards, and clearly a mistype). There was a single instance of a dash. The two next in frequency were the exclamation mark (30 instances) and an emoticon (9 instances), and I'll discuss these later.

What we are seeing here, then, is a stylistic shift. A new variety of English has emerged in these Internet settings, and motivated new patterns of usage, which include a realignment of some semantic values in punctuation. There are also pragmatic factors underlying the development – ergonomic factors to do with the ease and speed of typing, and fashion factors reflecting the informality, spontaneity, and playfulness associated with electronic communication. A traditional view of punctuation is not going to help in explaining what's going on electronically; nor, of course, is an account of what's happening on the Internet going to help in relation to traditional writing. From a teaching point of view, the primary aim must be to ensure that students learn – if they don't instinctively recognize it – that the two domains are stylistically distinct, that they understand the nature of the linguistic differences, and that they become 'masters of punctuation', able to translate from one medium to the other as occasion demands.

At the same time, we mustn't overstate the differences. The Internet is a very diverse medium, with participants of all ages, social backgrounds, and temperaments, so we will find that some users punctuate their sentences in exactly the same way as they would do offline. The notions of a hierarchy and system in punctuation apply with equal force to both. And several punctuational features show little variation in usage as we move between online and offline domains, as is clear if we examine the two long-recognized options at sentence-level in the punctuation hierarchy: the exclamation mark and question mark.

20

Exclamation marks!!

It's time you went home!

In Chapter 4, I noted the arrival in English of the 'point of admiration' during the late fourteenth century. The terminology soon evolved. By the seventeenth century we find it being called a 'note of admiration', 'admirative point', and 'sign of admiration', as well as 'wonderer' and 'note of exclamation'. There was evidently some uncertainty over the best way of capturing the meanings involved, judging by the definition in Randle Cotgrave's French/English dictionary of 1611, where he defines *admiratif* as 'Th'admirative point, or point of admiration (and of detestation)'.

Dr Johnson ignored the earlier variants and went for 'exclamation', which he defined as 'A note by which a pathetical sentence is marked thus !' (*pathetical*: 'affecting the passions'), and this seems to have influenced the grammarians Bishop Lowth and Lindley Murray – both of whom call it an 'exclamation point' – and everyone else after them. This is the usage which became dominant in the USA. In Britain, 'exclamation mark' became the norm. But the nineteenth century did see several further alternatives. In the anonymous (though attributed to Percival Leigh) *Comic English Grammar* (1840), the author says that 'the notes *of admiration* which we so often hear in theatres' are called 'notes of hand'. Goold Brown, in his *Institutes of English Grammar* (1890), calls the mark an 'ecphoneme'. And, as I mentioned earlier (p. 73), in Henry Alford's *The Queen's English* (1864) we see the printers blamed for inserting 'shrieks' all over the place. The newspaper world around the end of that century added several more, such as 'astonisher', 'gasper', 'screamer', 'startler', and 'shout'. In computer jargon, the list goes on and on: 'bang', 'pling', 'wham', 'smash', 'yell', 'cuss', 'boing', 'wow' ...

No other punctuation mark has attracted such criticism in modern times as the exclamation mark. The antagonism isn't restricted to pedantic stylists. Some very well-known authors have taken against them. Mark Twain opens his essay 'How to Tell a Story' (1897) by warning comic writers against the depressing habit of shouting at the reader, including the use of 'whooping exclamation-points', which, he says, makes him 'want to renounce joking and lead a better life'. And there's a much-quoted remark attributed to F Scott Fitzgerald: 'Cut out all these exclamation points', adding 'An exclamation point is like laughing at your own joke.' Repeated marks attract particular criticism. One of the characters in Terry Pratchett's Discworld novel *Eric* (1990) insists that 'Multiple exclamation marks are a sure sign of a diseased mind.'

The antipathy seems to have set in during the late nineteenth century, as part of a general feeling that writers, editors, and printers had rather overdone their preference for heavy punctuation. We see exclamation marks littering the pages in editions of Shakespeare, for instance. Take this line from *Romeo and Juliet* when the Nurse tries to wake Juliet (4.5.12). Modern editions (such as Arden, Oxford, Penguin) print it thus:

What, dressed, and in your clothes, and down again?

The Albion edition of the plays (1889) prints it thus:

What, dress'd! and in your clothes! and down again!

This was typical of the popular writing of the day. *Punch*, my first port of call for data about linguistic trends in the nineteenth century, gives us evidence in its very first issue in 1841, parodying the popular cheap novels of the day. Mr Punch plans to write a best-seller, 'terse and abrupt in style', which he calls *Clare Grey: A Novel*. In this extract from Volume III, Tom, back from the wars, has just heard that his lady-love Clare is marrying Job Snooks:

> Can't be—No go—Stump up to church—Too true—Clare
> just made Mrs. Snooks—Madness!! rage !!! death!!!!

And it is in the pages of *Punch*, especially in the cartoon captions, that we often see the exclamation replacing entire utterances, as in my illustration from A A Milne (p. 30).

Multiple exclamations, along with dashes, were always a feature of informal letter-writing between intimates, where we see a natural 'inflation' taking place as someone's letter proceeds. If writers use such a mark to express emotional level 1, at the beginning of their letter, there's a likelihood it will be increasingly repeated as their news unfolds:

> I'm fine! …
> You'll never guess what happened!! …
> I met Julian again!!! …
> And he wants to come over!!!!

Once you're on the exclamation bus, it's difficult to get off. And if you try to, you can easily convey the opposite of what you intended.

> I'm fine! …
> You'll never guess what happened!! …
> I met Julian again!!! …

And he wants to come over!

A one-exclamation-mark meeting now suggests a much less exciting prospect. And a zero-exclamation-mark would sound even worse:

And he wants to come over.

We'll see this inflation problem arise again in relation to the Internet.

The appeal of the exclamation has continued into the online era. Indeed, frequent and multiple use is one of the defining features of Internet orthography. It's the most-used alternative to zero as a sentence-ending in fast-moving online exchanges, as illustrated by the IATEFL chatbox in the previous chapter, where it closed nearly a third of the messages. Multiple use is fostered by the ease with which the mark can be produced on a modern keyboard, simply by holding down the key. Messages with half-a-dozen exclamations aren't at all unusual, and I've seen instances, when a sender has got really excited about something, of a sequence in which entire lines are taken up by them. This could never have happened in the early typewriter era, where the machines had no separate key for an exclamation. To type one you had to type a period, then back-space and hold the shift key down while you typed an apostrophe. Not very user-friendly.

Who are the frequent users of exclamations? There's a history of associating them with youth and gender. Several studies since the 1970s have analysed male and female writing from this point of view, and usually found that women use exclamations far more than men, whether in traditional writing or online. For example, in a small but illuminating study for the online *Journal of Computer-Mediated Communication* (2006), Carol Waseleski examined the use of exclamations in posts made to two electronic discussion lists. She found that women used them far more often than men – 73 per cent of all exclamations.

That's the easy bit. The difficult part comes when we try to explain why this is so. People who hear of this result usually jump to the conclusion that it must be because women are more emotional or excitable than men, so they will exclaim more often. However, Waseleski's study showed that this was not the case. Less than 10 per cent of the exclamation-pointed sentences indicated strong emotions, whether positive or negative, and where they did, they were equally distributed between the sexes. Indeed, there was a hint that the men were more excitable than the women, especially when it came to 'flaming' (angry Internet exchanges). Rather, the women used the mark more often when thanking, appreciating, welcoming, and generally contributing to what has been called a 'supportive' style of communication.

The dangers of superficial generalizations become apparent when we consider the range of meanings that an exclamation can convey: apology, challenge, agreement, call to action, statement of fact, friendship, argument, hostility, sarcasm, thanks … the list seems endless. Here's a short selection of contexts where the mark would be routinely used these days:

- interjections – *Oh!*
- expletives – *Damn!*
- greetings – *Happy Xmas!*
- calls – *Johnny!*
- commands – *Stop!*
- expressions of surprise – *What a mess!*
- emphatic statements – *I want to see you now!*
- attention-getters – *Listen carefully!*
- loud speech in dialogue – *I'm in the garden!*

- ironic comments – *He paid, for a change!* or ... *for a change (!)*
- strong mental attitudes – *'Hardly!' he thought*

A complete list of situations would be impossibly long, as it would need to identify all the emotions that could motivate the use of the mark. But the last two contexts show how easy it is to make a false generalization, such as 'exclamations show that the speech is louder'. There's no sound at all in the last example. Nor was there when Christopher Robin realized that Pooh was right (p. 30).

With so many meanings at its disposal, it's hardly surprising that exclamations are frequent, especially in writing where a strong element of social bonding is present. This is why they have become so common on the Internet. As I'll discuss later in relation to emoticons, there's an inevitable distancing effect that accompanies the detached appearance of online exchanges, which lack the facial expressions and tones of voice that express attitude in any face-to-face spoken conversation. This clashes with the expectations of social networking exchanges, forums, emails, instant messages, text-messages, and other activities where people want to express warmth and personality. Any device that will add solidarity and rapport is thus very welcome, and exclamations seem to be the punctuation of choice to enable this to happen. As David Shipley and Will Schwalbe say, in their book *Send: Why People Email So Badly and How to Do It Better* (2007):

> Because email is without affect it has a dulling quality that almost necessitates kicking everything up a notch just to bring it to where it would normally be.

But of course the overuse of any linguistic feature can lead to precisely the same kind of dulling effect. The ideal is to find some sort of balance.

In the twentieth century, the concern over excessive or inappropriate use of exclamation marks stems chiefly from the attitude of Henry Watson Fowler, in his various writings, and especially in *A Dictionary of Modern English Usage* (1926). (Surprisingly, the other big influence on style in that century, Ernest Gowers's *Plain Words* (1948) has nothing to say about exclamation marks, in its section on punctuation.) In the entry on 'stops', Fowler condemns the 'excessive use of exclamation marks [as] one of the things that betray the uneducated or unpractised writer', and elsewhere he adds that it shows the kind of writer 'who wants to add a spurious dash of sensation to something unsensational'. He excludes the case of poetry, but in prose he advises everyone to confine the use of the mark to what grammar recognizes as exclamations, and to avoid it after statements, questions, and commands.

Fowler gives a list of what he considers to be the grammatical cases (the following examples are from his book). They are: interjections (*oh!*), expletives (*heavens!, my God!*), sentences introduced by *what* and *how* (*What a difference it makes!, How I love you!*), wishes (*God forbid!*), emotional ellipses (*If only I could!*), emotional inversions (*A fine friend you have been!*), and apostrophes (in the rhetorical sense of 'address', as in *You little dear!*).

If Fowler had left it at that, the situation would be fairly clear. But he knows that 'the matter is not quite so simple', and he breaks his principle by accepting the necessity of adding an exclamation mark to statements 'to convey that the tone is not merely what would be natural to the words themselves, but is that suitable to scornful quotation, to the unexpected, the amusing, the disgusting, or something that needs the comment of special intonation to secure that the words shall be taken as they are meant'. He illustrates from such sentences as:

> You thought it didn't matter!
> Each is as bad as the other, only more so!
> He puts his knife in his mouth!

These are acceptable, he says. But he then disallows:

> This is a lie!
> My heart was in my mouth!
> Who cares!

He comments about the latter: 'the words themselves suffice to show the tone', and so an exclamation mark would show 'only that the writer does not know his business'.

But anyone who tries to use this distinction as a guideline for good practice is soon going to get into trouble, as *any* sentence can be given a special intonation to express an emotion that goes beyond what the words convey. 'This is a lie' could be said in several tones of voice. 'Who cares' could appear as a genuine enquiry – 'Who cares?' Indeed, one of my own books had a title which played on exactly this intonational ambiguity: *Who Cares About English Usage?*

That's the problem with the pedantry that surrounds this topic: it's easy enough to complain about excessive use; it's not to easy to write rules that say when such marks are appropriate and when they aren't. Never use five exclamation marks? Tell that to the Ghost at the Opera House in Terry Pratchett's Discworld novel *Maskerade* (1995), who sends the message:

> Ahahahahaha! Ahahahaha! Aahahaha! BEWARE!!!!!

The punctuation doesn't impress the musical director at the opera house, Salzella:

> What sort of person sits down and writes a maniacal laugh? And all those exclamation marks, you notice? Five? A sure

sign of someone who wears his underpants on his head.

Opera can do that to a man.

It's a character note, nonetheless. As it would be for the demon who put the notice on the door to Hell in Pratchett's *Eric* (*You Don't Have To Be 'Damned' To Work Here, But It Helps!!!*), eliciting Rincewind's wry comment that I mentioned earlier: 'Multiple exclamation marks are a sure sign of a diseased mind.' When we note the way some authors revel in the use of exclamation marks, it's clear that literary usage sends us mixed messages. The Twains and Fitzgeralds of this world are the ones most quoted; but there's another side, when we see these marks used wisely and well. To follow advice that says simply 'cut them out' is just plain daft, as it eliminates virtually everything we would ever want to read. And it would put us in a very awkward position as we live our daily lives.

Exclamation marks are unavoidable these days. They litter our roads, warning of danger ahead. They alert us to urgent electronic messages. They appear as an identity mark above a character's head in some video games. And they are there in all sorts of specialized settings, such as mathematics, computer languages, and Internet slang. In phonetics, the mark is a symbol representing an alveolar click sound (as in *tut tut*). In comics, it usually shows a character's surprise or shock, often by the symbol appearing alone in a bubble, in varying sizes (depending on the intensity of the moment). In chess notation, along with the question mark it is part of a family of semantic contrasts: *!* indicates a good move; *!!* a brilliant move; *?!* a dubious move; and *!?* an interesting but risky move.

The exclamation mark can even get into proper names. Places include *Westward Ho!* in Devon and an intriguing family of names in Quebec: the tiny parish municipality of *Saint-Louis-du-Ha! Ha!* and its local river (*Rivière Ha! Ha!*) and bay (*Baie des Ha! Ha!*) – a *haha*, according to local historians, being an old French word for an unexpected obstacle (presumably encountered when the area was first being explored). *Oklahoma!* has one too, in the name of the musical – though the innovation caught Helene Hanff by surprise. She records, in *Underfoot in Show Business*, how she was working at the Theatre Guild on the press release for the new show, to be called *Oklahoma*. She and a colleague had mimeographed 10,000 sheets when there was a phone call. This is how she tells it:

> Joe picked up the phone and we heard him say, 'Yes, Terry,' and 'All right, dear,' and then he hung up. And then he looked at us, in the dazed way people who worked at the Guild frequently looked at each other.
>
> 'They want,' he said in a faraway voice, 'an exclamation point after "Oklahoma." '
>
> Which is how it happened that, far into the night, Lois and I, bundled in our winter coats, sat in the outer office putting 30,000 exclamation points on 10,000 press releases
> …

Among people, there is a US dance-punk band called *!!!* – pronounced (it would seem from their website) 'Chk Chk Chk' – a motif that continues in the title of their album *THR!!!ER*, released in 2013. Among individuals, pride of place has surely to go to the writer Elliot S! Maggin, known to enthusiasts of Superman, Batman, and other comics. Maggin recounts the story of his middle initial like this:

> I got into the habit of putting exclamation marks at the end of sentences instead of periods because reproduction on pulp paper was so lousy. So once, by accident, when I signed

a script I put the exclamation point after my 'S' because I was just used to going to that end of the typewriter at the time. And Julie [his editor, Julius Schwartz] saw it, and before he told me, he goes into the production room and issues a general order that any mention of Elliot Maggin's name will be punctuated with an exclamation mark rather than a period from now on until eternity.

And so it came to pass.

One of the main indications of the ambiguity surrounding the use of the exclamation mark is its overlap with the question mark. It's an ambiguity within grammar as well as punctuation, and in speech as well as writing, reflected in such utterances as 'Are you asking me or telling me?' Sometimes the answer is 'both': a person can query and be surprised at the same time. This is what led to the typographical experiment to devise a new combined mark. Martin K Speckter, an adman with a strong personal interest in typography, suggested it in an article in *Type Talks* in 1962. He had noticed that copywriters often used the two marks in the sequences *?!* and *!?* and thought it would be useful to link them into a single symbol (‽). What to call the new mark? Suggestions included 'emphaquest', 'interrapoint', 'exclarogative', 'consternation mark', 'exclamaquest', and other blends, but the one he chose (incorporating an earlier slang term for an exclamation) was *interrobang*. It attracted a flurry of interest, but not enough to change traditional printing practices, and it largely disappeared from view during the 1970s. However, it is still encountered as a cult usage online, and it even exists as a Unicode character, so it may yet have a future. In the meantime we are left with the two old stalwarts.

Interlude: Inverting exclamation

¡ ⹁

Innovation in the use of the exclamation mark has a long history. John Wilkins, in his *Essay Towards a Real Character and a Philosophical Language* (1688), a work that in its detail anticipated Roget's *Thesaurus*, decided that the normal set of punctuation marks wasn't enough to handle all the meanings people want to express. In his view, the main deficiency was in relation to irony:

> the distinction of meaning and intention of any words,
> when they are to be understood by way of Sarcasm or scoff,
> or in a contrary sense to that which they naturally signifie.

In Chapter 9 of Part 3, 'Concerning Natural Grammar', he observes:

> And though there be not (for ought I know) any note
> designed for this in any of the Instituted Languages, yet that
> is from their deficiency and imperfection,

and he concludes:

> there ought to be some mark for direction, when things are
> to be so pronounced.

So, in Chapter 14, as part of his new writing system, he proposes an inverted exclamation mark. It never caught on, though it has had a recent resurgence online (see Chapter 33).

21

Next, question marks?

It's time you went home?

By contrast with its exclamatory cousin, the question mark has attracted little notice over the years. This is because people think it has just one, obvious, semantic function: to show that somebody has asked a question. And they feel that the concept of 'asking a question' is so basic and straightforward, so well grounded in English grammar, that uncertainty over its use could never arise. Gertrude Stein held that view (as we'll see at the very end of this book). There isn't even much variation in terminology, over the centuries, apart from an early use of 'asker' and a scholarly use of 'eroteme' (from a Greek word meaning 'question'). Everyone seems to have focused on the terms 'interrogation' or 'question', so we find expressions such as 'mark of interrogation', 'interrogative point', and the interesting (but short-lived) nineteenth-century use of 'question-stop'. Today, 'question mark' has no competition.

Are people right to think in this way? Is it so straightforward? Yes and no. The main use of the question mark is indeed much more clear-cut than in the case of the exclamation mark. But there are a few complications, partly arising from the imperfect relationship between writing and speech, and partly from the way fashions in English grammatical usage have changed in recent years. Moreover, the changes seem to be on the increase. So this chapter turns out to be just as long as its predecessor.

What do I mean by 'well grounded in English grammar'? The grammar-books present us with a set of rules that are clear and concise, recognizing the following question-types.

- *Yes/no*-questions, as the name suggests, prompt the answer *yes* or *no* (or of course *I don't know*, etc). They're formed by changing the order of the subject and verb:

  You are going to town. > Are you going to town?
  They were ready. > Were they ready?

- *Wh*-questions (also called *open-ended* questions) begin with a question-word such as *what*, *why*, or *how*, and again change the word-order:

  What are they doing?
  Where did they put the book?

- Alternative questions, a sub-type of *yes/no*-questions, present an either/or situation, where the answer can't be *yes* or *no*:

  Are you awake or asleep?

These question-types rarely present any problems of punctuation. It's been standard practice since the eighteenth century to end them with a question mark, and it would be considered a basic error if one were omitted. Only a very daring literary user gets away with it (such as Gertrude Stein or James Joyce). But some punctuational issues do arise in relation to a fourth question-type.

- The tag question, which can be positive or negative, makes an assertion, and then invites the listener's response to it:

> They're going, are they?
> They're going, aren't they?

The meanings here are trickier, as they reflect the intonation with which they can be spoken. If I use a rising tone (í), I'm asking you. If I use a falling tone (ì), I'm telling you.

> It's three o'clock, ísn't it? (*asking*)
> It's three o'clock, ìsn't it? (*telling*)

It's this last example that gives us a problem, for if someone is 'telling' us, what need of a question mark? To make the difference between these last two sentences clear in writing, therefore, we will often see this:

> It's three o'clock, isn't it? (*asking*)
> It's three o'clock, isn't it. (*telling*) *or even* It's three o'clock, isn't it!

But the orthographic distinction isn't standard, so that we often have to look carefully at the context to work out which meaning a writer intended, and it isn't always clear. It's one of the pitfalls over the use of the question mark that writers need to be aware of.

Here's another example of the same kind. I saw this request on a classroom door:

> Would the last student to leave this room please turn off the light.

This looks like a question, but it has the force of a command. There was no question mark at the end. Should there have been? The force of the request would have been very different if it had read:

> Would the last student to leave this room please turn off the light?

This turns it into a genuine question, offering the option of 'yes' or 'no'. We might interpret such a version in various ways – more inviting, perhaps, or more of a desperate plea! But we don't usually find a question mark in such circumstances. The writer is telling, not asking.

What we're seeing, in these cases, is an echo of the old controversy: does punctuation reflect grammar or pronunciation. The question mark began as a way of giving preachers a useful graphic cue about when to adopt a questioning tone of voice. By the end of the eighteenth century it had been firmly tied to grammatical constructions. Today, punctuation is often used as a way of by-passing grammar and directly representing pronunciations that reflect the intentions lying behind a sentence. It's this pragmatic function that accounts for the asking/telling issue, and it appears again in the commonest contemporary trend: the punctuation of 'uptalk'.

You're familiar with uptalk? It's the use of a high rising tone at the end of a statement? As a way of checking that your listener has understood you? The phenomenon began to be noticed during the 1980s, associated chiefly with the speech of young New Zealanders and Australians, and was transmitted to a wider audience through the Australian soap *Neighbours*. At the same time, an American version, associated initially with young Californians (you know?), was being widely encountered through films and television. At first largely confined to young women, it spread to young men, and since has been working its way up the age-range. Although disliked by many, its value lies in its succinctness: it allows someone to make a statement and ask a question at the same time. If I say 'I live in Holyhead?', the rising intonation acts as an unspoken question ('Do you know where that is?'). If you know, you will simply nod and let me continue. If you don't, my intonation offers you a chance to get clarification ('Where is that, exactly?'). I don't have to spell out the options. Uptalk has also become a fashionable way of establishing rapport, with the intonation offering the other participants in a conversation the chance to intervene.

The feature wasn't new. Several regional accents of the British Isles have long been associated with a rising lilt on statements, especially in the Celtic fringe. That's probably how it got into the antipodean accent in the first place. And there are hints of its presence in earlier centuries. Joshua Steele, in his essay on *The Melody and Measure of Speech* (1775), was the first to transcribe intonational patterns using a musical notation, and he noticed it. It would be very useful, he says, to develop an exact notation to describe 'how much the voice is let down in the conclusion of periods, with respect both to loudness and tone, according to the practice of the best speakers … for I have observed, that many speakers offend in this article; some keeping up their ends too high'. Evidently he didn't like it either.

But, like it or not, statements spoken in a questioning way are here, and so the intention behind them needs to be shown through punctuation whenever people wish to reflect this kind of mutually affirming dialogue in their writing. In the absence of an accepted new punctuation mark to do the job, writers have had to rely on the traditional question mark. We're unlikely to find question marks at the end of statements in written monologues, or in representations of formal conversations; but in places where informality and rapport are the norm, such as Internet chat, they are on the increase. We see messages like these tweets:

> I wonder when they'll give an Oscar to an LGBTQ actor for their brave and risky portrayal of a struggling straight person? [lesbian-gay-bisexual-transgendered-questioning]

Maybe we should report weather related brewery closures like the morning TV news reports school closures?

We can imagine the rising tones as these sentences reach their close.

This extended use of the question mark is in fact anticipated in a range of earlier uses expressing such attitudes as uncertainty, doubt, sarcasm, and lack of conviction. The mark is usually placed in parentheses adjacent to (before or after) the word that is its semantic focus:

(a) So I ought to be with you by (?) seven.
(b) This was written by Floura (?) Smith
(c) He claimed that the vote would go our way without any trouble. (?)
(d) She arrived in a new (?) dress.

We have to be careful about mid-sentence placements, as they can be ambiguous. What is being queried in (d), for example: the newness or the dress itself?

The range of meanings is so wide that there's sometimes an overlap with the semantic range conveyed by the exclamation mark. In (a), (b), and (c), replacing the question mark would convey a clearly different meaning:

(c1) This was written by Floura (?) Smith (is that her name?)
(c2) This was written by Floura (!) Smith (what a stupid name)

But in (d), there's hardly any difference, as the ironic intention could be conveyed equally well by either:

(d1) She arrived in a new (?) red dress.
(d2) She arrived in a new (!) red dress.

It's presumably this overlap in meaning that led early typesetters to confuse the two functions when the marks were
first used. For example, this is how the First Folio prints one
of Hamlet's famous speeches (*Hamlet* 2.2.203):

> What a piece of worke is a man! how Noble in Reason? how
> infinite in faculty? ...

The whole speech is a series of exclamations; Hamlet isn't
questioning anything. But apart from the first sentence the
printer took everything else as a series of questions.

From time to time, people become dissatisfied with the
broad application of the question mark and try to narrow it
down, usually by proposing distinct marks for the different
kinds of question. Rhetorical questions have attracted particular attention, as – not requiring any answer – they are
so different in kind. An Elizabethan printer, Henry Denham,
was an early advocate, proposing in the 1580s a reversed
question mark (⸮) for this function, which came to be called
a *percontation* mark (from a Latin word meaning a questioning
act). Easy enough to handwrite, some late sixteenth-century
authors did sporadically use it, such as Robert Herrick. Here
are the opening lines of an elegy to his friend John Browne,
who died in 1619:

> Is, is there nothing cann withstand
> > The hand
> Of Time: but that it must
> Be shaken into dust⸮

But printers were unimpressed, and the mark never became standard. However, it has received a new lease of life online, as we'll later see some people using it as way of showing an ironic or sarcastic question.

As a mark high up the punctuation hierarchy, the question mark, like the exclamation mark and the period, acts unambiguously as a sign of separation – to show where one sentence ends and the next begins. That's why a period was included within the symbol (and reflected in the term *question-stop*). This means it can be used without ambiguity even in a sequence of elliptical sentences:

> Will the event be in London? in Tokyo? in Rio?

It should be noted, though, that in such a case the question mark loses its full force as a sentence separator. Normally the next sentence after a question mark begins with a capital letter. But not here. If we try to use capitals:

> Will the event be in London? In Tokyo? In Rio?

we lose the structural parallelism between the three locations.

It's even more awkward if the list is presented vertically. Writers feel uncomfortable with all three of the options:

Will the event be	*Will the event be*	*Will the event be?*
in Tokyo?	in Tokyo	in Tokyo
in London?	in London	in London
in Paris?	in Paris	in Paris
in Berlin?	in Berlin?	in Berlin

The first raises objections of visual clutter. The second makes it appear that there's something questionable about Berlin. And the third makes it look as if the locations are outside the scope of the question mark. In such a case, the only solution is to rephrase, and avoid the problem.

Other issues of punctuation usage regarding the question mark are all to do with what happens when a questioned sentence is included within another sentence. If it's an indirect question (reported speech), there's no problem: the mark isn't used.

She asked me where I had left the books.

Usage had vacillated during the seventeenth century, until Lindley Murray made it absolutely clear:

A point of interrogation should not be employed, in cases where it is only said a question has been asked, and where the words are not used as a question.

That was that. But what happens when the words *are* used as a question, and are included within another sentence?

If the question is placed inside the sentence, but not at the end, the answer is straightforward, as the parentheses or inverted commas (or both) express the separation well:

He wrote a comment 'Is this your book?' on the cover.
He wrote a comment (Is this your book?) on the cover.
He wrote a comment ('Is this your book?') on the cover.

But if the questioning utterance occurs at the end of the sentence, writers often wonder whether to add the sentence-ending mark that would be appropriate to the sentence as a whole:

(a) He wrote the comment 'Is this your book?'.
(b) Did you see the comment 'Is this your book?'?
(c) How on earth did he write the comment 'Is this your book?'!

Usually, style guides recommend dropping the period in (a),

on the grounds that the period is already a part of the question mark. But some keep the double marking in (b) and (c), on the grounds that there are two meanings being expressed, each of which requires its own mark. People vacillate over (b). If the visual appearance is unacceptable, then writers are recommended to rephrase:

Did you see the words 'Is this your book?' on the cover?

A similar situation occurs if the question mark is part of a title that is printed in italics. There's no problem when the title is a statement:

Did she sing *I'm singing in the rain*?

But there is a problem if it's a question:

Did she sing *Where have all the flowers gone?*?

Nobody is likely to tolerate the juxtaposition of two question marks in different fonts. It's at this point that authors and printers begin to weep, for there is no solution other than rephrasing. And there's no solution in handwriting either, unless we've mastered two (roman and italic) hands. And even if we have, would readers really notice the contrast?

This is an important general point. It isn't the case that punctuation can solve all the problems of graphic representation thrown up by the multifarious subjects that we want to write about. It isn't a perfect system. And an important aim of teaching is to draw students' attention to the places where the system breaks down, and to suggest ways around the difficulties.

Students also need to note that, as with exclamation marks, there are a number of specialized uses, such as the chess notations described in the previous chapter. We see special uses of the question mark in computer programming and in Uniform Resource Locators (URLs) when they include a query string. This example, from the Shakespeare's Words website, tells us that someone has searched for Act 1 Scene 1 in Play Number 3:

http://www.shakespeareswords.com/Plays.aspx?Ac=
1&SC=1&IdPlay=3

In linguistics, we see it as an alternative symbol for the glottal stop and also to mark a doubtfully acceptable sentence, such as *?I gave a nudge to John.*

It's also important to develop a sense of frequency norms to avoid any charge of excessive use. The issue isn't as dramatic as in the case of exclamation marks. On the whole, people don't use question marks repeatedly to the same extent. And multiple question marks (*Really???*) are much less commonly encountered than multiple exclamation marks, though of course we'll see a sprinkling in informal letter-writing and in excitable Internet situations. In the Pooh example on p. 30 there is a single vs double use conveying Christopher Robin's dawning realization of what Pooh has said. That's clever writing. But I haven't found many instances where the semantic distinction is so well motivated.

It's theoretically possible to have an entire text with every sentence ending in a question mark. At least, I used to think it was just a theoretical matter. Not any longer, after reading Padgett Powell's surreal *The Interrogative Mood* (2009). His book begins:

Are your emotions pure? Are your nerves adjustable? How do you stand in relation to the potato? Should it still be Constantinople? ...

Fifty pages on, he is still asking:

> If you could be instantly fluent in a language you do not
> now speak, what language would it be? Can you change a
> tire by yourself? Have you ever petted a vole or a shrew? Do
> you partake of syrups?

Fifty pages more:

> What is the loudest noise you have ever heard? Have you
> done any mountain climbing? Would you eat a monkey?
> What broke your heart?

And it ends, after 164 pages and a couple of thousand
questions:

> Are you leaving now? Would you? Would you mind?

'If Duchamp or maybe Magritte wrote a novel', comments
novelist Richard Ford in the accompanying blurb, 'it might
look something like this.' And we do in fact see question
marks being used artistically sometimes – such as in concrete
poetry.

Interlude: Concrete questions

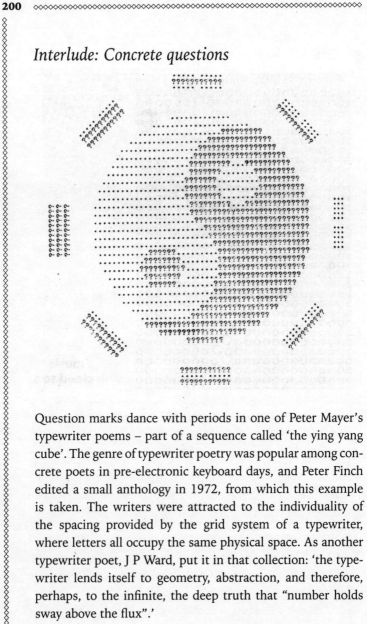

Question marks dance with periods in one of Peter Mayer's typewriter poems – part of a sequence called 'the ying yang cube'. The genre of typewriter poetry was popular among concrete poets in pre-electronic keyboard days, and Peter Finch edited a small anthology in 1972, from which this example is taken. The writers were attracted to the individuality of the spacing provided by the grid system of a typewriter, where letters all occupy the same physical space. As another typewriter poet, J P Ward, put it in that collection: 'the typewriter lends itself to geometry, abstraction, and therefore, perhaps, to the infinite, the deep truth that "number holds sway above the flux".'

22

Semicolons; or not

Like exclamation marks, semicolons have had a bad press –
but for different reasons. Several authors have taken against
them, especially novelists, mainly I suspect because they are
chiefly associated with the more complex sentences of formal
writing, and are felt to be out of place when inserted into a
free-flowing, informal dialogue. An often-quoted antagonist
is Kurt Vonnegut. He writes, at the beginning of Chapter 3 of
*A Man without a Country: A Memoir of Life in George W. Bush's
America* (2005):

> Here is a lesson in creative writing.
>
> First rule: Do not use semicolons. They are transvestite
> hermaphrodites representing absolutely nothing. All they
> do is show you've been to college.
>
> And I realize some of you may be having trouble
> deciding whether I am kidding or not.

He wasn't kidding. He uses no semicolons in his book – until
the very last chapter. There, at the end of a piece on the way
our brains deal with imagination, we read a much less-quoted
remark:

> Those of us who had imagination circuits built can look in
> someone's face and see stories there; to everyone, a face
> will just be a face.
>
> And there, I've just used a semi-colon, which at the
> outset I told you never to use. It is to make a point that I

did it. The point is: Rules only take us so far, even good rules.

Rules only take us so far. That sentence should be the motto for any work on punctuation.

There's a preference for short sentences, these days, when representing the colloquial character of everyday conversation, and when sentences do get longer, writers generally capture their rhythms by opting for dashes and ellipsis dots. Semicolons are no longer felt to do this job well. However, this is a modern response. Nineteenth-century novelists and short-story writers used them without a second thought. Here's Tom Jarndyce describing the horrors of going to law (Chapter 5 of Charles Dickens's *Bleak House*):

> 'For,' says he, 'it's being ground to bits in a slow mill; it's being roasted at a slow fire; it's being stung to death with single bees; it's being drowned by drops; it's going mad by grains.'

And poets have always found it a useful mark, ever since it arrived in English during the later decades of the sixteenth century. Ben Jonson took to it with enthusiasm, for example, as did John Donne.

Why was it so useful? Because it offered a way of conveying a meaning that had not been easily expressed before. When sentences are separated by periods, each topic comes across as semantically distinct. Two separate events are being reported in this summary of a conference schedule:

> Smith is going to speak about cars. Brown is going to speak about bikes.

There is no relationship being suggested between Smith and Brown. But imagine now that Smith and Brown are colleagues who have been working on a joint transport project, and they're each contributing to a report about their work. How do we maintain their independence, yet show they're in a relationship with each other that is different from the other conference speakers? The semicolon provides a solution:

> Smith is going to speak about cars; Brown is going to speak about bikes.

The semicolon allows us to join two independent sentences together when we feel they are semantically linked in some way. It is, in short, a device of coordination. And as such, we can think of its primary function as being the punctuation equivalent of the main coordinating conjunction, *and*.

> Smith is going to speak about cars and Brown is going to speak about bikes.

We'll often see sentences like that, with *and* linking the two constructions (*clauses*). But we'll also see them written like this:

> Smith is going to speak about cars, and Brown is going to speak about bikes.

Why the comma? It helps us to avoid a miscue. As we read, we don't actually know what's going to follow the *and*. It might be another linked noun:

> Smith is going to speak about cars and trucks ...

The comma makes it clear that the first clause is finished, and that what follows is going to be another clause.

So that's the essential choice the punctuation system gives us: semantically independent sentences vs semantically linked sentences. And there are only these two choices. The meaning of the colon is very different, as we'll see in the next chapter. And a comma is ruled out. We cannot write:

> Smith is going to speak about cars, Brown is going to speak about bikes.

This (sometimes called a 'comma splice') would make the reader think there was more to come, in the form of a list – a really bad miscue. It is, however, a common punctuation error, often unnoticed while we're writing, but usually obvious if we take the trouble to read aloud what we've written.

Once we see that the role of the semicolon is to unite and divide at the same time, we can see how it can be used to show a relationship between units other than complete sentences. Let's stay with *Bleak House*. In Chapter 6 we see Dickens uniting (yet keeping separate) elliptical sentences:

> Harold Skimpole loves to see the sun shine; loves to
> hear the wind blow; loves to watch the changing lights
> and shadows; loves to hear the birds, those choristers in
> Nature's great cathedral.

And in Chapter 8, we see Dickens linking phrases in his description of Chesney Wold:

> As to the House itself, with its three peaks in the roof; its
> various-shaped windows, some so large, some so small,
> and all so pretty; its trellis-work, against the south front
> for roses and honey-suckle, and its homely, comfortable,
> welcoming look.

This is where the semicolon comes into its own. It allows a huge amount of detail to be compressed into a single sentence. People admire Dickens's atmospheric sense of detail, the way he paints a vivid picture in a single sentence. The semicolon is one of the devices that enables him to do it.

The example also shows how the semicolon operates in the punctuation hierarchy, lying between the period and the comma. The same effect can't be achieved by relying on commas alone. Indeed, if we do that, the result is increasing confusion:

> As to the House itself, with its three peaks in the roof, its
> various-shaped windows, some so large, some so small,
> and all so pretty, its trellis-work, against the south front
> for roses and honey-suckle, and its homely, comfortable,
> welcoming look.

We need to breathe, to assimilate the different views as Dickens makes our eyes travel over the house; and the semicolon shows us where.

A similar organizational function appears when we look upwards in the hierarchy, towards the period. Note what is going on in this extract, also from Chapter 8, as Mr Jarndyce explains the workings of the law to Esther:

> Equity sends questions to Law, Law sends questions back
> to Equity; Law finds it can't do this, Equity finds it can't
> do that; neither can so much as say it can't do anything,
> without this solicitor instructing and this counsel appearing
> for A, and that solicitor instructing and that counsel
> appearing for B; and so on through the whole alphabet, like
> the history of the Apple Pie.

This is rhetorically very complex, but perfectly clear. And its clarity comes from the way the semicolon links not individual sentences, but pairs of sentences. Again, if the commas and semicolons were replaced by periods, the effect would be totally different. It's not that the irony is lost; simply that the reader has to work harder in order to see it:

> Equity sends questions to Law. Law sends questions back
> to Equity. Law finds it can't do this. Equity finds it can't do
> that.

This is always the best way to discover the function of
the semicolon: replace it by something else, and see what
happens.

To summarize: the semicolon allows us to see more clearly
the structure of a complex sentence, especially one which is
packed full of detail. It takes some of the load off the comma.
There's nothing semantically confusing about the sequence
of adjectives and nouns in the following sentence; but the
second version is much easier to read:

> The menu offered us orange or apple juice, a boiled, fried,
> or poached egg, toast, and tea or coffee.

> The menu offered us orange or apple juice; a boiled, fried,
> or poached egg; toast; and tea or coffee.

Note that, in the interest of preserving the parallelism
between the items in the list as a whole, we sometimes find
the semicolon closing an item that consists of just one word.

The trick, in using the semicolon, is to maintain grammatical parallelism. The semicolon happily links two sentences,
or two phrases, or even two words – but they are always two
units of the same grammatical kind. It begins to feel uncomfortable when we try to make it link units at different levels:

> The menu offered us orange or apple juice; a boiled, fried,
> or poached egg; toast; and I had coffee.

The reason is that *I had coffee* is a separate topic. It's no longer
an item on a menu list. As such, it would be better presented
as an afterthought, using a dash or ellipsis dots:

> The menu offered us orange or apple juice; a boiled, fried,
> or poached egg; toast – and I had coffee.

It's often been reported that the semicolon is going out of fashion, and the evidence (from the study of large collections of written material) does support a steady drop in frequency during the twentieth century. (They're much more common in British English than American English.) A typical finding is to see that 90 per cent of all punctuation marks are either periods or commas, and semicolons are just a couple of percent. The figure was much higher once. The semicolon had its peak in the eighteenth century, when long sentences were thought to be a feature of an elegant style, heavy punctuation was in vogue, and punctuation was becoming increasingly grammatical. The rot set in during the nineteenth century, when the colon became popular, and took over some of the semicolon's functions. The economics of the telegraph (the shorter the message, the cheaper) fostered short sentences. And today it has virtually disappeared from styles where sentences tend to be short, such as on the Internet. Some online style manuals are unequivocal. For example, Michael Miller writes in *Web Words That Work: Writing Web Copy That Sells* (2013, Chapter 14):

> you don't want to include more than a single thought in
> any one sentence; social media does not welcome such
> complexity. Avoid semicolons, dashes, and all other
> enablers of compound sentences. If you have two clauses or
> thoughts to get across, put them in two separate sentences.

There are many such cautions expressed these days. We have to take them with a pinch of salt, though, as the writers often break their own rules. Note the two thoughts separated by a semicolon in the above quotation, for instance. But such manuals are nonetheless influential.

It may be less fashionable than it was, but the semicolon still offers a unique semantic option: conveying a closer relationship than is expressed by the period. The writer is telling the reader: I want you to see that these thoughts relate to each other. And when we put it like that, we can see how easy it is for the mark to be misused. There's a limit to what the reader can take on board at any one time (that is, in any one sentence). We have no problem seeing a semantic relationship between two linked units, or even three; but if a sentence contains four or more, the strain on our comprehension is considerable. We are being asked to see the connection between too many separate thoughts, and we simply cannot do it.

This is one reason why I find it difficult to read certain authors who rely on the semicolon, such as William Hazlitt. Here's an example from his essay 'On Poetry in General' (1818). It's clear, from the use of the colon after the opening clause, that he sees everything which follows to be semantically linked, but it's impossible for us to maintain a coherent sense of connection as we read on:

> The storm of passion lays bare and shows the rich depths of the human soul: the whole of our existence, the sum total of our passions and pursuits, of that which we desire and that which we dread, is brought before us by contrast; the action and reaction are equal; the keenness of immediate suffering only gives us a more intimate participation with the antagonist world of good; makes us drink deeper of the cup of human life; tugs at the heart-strings; loosens the pressure about them; and calls the springs of thought and feeling into play with tenfold force.

Summarize that sentence! We follow the movement of the thought well enough, but any semantic role the semicolon might have had is soon lost, and we end up treating the mark as if it had no more value than indicating a slightly longer pause than a comma.

The same sort of uncertainty sometimes surfaces in modern novels. Here's the opening paragraph of Evelyn Waugh's *Brideshead Revisited* (in its 1959 revision):

> 'I have been here before,' I said; I had been there before; first with Sebastian more than twenty years ago on a cloudless day in June, when the ditches were creamy with meadowsweet and the air heavy with all the scents of summer; it was a day of peculiar splendour, and though I had been there so often, in so many moods, it was to that first visit that my heart returned on this, my latest.

Waugh seems to be trying to convey a stream of memories, but it's difficult to see a principle behind the use of the semicolons to do it, as opposed to using periods after *said* and *summer* and a dash or ellipsis dots after *before*. The semicolons are performing different functions in the same sentence – never a good practice.

These examples illustrate the kind of writing that has led some authors to assert that the semicolon is unnecessary, and to write a book without one, as George Orwell claimed to do in *Coming Up for Air* (1939). When he returned his proofs to his publisher (Roger Senhouse, of Secker and Warburg), he added:

> Did you know by the way that this book hasn't got a semicolon in it? I had decided about that time that the semicolon is an unnecessary stop and that I would write my next book without one.

In fact, as Peter Davison points out in his Penguin Classics edition, the surviving set of proofs does have three instances, though whether this was deliberate writing or patchy proof-reading remains unclear.

There's a second reason for the suspicion of semicolons which is nothing do with the frequency of their use. Its role, I said above, is to convey a semantic relationship. But what is the nature of that relationship? The primary meaning seems to be one of 'addition': we can replace many semicolons by *and* (or *and then*). But not all. If I look carefully at the style of a moderate semicolon user (me), we see it conveying a range of other meanings, such as these examples from earlier in this book:

- an adversative meaning, where the semicolon would have to be replaced by *but* or *whereas*:

  In one line, they might suggest a pause; in another they might not.

- a restatement, where it might be replaced by *that is*:

  The whole speech is a series of exclamations; Hamlet isn't questioning anything.

- a result, where it might be replaced by *as a result*:

  Only a tiny elite of monks, scribes, and other professionals knew how to write; so there was no popular expectation that inscriptions should be easy to read.

In this last example, the resultative meaning is actually made explicit by the word *so*.

The consequence of this semantic diversity is that readers are faced with the need to make a decision. Is the semicolon expressing addition, contrast, identity, result, or any other of the meanings that English conjunctions can express?

Usually, the context makes it clear. And often the writer who is aware of the issue will reinforce the desired meaning by the use of a conjunction (as I did with *so*). But a writer who is not aware could easily slip into using a semicolon where it remains unclear what the semantic relationship between the two sentences is. To return to my opening example, what is actually going on behind this sentence?

> Smith is going to speak about cars; Brown is going to speak about bikes.

If Smith and Brown are collaborators, the likely meaning is 'addition'. And we might expand it as follows:

> Smith is going to speak about cars; and Brown is going to speak about bikes.

But what if they are rivals or competing for an audience? Now the expansion goes in a different direction.

> Smith is going to speak about cars; but Brown is going to speak about bikes.

> Smith is going to speak about cars; so Brown is going to speak about bikes.

In short, writers should not react to a semicolon as if it were an isolated piece of punctuation. Its use or non-use should be governed by a sensitive appreciation of its role in relation to the discourse as a whole, in which semantics – not grammar – is the primary consideration. A practice of total avoidance of what can at times be a useful semantic option seems to me to be as counter-productive as the practice of overusing them.

As with other punctuation marks, the semicolon has a range of specialized separating uses, such as in mathematics, where it can mark a boundary between expressions. In computer programming, it usually acts as a statement separator – reflecting its use in grammar. A similar use appears with some email systems, where it separates the different recipients of a message. And it surfaces as the symbol for a wink in emoticons.

In law, it's taken very seriously. In 2004, in a San Francisco court, a conservative group challenged a statute allowing gay marriage (Proposition 22, Legal Defense and Education Fund). It asked the judge to

cease and desist issuing marriage licenses to and/or solemnizing marriages of same-sex couples; to show cause before this court.

The plea was rejected because of the punctuation. Judge James Warren explained:

The way you've written this it has a semicolon where it should have the word 'or'. I don't have the authority to issue it under these circumstances.

And he added: 'That semicolon is a big deal.'

Just how big a deal it can be was also illustrated by one of the most famous punctuation incidents of all time. It took place in France, but it was reported widely in the British local and national press. This is how *The Standard* (London) told the story in its edition of 7 February 1837:

A duel with small swords lately took place in Paris, between two well known jurisconsults of the Law School, on account of a passage of the Pandects. The one who contended that the passage in question ought to be concluded by a semicolon was wounded in the arm. His adversary maintained that it should be a colon, and quoted in support of his opinion the text of *Trebonius*.

We might expect the two marks to have been equally matched, as they function at roughly the same level in the punctuation hierarchy. But the colon won, it seems.

Interlude: Semicolonophilia

The repeated semicolonophobia of writers like Kurt Vonnegut has brought an equal and opposite reaction, and prompted a profusion of metaphors. In *The Vocabula Review* (July 2009), Janet Byron Anderson described it as 'the mermaid of the punctuation world – period above, comma below'. And in a *New Yorker* article (19 July 2012), Mary Norris reports a viola-playing friend describing the semicolon as 'a comma with vibrato'. Virginia Woolf would approve. As would Mrs Albert Forrester, in Somerset Maugham's short story 'The Creative Impulse'. She's described as having 'a humour of punctuation':

> in a flash of inspiration she had discovered the comic possibilities of the semi-colon, and of this she had made abundant and exquisite use. She was able to place it in such a way that if you were a person of culture with a keen sense of humour, you did not exactly laugh through a horse-collar, but you giggled delightedly, and the greater your culture the more delightedly you giggled. Her friends said that it made every other form of humour coarse and exaggerated. Several writers had tried to imitate her; but in vain: whatever else you might say about Mrs Albert Forrester you were bound

to admit that she was able to get every ounce of humour out of the semi-colon and no one else could get within a mile of her.

In the *New York Times* (18 February 2008) there was an article about an anti-litter ad that had been seen on a New York subway train, which included the lines:

Please put it in a trash can;
that's good news for everyone.

The use of the semicolon received widespread (and largely positive) publicity, and made headline news:

Celebrating the Semicolon in a Most Unlikely Location

Several expressions of support have appeared in newspapers and online. In 2008, US lexicographer Erin McKean set up a Semicolon Appreciation Society. There is a Facebook page: Great Moments in Semicolon History. Innumerable chests are covered by T-shirt designs that applaud the semi-colon. And I've seen several variants of the message: Keep Calm.

23

Colons: the chapter

After all the fuss surrounding semicolons, colons offer us a more relaxing encounter. Many people have loved or hated semicolons; but not so many develop an emotional relationship with colons. There are some colon T-shirts, but I don't often see people wearing them. Perhaps it's because of the word's ambiguity. A slogan to 'look after your colon' is more likely to be about cancer than punctuation.

When the colon arrived in English at the end of the sixteenth century, writers and printers had a clear idea about how to use it. As described in Chapter 6, they placed it within a hierarchy of pauses, expressing a silence shorter than the period but longer than the semicolon and comma. This is more or less how it's used in Shakespeare's First Folio (there's quite a lot of variation among the typesetters), such as in these examples from *Hamlet*:

> To be, or not to be, that is the Question:
> Whether 'tis Nobler in the minde to suffer
> The Slings and Arrowes of outragious Fortune;
> Or to take Armes against a Sea of troubles,
> And by opposing end them: to dye to sleepe ...

We see the problem in the last line. Every modern edition would replace that colon by a period, and start a new sentence:

> And by opposing end them. To die, to sleep ...

From a rhetorical point of view, the colon in that line had exactly the same pausing value as the one in the opening line. And as long as pronunciation ruled punctuation, it would have been interpreted in that way. It didn't matter what the constructions were on either side of it. The important thing was the length of the pause. So we see it followed by a new sentence (above), and also by parts of sentences, such as a phrase, repeated words, and even single words:

Nor I my Lord: in faith.
I humbly thanke you: well, well, well.
Fye upon't: Foh.

We can also sense an uncertainty over the use of this new mark, especially in relation to other punctuation marks:

(As I perchance heereafter shall thinke meet
To put an Anticke disposition on :)

This isn't an ancient example of an emoticon. It shows a typesetter unsure whether a closing parenthesis is sufficient to signal the required pause.

The other point to note about early use of the colon is that there was no limit to the number that might appear in a single sentence. So we find Polonius announcing the impending arrival of the Players to Hamlet in this way:

The best Actors in the world, either for Tragedie, Comedie, Historie, Pastorall: Pastorall-Comicall-Historicall-Pastorall: Tragicall-Historicall: Tragicall-Comicall-Historicall-Pastorall: Scene indivible, or Poem unlimited.

This is very different from present-day use, as we'll see.

As soon as the grammarians took control of punctuation, the situation changed. They attempted to define rules for the use of the colon, but the advice was vague. Here's Lindley Murray:

> The Colon is used to divide a sentence into two or more parts, less connected than those which are separated by a semicolon; but not so independent as separate distinct sentences.

The problem is clear: how are we to define the degree of connection between colon and semicolon? Usage throughout the nineteenth century shows that people had no idea how to decide, as we find many examples of writing where the marks are used inconsistently and interchangeably. Here's a poetic example, which I choose because it presents the variation very clearly. It's a transcription of a manuscript of the last poem written by Edgar Allan Poe: 'Annabel Lee' (1849). This is the beginning of the first stanza:

> It was many and many a year ago,
> In a kingdom by the sea,
> That a maiden lived whom you may know
> By the name of Annabel Lee;--
> And this maiden she lived ...

And here are the middle lines of the last:

> And the stars never rise, but I feel the bright eyes
> Of the beautiful Annabel Lee:--
> And so, all the night-tide ...

The metre and the surrounding grammatical context are the same, yet there is a punctuation shift. Now we could of course argue until daybreak about whether there is something significant in this; but any subtle interpretation would be well beyond the perception of the average reader, who is left with the impression that the choice between the colon and semicolon is perhaps phonetic, perhaps grammatical, perhaps semantic – or simply a matter of taste. Similarly, the use of an associated dash, seen in this extract, was widespread in earlier centuries, especially in British English, but practice varied enormously. It's largely disappeared from print nowadays, though it remains popular in informal handwriting. It's even been given a name – the *colash* – part of a small family of old usages that includes the *commash* (,-) and the *semicolash* (;-).

During the nineteenth century, usage preferences began to accumulate, so much so that pundits at the beginning of the twentieth century felt able to make rules that they felt would work. Henry Fowler summed it up in typically daring metaphors:

> the time when it was a second member of the hierarchy, full stop, colon, semicolon, comma, is past … [it] has acquired a special function, that of delivering the goods that have been invoiced in the preceding words; it is a substitute for such verbal harbingers as *viz, scil., that is to say, i.e.,* &c.

He was right about the first point. And he was almost right about the second. The primary function of the colon is indeed to 'deliver the goods'. But this isn't its only function.

Let's explore 'delivering the goods' a bit further. The metaphor hides various nuances.

- What comes after the colon can be an explication of what comes before. We may replace it by *as follows*.

    > The issue can be briefly summarized: either we go or we don't.

    > The second part is essential to the discourse. If the sentence were to stop at *summarized* we would feel

semantically short-changed. This makes it an ideal
introducer for examples (as in this book).

- What comes after the colon can be a rephrasing of what
comes before. We may replace it by *namely*.

> Everyone accepted John's point: we had no choice
> but to go.

Here the second part is less central to the discourse. If
the sentence were to stop at 'point', it would still make
sense. What follows the colon is more a reminder or
summary of what has already been said.

- What comes after the colon is a rhetorical contrast with
what comes before. We may replace it by some such
phrase as *in contrast*.

> The difficult is done at once: the impossible takes a
> little longer.

It is an antithesis, and it displays an interesting semantic
asymmetry. The first part can do without the second; but
the second can't do without the first.

What these examples have in common is the expression
of a very specific semantic relationship. This is what differen-
tiates the colon from the period and the semicolon, which are
both much more general in the meaning they convey. Consider the following three options:

- (a) I looked around the room. Mike was winking. Jane was
smiling.
- (b) I looked around the room. Mike was winking; Jane was
smiling.
- (c) I looked around the room. Mike was winking: Jane was
smiling.

The first is a simple narrative: one thing happened and then another. The second asserts a semantic association between Mike and Jane, which the previous context would have made clear: as illustrated in the previous chapter, Mike and Jane are part of the same story, connected in some way. The third does something different: the colon suggests a significant link between the two events. Telling a bit more of the story will help to make these distinctions clearer:

(a) I looked around the room. Mike was winking. Jane was smiling. Graham was grinning widely. Everyone could see what had happened …

(b) I looked around the room. Mike was winking; Jane was smiling. Graham, their next-door neighbour, was ignoring them, as he always did at parties. …

(c) I looked around the room. Mike was winking: Jane was smiling. It was great to see that my plan to bring them together had worked.

Jane was smiling *because* Mike was winking. It's a subtle point, but it's the sort of thing that sophisticated writers do.

The positions of the colon and the semicolon in the punctuation hierarchy have thus shifted over the centuries. In a pronunciation-dominated era, the colon outranked the semicolon. Now both marks function at the same level: one level down from the sentence-ending period, and one level up from the phrase-dividing comma. Some analysts rank the semicolon as somewhat higher, because it has a much wider set of functions:

- The semicolon has a broader semantic reach. The range of meanings conveyed by the semicolon, as we saw in the previous chapter, is wide and indeterminate. By contrast, the range of meanings expressed by the colon is limited and much easier to define.
- The grammatical function of the semicolon is to join

sentences (or elements of sentences) in a balanced way. By contrast, balance is not an issue when using the colon. What follows the colon is often not a sentence at all, but a phrase, an individual word, or a list of items:

> John got what he wanted for his birthday: a new pen.

> There was only one thing left to do: cry.

> Continue the sequence: 5, 10, 15, 20 ...

- We often encounter more than one semicolon in a single sentence; but it's rare to see more than one colon. Style guides advise writers not to use a sequence of colons in a single sentence. They usually just say it is 'bad style'; but the underlying reason is semantic. Explications within explications get confusing:

> Everyone accepted John's point: there were three options available to those who wanted to attend the conference: to drive, take the train, or catch one of the frequent buses: either the 3.30 from Oxford or the 4.10 from Reading.

We keep having to change perspectives as we read this sentence. The first explication (*there were three ...*) makes us refer back to *John's point*. The second (*to drive ...*) makes us refer back to *three options*. The third (*either ...*) makes us refer back to *frequent buses*. We are trying to read in a forwards direction, but the colons keep forcing us to make retrospective semantic connections. This isn't a problem if we have to do it just once in a sentence; but it becomes a strain when we have to do it repeatedly.

Perhaps because the colon has so few meanings, it has

developed a wide range of specialized uses marking separation – far more than the period and semicolon. It has an advantage over the period in being more visible, so we tend to see it more often when we need to separate numerals, as in times (3:40 pm), dates (1:3:14), and racing results in hours, minutes, and seconds (2:14:56), especially online and on electronic clock faces. The period could also perform this role, but as this mark is already used for specific mathematical functions (such as a decimal) there's a reluctance to extend it. We thus see a race result involving tenths of a second written with both symbols: 9:3.4 (9 minutes 3.4 seconds).

Other specialized uses are found in computer programs and mathematical settings. For example, it identifies a ratio in mathematics (3:4), and this has many applications, such as in map scales (1:5000). We see it on our computer screens as part of a drive letter (such as C:) or as a component delimiter in web addresses (http:// …). In print, it's widely used to separate main titles from subtitles, though typography often replaces this function on book jackets and in chapter headings, as we saw on p. 113. It's also standard practice to use a colon before speeches in play scripts (as on p. 140) or verbatim reports (as in the Hansard example on p. 133), and it's a regular way of introducing a quotation (as throughout this book). It can show a repeat in musical scores, a long vowel or consonant in phonetics, or a pair of eyes in an emoticon :). Idiosyncratic usage includes a double colon in some Internet game exchanges to show a parenthetical action or quotation within a narrative:

::curses and leaves the room::

At the same time, there's a great deal of house-style variation. Some publishers use it to separate place and publisher in bibliographies:

Crystal, D. 2012. *The Story of English in 100 Words*. London: Profile Books.

Some use it in indexes, separating a heading from its subheadings:

politics: in France 4, 11; in Germany 17, 44

Some use it to separate the numerals in section headings (3:12). Others use the period, or even the comma, for some of these functions. In bibliographies, for example, we will see such variants as:

London. Profile Books.
London, Profile Books.

From a grammatical point of view, the earlier examples in this chapter have one thing in common: the element preceding the colon would, in other circumstances, be a sentence. It is, technically, an independent clause.

Everyone accepted John's point: we had no choice but to go.
Everyone accepted John's point.

The only exceptions are when what follows a transitive verb (i.e. one where an object is required) is a quotation or direct speech. We will find people writing the following examples with the verb followed by a comma or no punctuation, but often a colon is used:

The subtitle read: 'The Pernickety Story of English Punctuation'.
John asked: 'Where are we going?'

Here, what follows is acting as the required object: 'The subtitle read X', 'John asked Y.' It's important to note this point of grammar, because one of the common errors in using colons is to insert one before a list in cases like this:

> The capital cities of Europe include: Paris, London, and Berlin.

While this sort of usage is common enough informally, it's considered bad practice in formal writing because 'The capital cities of Europe include' doesn't make sense. The point is worth emphasizing, because unwanted colons seem to be on the increase, for reasons that aren't clear. It may have something to do with the television practice in competitive shows to announce the winners with a dramatic pause before the names:

> The winners are — DRUM ROLL — Matthew and Sarah!

If we had to write this down, a better mark – given the informal setting – would be one or more dashes.

Related to this is the question of capitalization: should we use a capital letter after the colon? With quotations and direct speech, as we see, the answer is yes. It's yes also if what follows the colon is a series of sentences:

> Two things would follow: First, the rivers would overflow. Second, the low-lying villages would be flooded.

Showing that the sentences are parallel is felt to be the more important issue: *both* sentences relate back to *Two things*. Hence the following version is disturbing, as the orthography is sending us contradictory messages at the same time:

> Two things would follow: first, the rivers would overflow. Second, the low-lying villages would be flooded.

Where just one sentence follows, the answer is less clear, because usage varies:

> Everyone accepted John's point: We had no choice but to go.
> Everyone accepted John's point: we had no choice but to go.

The capitalized version is far more common in American English writing, but style guides differ. Publishers will have made their choices in their house styles. In other circumstances, the only advice is to make your choice and be consistent. Taste rules, once again. And if you don't like any of the above, the only solution is to rephrase.

Finally, it's useful to note cases where the use of a colon is semantically redundant, and the only reason to use it is tradition. I've already mentioned cases where it's dropped between a book-title and its subtitle, and where type size, font, colour, or layout makes the relationship between the elements clear. More commonly in everyday life we see it used after a salutation at the beginning of a formal letter.

> To whom it may concern:

> Dear Professor Smith:

This is standard practice in American English. British English traditionally uses the comma (though American influence is spreading). However, the stylistic issue isn't as critical as it used to be. The spacing conventions for letter-openings are sufficient to highlight any salutation, and punctuationless saluting is increasingly the norm. Most of the letters I receive these days – formal as well as informal – have neither colon nor comma. It's another manifestation of the move towards an uncluttered appearance in modern orthography.

Overall, the colon presents fewer problems of usage compared with other punctuation marks. In this it contrasts dramatically with the comma, which presents most of all.

24

Commas, the big picture

We are nearing the bottom of our punctuation hierarchy. To recapitulate:

- a text is divided into paragraphs (Chapter 15)
- a period (and sometimes other marks) separates sentences in paragraphs (Chapters 16–21)
- a semicolon separates two or more clauses (and sometimes other units) within sentences (Chapter 22)
- a colon separates two clauses (and sometimes other units) within sentences (Chapter 23).

That leaves us with three more levels:

- a comma may separate clauses, but also separates phrases (often single words) within clauses
- a space separates words (dealt with in Chapter 2)
- a hyphen and an apostrophe separate elements within words (Chapters 27–9).

These all present the writer with problems of usage.

Regardless of the approach to punctuation, the comma has always attracted particular attention. It's the longest section in traditional accounts, and the author invariably ends by making an apology for the inadequacy of his (I've not come across female grammarians or printers in researching this book) treatment. Here's William Cobbett, in Letter 14 to his son in *A Grammar of the English Language* (1829):

The comma marks the shortest pause that we make in speaking: and it is evident, that, in many cases, its use must depend upon taste.

In many cases, yes, but not in all. And what is taste anyway? If a lot of people have the same taste, in the way they use commas, what is it that unites them? There is evidently a certain amount of variation in the way commas are used, but it isn't infinite or totally idiosyncratic. In fact there are only a few cases where variation is possible, as we'll see.

Why is the section on commas the longest in any usage manual? It's because this mark is used more often than any other. Here are the totals found in a 72,000-word corpus (reported in the reference grammar published by Randolph Quirk and his associates in 1985, *A Comprehensive Grammar of the English Language*, p. 1613):

commas	4,054
periods	3,897
dashes	189
pairs of parentheses	165
semicolons	163
question marks	89
colons	78
exclamation marks	26

Obviously, such totals will reflect the genres included, so another survey of different material may alter the frequencies quite a bit, especially at the lower end. But the comma usually comes top. The reason is that it has a wider range of uses than any other mark. Most punctuation marks have a fairly restricted role: they separate sentences or the main parts of sentences (clauses). Commas can do this too, and additionally separate phrases and words. No other punctuation mark operates all the way down the grammatical scale.

I'll look at its use at the higher levels in this chapter, and in the next explore the way it's used at the lower levels.

Commas separate sentences? Not normally. Teachers would throw their hands up in horror at the thought. Any child who wrote:

> I went to the beach at the weekend, I had an ice-cream ...

would be likely to have the comma corrected. On the other hand, what would a teacher do if a (precocious) child came in the next day and said: 'Please, miss, why did you correct my comma when in my history book about Julius Caesar it says this?'

> I came, I saw, I conquered.

Read this chapter, would be my answer.

Punctuation has a differentiating function: it developed in order to allow writers to express differences of meaning. It would be pointless (*sic*) to have a punctuation mark that did exactly the same job as some other punctuation mark. One or the other would eventually die out, or would come to be associated with different kinds of users (such as British vs American). There will always be a few cases where there's an overlap in function – where users have a free choice between mark X and mark Y – but most of the uses will be distinct, and juxtaposing examples is the best way of seeing what the distinctions are.

That is why commas aren't usually used to join sentences. There are already marks which do that job very well – the period, the semicolon, and the colon, which allow us to make the broad distinctions of meaning I've discussed in previous chapters. Let me illustrate using dear old Smith and Brown of semicolon fame. We don't normally join two sentences like this:

> Smith is going to speak about cars, Brown is going to speak about bikes.

This is making the comma do a job it was not designed to do. And in marking it wrong, in a learner's writing, it's important to explain this. The comma has evolved to convey a set of meanings that is different from those conveyed by other marks. To use it in a place where one of those other marks should go is to mislead your reader.

Once again, we're talking semantics. Discussing the use of the comma in solely grammatical terms is not the solution. We have to dig deeper. This is why the traditional grammars were of limited help. If we know how to talk about grammar, the description of this next sentence is easy to make:

> Smith is going to speak about cars; and Brown is going to speak about bikes.

The semicolon is linking two independent clauses, the second one introduced by a coordinating conjunction. Now let's turn to this version:

> Smith is going to speak about cars, and Brown is going to speak about bikes.

The description is the same: the comma is linking two independent clauses, the second one introduced by a coordinating conjunction. Grammar is thus no help in showing us when to use the comma and when the semicolon. We have to talk about the kind of meaning that the marks are conveying. Semantics again.

What commas do is they allow us to show a closer semantic association between the two clauses than if we used the semicolon. Let's recapitulate the point made about semicolons in Chapter 22:

> Smith is going to speak about cars; Brown is going to speak about bikes.

The semicolon shows the clauses are linked, more than they would be if they were separated by a period; but the link is not very tight. Each clause could be used as an independent sentence without the other:

> Smith is going to speak about cars.
> Brown is going to speak about bikes.

The semantic link remains the same even if we reinforce the semicolon by a coordinating conjunction:

> Smith is going to speak about cars; and Brown is going to speak about bikes.

The value of a coordinator is that it makes explicit the nature of the semantic relationship between the two clauses, and this can vary. We can replace the *and* by one of the other words that have a coordinating function, such as *but*, *or*, and *so*.

Now look what happens when we use a comma. Immediately the semantic link between the two clauses is tighter, and this is usually reflected by other signs of tightness in the second clause, such as:

> Smith is going to speak about cars, and Brown will follow him by speaking about bikes.

> Smith is going to speak about cars, and we're really looking forward to his talk on this subject.

Here, words like *him*, *his*, and *this* refer directly back to *Smith* (grammarians call this effect *anaphora*), and bind the two clauses tightly together. It's no longer possible to use the second clause as an independent sentence:

> We're really looking forward to his talk on this subject.

The comma, in other words, mustn't be studied in isolation. It forms one of the ways in which we make a close semantic connection between clauses, and the closer that connection (shown by such devices as anaphora) the less likely we are to use a semicolon:

> Smith is going to speak about cars; and we're really looking forward to his talk on this subject.

The punctuation disrupts the flow. The other cues in the second clause (*his, this*) are signalling that the writer sees it closely related to the first. The semicolon is signalling that the relationship is more distant. The writer can't have it both ways.

It's the tightness of that link which explains why, in a few instances, we *can* link independent sentences by a comma. This happens when the tightness is signalled by other features, usually by the sentences being completely parallel in construction and the rhetorical effect of the whole being greater than the sum of the parts. That's why we see it in relation to Julius Caesar – and also here, in this fragment of Winston Churchill's speech to the House of Commons on 4 June 1940:

> ... we shall fight on the beaches, we shall fight on the
> landing grounds, we shall fight in the fields and in the
> streets, we shall fight in the hills ...

This shows how a rhetorical motive – he is in the last, climactic paragraph of his discourse, and the end of the speech is just seconds away – can use the comma to link any number of sentences. That's why I said 'don't normally join' above. But you have to be an experienced language user to use this strategy effectively.

The tightness of the semantic link shown by a comma is also why we can use it in a much wider range of constructions. Semicolons reinforce the link between clauses that coordinate ideas. Commas do this too, as we've just seen, but they also reinforce clauses where one idea is subordinated to another, as shown by the use of subordinating conjunctions:

> Smith is going to speak about cars, because it's a subject he loves.

> Smith is going to speak about cars, whether we want him to or not.

Again, we wouldn't expect to see these clauses joined by a semicolon:

> Smith is going to speak about cars; because it's a subject he loves.

> Smith is going to speak about cars; whether we want him to or not.

Mixed messages again.

The focus in these examples is on the second clause. That's always how it is. Imagine Hilary writing to her friends about the forthcoming conference. She reaches the end of the first clause:

> Smith is going to speak about cars

She now has to decide how much she wants her next thought to be linked to this one. If she wants to make a totally separate remark, she will use a period. If she wants to show a balanced contrast, she will use a semicolon. If she wants to introduce a list, she will use a colon. And if she wants to immediately say more about Smith, his speaking, or his cars, she will use a comma – or no punctuation at all.

We must consider this last option, before moving on to the other. 'No punctuation' is the ultimate marker of semantic tightness. With only word spaces left, the words between clauses now look the same as the words within the clauses.

> Smith is going to speak about cars and Brown is going to speak about bikes.

If the clauses are short, this presents no problem to the reader, who can take in the structure of the sentence at a glance. But the usage has to be motivated, of course. Why would a writer *want* to bind the two clauses together so tightly? Well, imagine a scenario where Hilary rushes into a room in a state of great excitement, because she has just learned the exciting news. There's no pause. And if this excitement were to be represented in writing, there's no time for a comma.

Comma omission is most likely when the semantic link is one of 'and'. It's a reflection of the normal way in which people narrate – a strategy that is found in young children from the age of three, when they first learn to coordinate sentences:

> Mikey did go in the garden and – and – he did go on the swing and – and – and – he wented high up ...

It's also the commonest way of linking sentences in the early stories that children write. And it continues into adult spoken narrative style: any story will contain more instances of *and* than any other conjunction. But if we start to be more subtle in our connecting, making a contrast using *but* or *and yet*, then writers usually insert a comma:

> Smith is going to speak about cars, but Brown is going to speak about bikes.

It's less easy now to imagine someone rushing in and telling this story (and thus, omitting the comma). The focus is now more meditative, on the contrast between the two events. The comma reinforces the meaning conveyed by *but* and draws our attention to it. Why go to the trouble of drawing the readers' attention to a semantic contrast if you're then going to make it more difficult for them to see the contrast (by omitting the comma)? Mixed messages again.

Any grammatical construction that binds two short clauses tightly together will motivate the omission of the comma. Look what happens when we leave out parts of the second clause, as here:

> Smith is going to speak about cars and wants a room with a projector.

A comma is less likely, as we need to read in the subject of the first clause (*Smith*) and this forces the two parts together. We might find a comma if the writer saw the second clause as some kind of afterthought, in which case a dash would be a more effective way of conveying this meaning:

> Smith is going to speak about cars – and wants a room with a projector.

Still, if the meaning warrants it, a comma can nonetheless have a reinforcing function:

> Smith waited for a few seconds, and then began to speak.

We can imagine an actor reading this novel-fragment aloud and pausing dramatically after *seconds*.

I've used the word 'short' several times in the last few paragraphs. The question of length. This is the factor that has disturbed everyone from Lindley Murray to Henry Fowler – and which caused all of them to throw in the towel when it came to formulating rules to explain the use of the comma.

The longer the clauses being connected – and especially the longer the opening one in a sequence – the more we're likely to introduce a comma to help the reader see the overall structure of what we're saying.

> Smith is going to speak about cars using the same pictures that he had when he gave the talk in Edinburgh last year, and Brown is going to speak about bikes.

The function of the comma is now not so much grammatical as psycholinguistic. It gives the reader time to assimilate, time to mentally breathe.

Length would have been one of the factors that lay behind the worry of Cobbett (and others) about taste. It's at the heart of comma uncertainty, and we'll see it surfacing again in the next chapter. The reason that it's so central is because it unites the two approaches to punctuation that have dominated thinking in this field: the elocutional and the grammatical. The longer a construction, the more difficult it is to speak aloud; and the longer a construction, the more content it contains, and thus the more difficult it is to assimilate. But what one person might feel is 'long' another might feel is 'not so long'. That's where individual differences ('taste') enter in. One person says, 'I need a comma to make the meaning of this sentence clear'; another finds the same sentence perfectly understandable without a comma. It's because they have different processing abilities.

We're now entering the world of psycholinguistics. We know that there are limits governing how much we can hold in working memory at a time. Psycholinguist George Miller once defined it as 'the magic number seven, plus or minus two'. The formula should be seen as no more than a guideline, as it is affected by many factors; but it's a valuable mnemonic. And it shows how different people are.

There's an experiment anyone can do. Ask someone to repeat after you a list of items, such as a string of numbers between one and ten, increasing the length of the task by one each time. Say the items steadily, with a slight pause between each one:

You	*Listener*
Four	Four
Six, two	Six, two
Eight, one, three	Eight, one, three

The aim is to note when the listener finds it difficult to repeat the string confidently and correctly. Many people start to have trouble at around five elements, and seven seems a top limit for most, but some can handle up to nine with ease.

Now take the task to a more advanced level. If your listeners have failed at repeating six or seven items in a row, ask them if they would like to repeat eight items accurately. They will say yes, but wonder how. What you do is group the eight items into two sets of four, and speak them without pausing between the digits, a bit like reading out a long telephone number:

eight one three four / two nine six one

Most people can handle that. The rhythm and intonation help them keep such long strings in their head. And if we were to show this in writing, we could do so like this:

eight one three four, two nine six one

If we now look at sentences where there is variation over the use of the comma, we'll find that the point of greatest uncertainty comes when the first clause approaches five semantic units (content words, along with any grammatical modifiers, such as prepositions or articles). There's no problem if the opening clause contains two semantic units (I'll underline each unit in the first one):

Smith will speak and Brown will listen.
  1   2

It would be unusual to see a comma here. Similarly with three semantic units:

Smith will speak about cars and Brown ....
  1   2   3

or four:

Smith will speak about cars on Monday and Brown ...
  1   2   3   4

But uncertainty sets in when we get to five:

Smith will speak about cars on Monday in Edinburgh and Brown ...
  1   2   3   4   5

And if the first sentence gets longer than this, most people will feel the need of a comma.

Note that we can increase the length of the first sentence in other ways, such as by adding adjectives or other forms of modification.

Smith will speak about cars and Brown will listen.
  1   2   3

Smith will speak about second-hand cars and Brown ...
  1   2   3   4

Smith will speak about available second-hand cars and Brown ...
  1   2   3   4   5

As we reach the 'magic number five', the need to breathe sets in again.

These are adult intuitions. With children, it takes time for their working memories to develop in order to handle such complex sentences. They will therefore be more likely to introduce a comma in places where an adult wouldn't feel it necessary. Teachers who see 'too many commas' in young writers thus need to be aware that the extra commas may actually be helping them express themselves, as they attempt more complex constructions, and that it takes time to develop a mature comma-using style.

Keep all this in mind as you read the next chapter. Because everything that I've said here in relation to the linking of sentences applies equally when we consider the way commas are used to link constructions lower down the grammatical scale: phrases and words.

25

Commas, the small picture

Grammar always offers us choices. People often ask why grammar is so complex. The answer is simple: because we want to express complex thoughts. If all we wanted to say was 'Me Tarzan. You Jane', it wouldn't be complex at all. But we need to do much more than this.

The choices are particularly apparent in a narrative where we string sentences together. We like to vary the way we say things. Only in the simplest early readers do we see repeated constructions:

Peter can see a pig.

Jane can see a horse.

Mummy can see a cow. ...

The primary options for change occur at sentence ends. So, to return to the example in the previous chapter, when Hilary begins her report about Smith and decides to go for a tightly linked second part, she will use a comma, but what follows can be several grammatical constructions, such as:

Smith is going to speak about cars, and he'll need an hour.

Smith is going to speak about cars, which will need an hour.

Smith is going to speak about cars, needing an hour.

As long as the second construction continues to act as a clause – containing a (finite or non-finite) verb – we need the comma. If we omit it, there's a real chance of ambiguity. In the last sentence above, it's Smith that needs the hour. But in the following version it's the car:

> Smith is going to speak about cars needing an hour to warm up before they can be driven at speed.

This is one of the cases where the presence or absence of a comma is nothing at all to do with taste. It depends on what you mean. Do you want to say something more about *cars* or not? If you don't, you'll keep the comma in. If you do, you'll omit it, to show you're thinking about cars in a more specific way.

This ability to be specific or not is a major feature of English grammar, and shows up both in the way we speak (through our intonation) and in the way we write (through punctuation). It can make all the difference in the world. How many sisters does Mary have in this unpunctuated sentence?

> my sister who lives in China has sent me a letter

It depends. If we punctuate it like this, she has just one sister:

> My sister, who lives in China, has sent me a letter.

If we punctuate it like this, she has an indeterminate number of sisters:

> My sister who lives in China has sent me a letter. (My other sister(s) haven't.)

The comma-less clause *who lives in China* makes you think of *sister* in a very specific way. Grammars therefore say such clauses – called *relative clauses* – have a 'restrictive' or 'defining' function. And when they are surrounded by commas, we see them having a 'non-restrictive' or 'non-defining' function.

The contrast is very frequently used in everyday writing. Again, it can make all the difference in the world. Did John see his parents or not?

> John didn't visit his parents, because his brother would be there. (He didn't go.)

> John didn't visit his parents because his brother would be there. (He did go, but for some other reason.)

And how did John talk about his relationship with Mary?

> He spoke about it naturally. (In a natural way, as if nothing had happened.)

> He spoke about it, naturally. (Of course he did.)

This is one of the reasons why people who say 'we can do without the comma' are wrong. For example, in February 2014 the *Mail Online* had an article headed 'The death of the comma?' It was reporting an American linguist, John McWhorter, who was predicting the obsolescence of the comma, on the grounds that you could

> take them out of a great deal of modern American texts and you would probably suffer so little loss of clarity that there could even be a case made for not using commas at all.

He seems to have been thinking chiefly of cases like the serial comma, which I discuss in the next chapter, and where clarity is indeed hardly ever affected. But when we consider cases like the distinction between restrictive and non-restrictive, it's clear that abolishing the comma would make us unable to express succinctly and unambiguously an important semantic distinction.

That is the point: succinctly and unambiguously. It would of course be possible to rephrase my sentences about the sisters to avoid having to rely on the punctuation. But why should we do this? The result would be wordier. And it would go against the main reason for having punctuation in the first place: to help represent speech. The contrast between restrictive and non-restrictive is clearly expressed through English intonation, and it's only natural to want to write this down.

These are all cases where the comma has a double function: it separates but it also specifies – expressing a meaning which its absence would not convey. As we look at lower levels of grammatical construction, we see it chiefly having only a separating function. So we wouldn't expect to see it used between the elements of a clause, even if we wanted to pause between them in reading aloud:

> The detective in charge of the case / doesn't want to keep on questioning / this new group of witnesses / until the early hours of the morning.

A comma is not used to mark the change-points between subject, verb, object, and adverbial (shown by /). This is one of the big differences between modern punctuation and earlier practice. In Lindley Murray's day, a comma between subject and verb or between verb and object was often used when the element was at all complex. Here are two examples from his *Grammar*:

> A conjunction added to the verb, shows the manner of being ...

> These writers assert, that the verb has no variation from the indicative ...

This would be considered an error today.

The only case which presents a difficulty at this level of grammar is in relation to the optional adverbial. (When I say 'optional', I mean it can be left out without the sentence becoming ungrammatical.) This is a mobile element of structure: it can be used initially, medially, and finally in a clause. So, if we begin with the 'bare' sentence *John entered the room*, we can have:

Quickly John entered the room.

John quickly entered the room.

John entered the room quickly.

When the adverbial is short, there's no grammatical or semantic reason to include a comma. The sentences mean the same whether we insert a mark or not:

Quickly, John entered the room.

John, quickly, entered the room.

John entered the room, quickly.

The rhythmical effect is very different, though. So the option is open to any author who imagines these words spoken with a particular pronunciation and who wants to reproduce this effect in writing. Anyone with a penchant for heavy punctuation (often for the pragmatic reason that it it has been hammered into them in school) will of course opt for commas regardless of sentence length or pronunciation. Anyone with a penchant for light pronunciation (often for the equally pragmatic reason that they want their writing to look as uncluttered as possible) will opt for their omission. And there are all kinds of intermediate positions. This is the main domain where 'taste' operates.

But we mustn't ignore semantic factors. A lot depends on the subject-matter. We're more likely to see a comma in a story where the action is proceeding slowly, or where the writer wants to make you think, create a particular atmosphere (of looming menace, of impending doom), slow down the pace, or is simply acting like a camera panning around a view.

Gradually, the first light of dawn illuminated the room.

Equally, the gun may have been in the desk.

Regrettably, you have no future (Mr Bond).

Outside, several children were playing.

We're less likely to see a comma after initial adverbials where the action or the emotion speeds up:

Suddenly a dog barked.

Obviously I'll go with you.

Please don't do anything silly.

If commas are used here, they convey a more dramatic implication, which could be differentially expressed through a dash or ellipsis dots:

Please, don't do anything silly. (A more forceful appeal?)

Please ... don't do anything silly. (The speaker is dying?)

Please – don't do anything silly. (The speaker is being authoritative?)

These are of course just some of the many semantic possibilities. And the same considerations influence usage medially and finally:

> I think, ideally, you should go.
> I don't honestly know.
>
> That's true, geographically.
> Come here immediately.

And so we might reflect on the likelihood or otherwise of:

> Come here, immediately.
> Come here ... immediately.
> Come here – immediately.

This is where teaching punctuation gets really interesting. I've seen a class of youngsters enthusiastically discussing what would happen if one of these marks were used in a story rather than the others.

It's a really useful teaching exercise, when exploring comma usage, to collect a large number of single-word adverbials like this, and try them out in different contexts – something I haven't got the space to do in this book, where my illustrations have to be selective. When there are no clear-cut rules to guide usage, all we can do is build up an intuition of what good practice is like by reflecting on as many instances as possible. This can come unconsciously just from reading a lot; but the issue can be neatly focused by presenting the learner with a judicious selection of examples.

As the length of the adverbial increases, with phrases and clauses replacing single words, the role of taste diminishes, but the above principles continue to apply. It would be unusual to see commas before short items such as the following:

> People took up new jobs afterwards.
> People took up new jobs after the war.
> Most people took up new jobs after the war was over.

But as the adverbial lengthens, and the number of semantic units in the sentence goes towards the 'magic number seven', we're likely to see a comma:

> Most people took up new jobs, after the peace negotiations had been brought to a satisfactory conclusion.

This is especially so if the first part of the sentence is itself complex:

> Thousands of people of all ranks and ages took up new jobs in a wide range of professions, after the peace negotiations had been brought to a satisfactory conclusion.

And it's virtually obligatory if a medial adverbial goes to such lengths.

> Thousands of people of all ranks and ages, after the peace negotiations had been brought to a satisfactory conclusion, took up new jobs in a wide range of professions.

Try reading that without the commas:

> Thousands of people of all ranks and ages after the peace negotiations had been brought to a satisfactory conclusion took up new jobs in a wide range of professions.

In all these examples, it's the sentence that counts. That is the 'main unit of sense'. Understanding the whole sentence is the aim. And punctuation helps us achieve that, when sentences are long.

But it's not just a question of length. As with the examples in the previous chapter, the tightness of the semantic relationship between the adverbial and the rest of the sentence is also a factor influencing us in our use of a comma. The tighter the link, the less likely the comma.

> John stopped reading the book when the light got so bad he couldn't continue.

This is a very tightly bonded adverbial, as seen by the dependence of *he* and *continue* on what went before. The thought in that adverbial could never stand alone:

> The light got so bad he couldn't continue.

But in this next sentence, the link is much looser:

> I stopped reading the book, although there was plenty of light in the room.

Here the thought in the adverbial could stand alone.

> There was plenty of light in the room.

The comma isn't obligatory, but inserting one certainly helps the reading process, whether internally or reading aloud, and we thus often see it used in such sentences.

The printer John Wilson, in his *Treatise on Grammatical Punctuation* (1844), reflects glumly:

> In punctuation there is scarcely any thing so uncertain and varied, as the use or the omission of commas in relation to adverbs and adverbial phrases, when they qualify sentences or clauses.

We can see now why there's such uncertainty. The main cases of divided usage arise when there is a clash between the criteria of length, semantic bonding, and auditory effect. A lengthy construction motivates a comma, whereas a strong semantic link doesn't. This sentence illustrates:

> I stopped reading the book about how to carry out an analysis of commas in a wide range of languages(,) when

I realized that it wasn't going to reach any satisfactory conclusion.

Style guides vary in their advice, in such cases. Writers with a strong sense of auditory style are much more likely to use commas, to point the way they want their sentences to be heard. And it's this competition between the criteria that lies behind all the other cases of comma uncertainty, especially the famous 'serial comma'.

26

Commas, the serial killer

In 2013 in the UK, the new Spelling Punctuation and Grammar test, introduced for children at the upper end of primary schools (around the age of ten) came in for a huge amount of criticism because of the linguistic inadequacy of the questions it set. This was Question 15 in paper 1:

'Which of the sentences below uses commas correctly?'
Tick one.

We'll, need a board, counters, and a pair of dice.
We'll need a board, counters and a pair, of dice.
We'll need a board, counters, and, a pair of dice.
We'll need a board, counters and a pair of dice.

What's immediately obvious to any punctuation-aware person is that the main alternative to the last example is missing:

We'll need a board, counters, and a pair of dice.

Was this just by chance? No. Further down the same test, we see Question 27:

Insert three commas in the correct places in the sentence below.

I need to pack a swimming costume some sun cream a hat sunglasses and a towel.

Only three? The examiners are clearly looking for this answer:

> I need to pack a swimming costume, some sun cream, a hat,
> sunglasses and a towel.

Their intention is made clear in the guidance notes. Markers are told: 'Do not accept the serial comma' – a comma before *and*.

In my blog at the time, I railed against the surfacing in exams of the 'ugly face of prescriptivism' – by which I mean the imposition of unauthentic rules on a language. Somebody at top level in government clearly doesn't like the serial comma and feels they have the right to impose this personal taste on everyone else. I would have failed that question, as I use the serial comma in my writing. So does Oxford University Press. All failures.

That's where the serial comma got its other name: the 'Oxford comma'. We see it in the set of rules devised by Horace Hart for the Press in 1893. This is the relevant section:

> Where *and* joins two single words or phrases the comma is
> usually omitted; e.g.
> The honourable and learned member.

> But where more than two words or phrases occur together
> in a sequence a comma should precede the final *and*; e.g.
> A great, wise, and beneficient measure.

There we are. The principle would apply equally if the conjunction were *or*. And generations of writers have followed this lead – though not, evidently, the teachers who taught the minister of education in 2013.

Why did Hart go for the comma? Because Lindley Murray did – along with all the other influential grammarians and printers who wrote on the subject in the late eighteenth and early nineteenth centuries. This was the era of heavy punctuation, and it carries over into the twentieth century. The leading American usage guide, William Strunk and E B White's *The Elements of Style* (1919), used the serial comma. It was so routine that, when Henry Fowler used it in his examples of lists, in his *Dictionary of Modern English Usage* (1926), he didn't even bother to comment on it.

So why was it used? David Steel explains it this way in his *Elements of Punctuation* (1786):

> Three or more adjectives, belonging to the same substantive, with or without copulatives, should be separated by commas.

He illustrates from the sentence:

> Ulysses was a wise, eloquent, cautious, and intrepid hero.

And he gives this explanation:

> *intrepid* is not more particularly connected with *hero* than *wise* or *eloquent* – all equally belong to the substantive, and ought to have the same degree of separation or connection.

This was the view maintained throughout the nineteenth century, by printers as well as grammarians. John Wilson addresses the issue in his 1844 *Treatise*. In his chapter on the comma, he mentions that some punctuators omit the serial comma, but he recommends it, and explains in a note:

> The propriety of using the comma will perhaps be obvious to any one who attentively examines the construction of such sentences, and who perceives that the last two words of a series are not more closely connected in sense with each other than with those which precede.

So there's a solid semantic reason why the comma should

be there. It reinforces the parallelism between all the items in a list. If we omit it, that sense of connectivity is reduced – though in examples like the *Ulysses* sentence not by much. That's why people readily omit it: they argue that it makes no difference to the meaning, and that the *and* does the connecting job of the comma anyway, as shown by such alternatives as *an old, comfortable chair* and *an old and comfortable chair*. Eric Partridge, for example, in *You Have a Point There* (1953) says commas in this position 'are excessive, for they perform no useful work'. As a result, because they can't see any semantic reason for it, they begin to use it inconsistently, allowing such random factors as the length of the words in the list or their sense of timing to influence whether they add one or not.

This is one of the reasons John McWhorter made his prophesy (quoted in the previous chapter) about the demise of the comma. He highlighted the inconsistency in the use of the serial comma, observing:

> Nobody has any reason for it that is scientifically sensible and logical in the sense that we know how hydrogen and oxygen combine to form water.

This is a bit unfair on the early grammarians, who were at pains to find logical reasons for its use, but it does represent the way attitudes towards the comma changed during the twentieth century. 'We are more sparing of commas nowadays', writes Ernest Gowers in his influential *Plain Words* (1948). And the remark is even more true today, turning up without revision in his granddaughter's new edition of his book (Rebecca Gowers, 2014).

Where did the idea to drop the comma come from? Most publishers retained it, on both sides of the Atlantic, following the guidance of Fowler, Strunk and White, and other manuals such as *The Chicago Manual of Style* (first edition in 1906). Its omission grew gradually during the early twentieth century, as part of the trend towards punctuation minimalism. Newspapers and magazines on the whole avoided it, to save space and (in the days when typesetting was painstakingly by hand) time and energy. Critics argued that an unnecessary comma was an intrusion that delayed the reader. And developing a clean look to the page was one of the ways in which a forward-looking publishing house could distinguish itself from the conservative practices of other presses. Smaller houses instructed their copy-editors to delete it from typescripts, unless it caused an ambiguity, and we see the practice spreading around English-speaking nations such as Australia and Canada. Cambridge University Press, anxious to distinguish itself from Oxford, routinely abandoned it. In my very first book for Cambridge, *Prosodic Systems and Intonation in English* (1969), we find such strings as 'grammar, vocabulary and segmental phonology'. That isn't what I wrote, but it didn't bother me.

As the century progressed, some publishers began to take a more equable view, acknowledging the fact that diversity was the norm. Judith Butcher, in her influential handbook for Cambridge University Press, *Copy-Editing* (§6.12), allows both practices:

> In lists of three or more items, a comma should be consistently omitted or included before the final 'and': red, white and blue; red, white, and blue.

And you will thus find the serial comma throughout all my later writing for that Press including the series of Cambridge general encyclopedias. But everything still depends on the publisher. The house style used by Profile Books omits them. In the introduction to my *Spell It Out* (2012), we read:

> we encounter a host of anomalies, variations and
> exceptions.

In my manuscript, it appears as:

> we encounter a host of anomalies, variations, and
> exceptions.

In the margin of the online copy-edited typescript, in bold blue under 'track changes', I see the message:

> Jane 23/2/12 16:38
> **Deleted**: ,

The death of my comma, precisely timed. (I was allowed to keep my serial comma in the present book, given its subject-matter!)

Every writer on punctuation in the twentieth century recognized the diversity of practice. Here's G V Carey in *Mind the Stop* (1939, Chapter 3) arguing that usage here is 'a matter of individual choice'. He belongs to what he calls the 'final comma school', as do I, and he gives a reason:

> because the 'no final comma' principle breaks down now
> and again through ambiguity, whilst the 'final comma'
> principle can be followed consistently with less risk of it, I
> personally vote for the latter.

Ernest Gowers belongs to the 'no final comma school'. After giving an example, he says:

> commas are always put after each item in the series up to
> the last but one

though he immediately acknowledges that 'practice varies'. Interestingly, he gets the reason wrong:

> Those who favour a comma there (a minority, but gaining ground) …

In fact, it was the other way round. Everyone from Murray to Fowler had used the serial comma. It was the omitters who were gaining ground.

Whatever the school you belonged to, everyone agreed that there were exceptions, and that avoidance of ambiguity must be the primary rule. If it's ambiguous to omit the comma, don't omit it. If it's ambiguous to insert the comma, don't insert it. We see both cases here:

- Adding the comma helps:

    > In the first part of the evening, the choir will sing two hymns, Old Man River and Shenandoah.

    How many items are being sung? Two or four? If you're not sure whether the named pieces count as hymns, you have no idea. Adding a comma before the *and* would show that they don't.

- Omitting the comma helps:

    > I'm inviting my brother, a playwright, and three actors to the party.

    How many people are coming to the party? If *playwright* is in apposition to *brother* (that is, the brother *is* the playwright), there are four. If it's a list, there are five. Omitting the comma before the *and* would push the sense towards the 'five' interpretation.

Any textbook on punctuation will draw your attention to examples like these. Their value is that they show total consistency to be impossible, when it comes to the serial comma, because of the complexity of English syntax. And we can generalize this point to the use of the comma in other syntactic domains. Even quite basic rules might have exceptions. Take the one I described in the previous chapter: no comma between subject and verb or between verb and object. That's a fairly strict rule today, but there are still exceptions. If a clause uses two instances of the same word, we see writers using a comma to help remove a source of possible confusion:

Whatever his name is, is of no concern to me.

And when commas are used in direct speech, there may be a comma between the verb and an object:

She said, 'I'm in the front room.'

The only rule that never has any exceptions is the one forbidding a comma within the elements of a phrase that has no serial content. We never find:

the, car
her beautiful, dress
I will, go
in, the garden

The only possible way to interrupt a phrase is if we include another unit within it, and then we need a different convention involving pairs of marks:

This is her beautiful (I do hope you agree) dress.

There are also some strictly controlled specialized settings where individual conventions apply, such as in bibliographies and indexes, where the comma separates surnames and first names (*Crystal, D.*). In mathematics it separates thousands, as in *14,236* (and in some places, decimals, see p. 136). Even here, though, we may see variation, such as the replacement of the comma by a space.

Exceptions and ambiguities exist, but we mustn't exaggerate their importance as a guide to general practice. With the serial comma, for every one case of possible ambiguity, there are ninety-nine where there's no ambiguity at all, and we are faced with a straight pragmatic choice. As Ernest Gowers says:

> The correct use of the comma – if there is such a thing
> as 'correct' use – can only be acquired by common sense,
> observation, and taste.

And, I would add, a linguistic perspective.

Interlude: Pun-ctuation

Punch could never resist a pun, and punctuation was no exception. In No. 16 for 1849 we read of a new proposal under the following heading:

STREET PUNCTUATION

We understand that an attempt is to be made to introduce a new system of Punctuation, on the principle of street stoppers, or street stops.

This will enable the publishers of School-books to bring out an Illustrated Work on Punctuation, in which a comma may be represented by an unac-comma-dating cabman, who, by refusing to move on, occasions a slight pause in the progress of traffic; while a coal-waggon at a stand-still, would be very fairly emblematical of a co(a)-lon or semi-co(a)-lon, as the case may be. An advertising van, would convey a good idea of a point, a dead stand-still, or full-stop. Notes of admiration could easily be shown by the astonished foot-passengers: notes of exclamation by the Omnibus-drivers in full cry at the impediment: and notes of interrogation, by the policemen inquiring why the drivers do not move on.

The traffic jams in Fleet Street (where *Punch* had its office) were a daily source of complaint.

27

Hy-phens

Any book that set out to cover every eventuality in punctuation would be unpickupable. I've therefore focused on the general principles behind punctuation and how to deal with the problems that feature frequently in its use. It has taken me three chapters to explore just the main uses of the comma. If I were to cover *all* the ways in which the comma can be used, I would end up having to write an entire grammar of English from a punctuational perspective, as every construction has to be punctuated, and commas operate at all levels of syntactic organization. Similarly, if I were to cover all variations in the use of the hyphen, I would have to write an entire dictionary, because each compound word has its own story. It is the most unpredictable of marks. Henry Fowler sums it up well in the opening sentence of his entry on hyphens in his *Dictionary of Modern English Usage*: 'chaos'.

The hyphen has an ancient history (the name is from an Ancient Greek word meaning 'together'), and the mark that it describes can be seen throughout the manuscript era in several functions, but usually to draw a reader's attention to the way words, or parts of words, separated through some accident (such as being unable to fit at the end of a line), needed to be brought together. In the sixteenth century, John Hart emphasized this linking role in his term for the hyphen: a 'joiner'. Hyphens became increasingly common in print from the 1570s, even though the term itself isn't recorded in English until the early 1600s.

We then see the hyphen becoming a standard feature of English orthography, with the same two broad functions that it has today: as a divider, to show a word-break at the end of a line, and as a linker, to mark the unity of a word containing distinct grammatical elements. But it took a while for a consistent practice to develop. It's clear from the way it is sprinkled around the publications of the Elizabethan period that there was a great deal of uncertainty over its use. For example, in Shakespeare's First Folio we see hyphens that we would never tolerate today, such as *for-sake*, *a-gaine*, and *yon-der*. And any word sequence that was felt to have a tight semantic link might be hyphenated, such as *red-plague* and *for her wealths-sake*.

With just two main functions to perform, we might expect hyphenation to be a straightforward matter. But repeatedly we see the usage pundits keeping their distance. Here is Ernest Gowers's elegant disclaimer: 'If I attempted to lay down any rules I should certainly go astray, and give advice not seemly to be followed.' He is alluding to a style book written for Oxford University Press by John Benbow in which we read: 'If you take hyphens seriously you will surely go mad.'

Nonetheless – and allowing for this possibility – we do need to give hyphens some serious consideration, especially as both functions give rise to variation and change. The hyphen that identifies a word-break at the end of a line is the easier matter to deal with. It presents few problems once we recognize that it's located at a syllable boundary and not after a syllable fragment. Monosyllabic words are straightforward: they are never broken. We don't see *str-ing* or *go-ne*. (The convention isn't self-evident, as is shown by the way children make such breaks when writing their first stories. It has to be taught.) The only usage issue relates to differences between

British and American practice over polysyllabic words.

British practice is to follow the way a word divides gram-matically or etymologically; American practice is to follow the way the word sounds. So if we see *bio-graphy* and *philo-sophy*, we can guess we are reading a British book following Hart's original rules; if *biog-raphy* and *philos-ophy*, it must be American (as in Webster's dictionaries) – though during the twentieth century some British dictionaries began to follow US practice, especially those aimed at a foreign learners' market. The issue was never serious, as most words divide in the same way (both principles would show *pun-ish*, for example) – and in any case it's largely of historic interest now, as we hardly ever see hyphenated line-breaks today, thanks to sophisticated typesetting on paper and software-governed typesetting on screen.

Word division at line-endings never bothered the usage pundits much, except when it gave rise to a facetious miscue (such as *the-rapists*). They left such matters to the printers. Henry Fowler devotes five pages in his *Dictionary* to examples of correct and incorrect hyphenation, and doesn't mention line-breaks at all. He, as everyone else, was entirely focused on the way hyphens are to be used, or not used, in word identification, where there are two central issues. Do we use a hyphen to separate the elements in a compound word? And do we use one to separate a prefix from the rest of the word?

There are three options if we decide to bring two (or more) elements together to make a compound word. We can write *flower pot* (spaced), *flower-pot* (hyphenated), or *flowerpot* (solid). These are the choices, bringing together two levels in the punctuation hierarchy: the word space and the hyphen. They are now in competition with each other. To space or not to space? That is the question. And if we decide on the latter: to hyphenate or not to hyphenate?

Most writers have no idea. They may have an instinctive preference or a long-standing habit for writing a word in a particular way, but they know that their choice may not be shared by other writers. And instinct never guarantees consistency. That's one of the reasons publishers employ copy-editors: they will check that a writer has hyphenated consistently and in accordance with the publishing-house style. And because publishers make different decisions over which words should be hyphenated, authors – especially those who have written for a variety of houses – are not going to have a clear intuition about what to do, and will generally be happy to leave that to the editors.

Even if you've spent the whole of your authorial or journalistic life with a single publisher, your intuition may let you down. This is because there are two factors influencing publishing practice: tradition, which fosters a firm's identity, and language change, which affects everyone. The concern for identity that we saw in the case of the serial comma is seen again here. British publishers opt for the hyphen much more than American houses do. Canadian and Australian publishers sometimes follow British practice, sometimes American. And within a country, there may be various policies. Oxford and Cambridge style guides make different decisions, for example. I normally write *no-one*. When in 2008 I put this in a book for CUP, the copy-editor changed it to *no one*. When in the same year I put *no one* in a book for OUP the copy-editor changed it to *no-one*. And changing language fashions can create havoc with style guides. In a later book for OUP my *no-one* was changed to *no one*.

Changes in fashion are the main reason why the obvious solution to any question about hyphenation – look it up in a dictionary! – won't always help. Look up *flower-pot* in the online *Oxford English Dictionary* and you'll see the heading:

flower-pot | flowerpot, without further comment. It's left up to you. And if you were in the habit of using the *Shorter Oxford Dictionary*, and had internalized its recommendations, you would have had a real shock in 2007, when the sixth edition was published and you saw that around 16,000 items had had their hyphens removed. Most of the changes had the hyphen replaced by a solid setting (*pigeon-hole > pigeonhole, cry-baby > crybaby, bumble-bee > bumblebee*), but quite a few ended up spaced (*test-tube > test tube, ice-cream > ice cream, hobby-horse > hobby horse*). Reactions ranged from the hysterical to the bemused. Some observers called it 'hyphengate'.

Why did the editors do this? They are partly reflecting changes in fashion. The chief editor, Angus Stevenson, commented at the time that the dictionary is reflecting the current dislike of the hyphen on the part of designers: 'The hyphen is seen as messy looking and old-fashioned.' And indeed, his view is reflected across the dictionary world. Certainly, most people would agree that there's something clean and modern about the first of the following alternatives (6th edition) compared with the conservative appearance of the second (5th edition):

If you buy too much ice cream with your pin money you'll end up with a pot belly.

If you buy too much ice-cream with your pin-money you'll end up with a pot-belly.

Apart from anything else, it's far easier to type the first version in the fast-moving Internet world. The position of the hyphen on a keyboard doesn't help.

But there's more to it than the pragmatic factors of fashion, aesthetics, and ergonomics. We still have to explain why some words have ended up spaced and some have ended up solid. Why is it *ice cream* and not *icecream*? And why *bumblebee* and not *bumble bee*? We might imagine it would be even faster to leave the space out. The reasons are all to do with semantics – the ease with which we visually perceive the meaning and the familiarity we have with the concept.

Legibility is affected when unfamiliar sequences of letters come before the eye, or the letter-sequence distracts us by making us think of an irrelevant word. So, for example, we are unlikely to find *arrowworm* or *lookingglass* because of the unfamiliar juxtaposition of the middle consonants, and both of these are indeed spaced in the new *Shorter Oxford*. Similarly, pairs of vowels can cause momentary uncertainty, so we are less likely to encounter *deicer*, *moreish*, *goahead*, or *toing and froing*, and never *antiinflation*, *belllike*, or *freeenterprise*. Irrelevant associations arise if we were to write *weeknight*, *walleyed*, and *tearoom*. Length can also be a factor. Readers don't like short elements (less than three letters), so when email first arrived it was spelled *e-mail* – never *e mail*. Similarly we see *U-turns* and *H-bombs*. Compounds that become lengthy (around ten letters or more) also prompt separation – so *commonsense*, *goodlooking*, and *backprojection* are often avoided. And we see a hyphen routinely when the typography is unusual, such as when the base of the word begins with a capital letter (*pro-English*), a numeral (*post-2000*), or a punctuation mark (*un-'hip'*).

But note the qualifications – 'usually', 'less likely', 'unlikely', 'often', 'routinely'. These are tendencies, not rules. And any of these tendencies can be overruled by the factor of familiarity, which explains a great deal of the variation in the history of hyphenation. A compound word is a semantic unit as well as a grammatical one: the meaning of the whole is different from the sum of the parts. But it takes time for the meaning of a new compound to become familiar, and this is reflected in changes in orthographic practice, as shown by looking at the historical citations in the *OED*. Typically, the first recorded examples are spaced: the two elements retain a trace of their separate identities. Then, as people get used to the new concept, we find the compound hyphenated as well as spaced. And eventually, once the original meanings have been lost sight of, we see it written solid. So, for example, we find *pigeon holes* in the sixteenth century, *pigeon-holes* predominating in the seventeenth, and *pigeonholes* growing in frequency in the twentieth. 'For sale: a type writing machine', says an ad in 1881, and soon after we get *type-writing* and then *typewriting*. As email became more familiar, it began to drop its hyphen, and *email* is now the most common form. Again, the underlying principle is a trend, not a hard-and-fast rule; but it makes sense. And it explains why it's necessary, every now and then, for a dictionary to change its recommendations. It is simply trying to reflect the new ways in which people are thinking of the words.

Here's a more detailed example of the way practices change. It's standard now to spell *today*, *tomorrow*, and *tonight* without a space or hyphen. But when the words first arrived in Old and Middle English they were seen as a combination of preposition *to* followed by a separate word (*dæg, morwen, niht*), so they were spaced. This usage was reinforced by Dr Johnson, who listed them as *to day* etc in his *Dictionary* (1755). But people began to think differently in the nineteenth century, and we see the big new dictionaries (such as Worcester's and Webster's) hyphenating the words. People began to get fed-up with this in the twentieth century. Henry Fowler came out against it in his *Dictionary of Modern English Usage* (1926):

> The lingering of the hyphen, which is still usual after the *to* of these words, is a very singular piece of conservatism.

He blames printers for its retention, in a typical piece of Fowlerish irony:

> it is probably true that few people in writing ever dream of inserting the hyphen, its omission being corrected every time by those who profess the mystery of printing.

'Lingering' was right. In fact we see instances of the hyphenated form right into the 1980s. In *Postman Pat's Thirsty Day* (1984), we read:

> 'It's a real scorcher to-day,' said Pat to Jess, as they drove along.

There's no hyphen in the 1996 printing.

Lingering is normal. Someone who is taught a particular use of the hyphen at age eight is likely to be still using it at age eighty-eight. Changes take a long time to become standard – about a century, in the case of the *today* forms, judging by what Mark Twain wrote in *The Atlantic Monthly* in 1880:

> No one now writes *to day* or *to morrow*, and few people write *some thing* or *some body*; instead, we use *to-day*, *to-morrow*, *something*, *somebody*, and that we shall eventually come to use *today* and *tomorrow* is clear from the increasing frequency with which these forms are even now seen in carefully conducted journals.

An accurate prophet.

Semantics is always the main factor to be considered in deciding about hyphenation. Any fashionable trend will be overruled if it leads to ambiguity. So a hyphen is essential to distinguish such cases as:

> I recovered/re-covered the book. [got it back/put a new cover on it]

> They've made a small arms/small-arms deal. [a little one/ handguns only]

> The remarks/re-marks are in the margin. [comments/new marks]

> We need some more expert/more-expert advisers. [additional ones/people who know more]

> I belong to an English teaching/English-teaching organization. [one from England/one that teaches English]

Puns abound, without punctuation. I know some high school teachers. Inadvertent puns too. I have a great grandfather.

Grammar is the next factor to be considered. Detailed accounts of hyphenation always attempt to find rules based on the grammatical structure of the compound – classifying them (or their elements) into nouns, verbs, and so on – but there are no rules, only trends. If it's a strong trend, this should certainly be pointed out, but with the qualification: 'not always'. For example, if the first element is an adverb, we see a well-established alternation. Before a noun, the adverb is attached with a hyphen; after a verb, it isn't:

> This is a well-known principle.
> The principle is well known.

The reason is to ensure that the word is recognized as an adverb, so the issue arises mainly in relation to words that look as if they could also be adjectives, as in *best-known* and *good-sized*. If the word clearly looks like an adverb, by ending in *-ly*, most traditional practice (Hart's *Rules*, once again) says: no hyphen. So we find both:

> This is a carefully drawn picture.
> The picture is carefully drawn.

Note: 'most' practice. Some style guides have allowed a hyphen, especially in Britain. But practice has increasingly followed the American preference for spaced words, which of course suits the present-day fashion to omit punctuation wherever it's semantically unnecessary.

Similarly, although prefixes and suffixes aren't usually hyphenated (*unhappy*, *powerful*), there probably will be a hyphen if there's a possible miscue (*co-worker*, *co-op*), and some prefixes tend to attract the hyphen more than others (such as *ex-husband*, *half-baked*). Usage here varies enormously, both regionally and institutionally. My despair over what to do with *no-one* is repeated regularly with *non-standard* and *neo-classical*.

Another example of a fairly clear-cut context is when a complex grammatical word-string is included within a larger construction, such as a noun phrase. Without the hyphens, the unusual word-strings can cause momentary confusion:

> I met the on the spot reporter. > I met the on-the-spot reporter.

> We are in a take it or leave it situation. > We are in a take-it-or-leave-it situation.

When the string is not included in a larger construction, the reason for the hyphen disappears:

> The decision was made on the spot. *not* The decision was made on-the-spot.

> I want you to take it or leave it. *not* I want you to take-it-or-leave-it.

But well-established compounds may break this rule, so that we can find *up-to-date*, for example, used in both contexts; and some compounds of three words or more, such as *father-in-law*, never lose their hyphens, whichever part of a sentence they appear in.

There are a few other contexts where a hyphen is predictable. We see one in established lists, such as compound numerals (*thirty-six*, *three-quarters*). We see one where there are strong phonetic reasons to bind the elements together, such as in reduplicated or rhyming words (*helter-skelter*, *bow-wow*, *tip-top*). We see one in coordinations (though in print the en-dash performs this role, p. 145), as in *an English–French treaty*. And hyphens are obligatory when we need to show a syntactic relationship that extends over an intervening word:

pro- and anti-government
nineteenth- and twentieth-century movements
business-men and -women
eighteenth- and nineteenth-century fashions

These are called 'hanging' (or 'floating') hyphens.

The hyphen has few other uses apart from its roles in line-breaking and compounding. But we do see it when writers want to convey prolongation or repetition with consonants or vowels:

D-d-d-do you mind [stammering, fear, teeth chattering, etc]
He-e-elp, Ye-e-es [calling, tentativeness, uncertainty, etc]
Ha-ha-ha, Boo-hoo-hoo [spasmodic articulations, as in laughs, giggles, sobs]

And hyphens also have a few technical functions. Dictionaries use them to show the way words di-vide in-to syl-la-bles – a technique also used by Victorian readers for young children (*Ja-net is talk-ing to Ri-chard*). Linguists use them to show word-elements (*-ed*, *ex-*). Numerical entities such as telephone numbers or dates use them (or dashes) to separate their elements (*6-7-1941*). URLs use them as a way of separating words (*www.this-is-an-example.com*) – an option that is much discussed in web forums, as their presence raises issues to do with the ease of remembering an address and the efficiency with which the address can be located by a search engine.

Sometimes there's no punctuational solution to be found. Nobody has yet come up with a generally acceptable way of adding an inflection after a word ending in a vowel. How would you report the way someone danced the samba all night: they – *sambaed*? *samba'd*? *samba-d*? *samba-ed*? All we can do, in such cases, is rephrase. Similarly, there isn't a way of joining a hyphen (or an en-dash) to a spaced compound, as in the *New York-Chicago* or *Chicago-New York* express, without leaving one part of the compound curiously isolated. As already mentioned, punctuation doesn't solve all the problems of representing speech in writing.

Finally, we need to note the issues associated with the hyphen when it comes to marking personal or cultural identity. People can get very cross if someone misses out the hyphen in their double-barrelled first name (*Marie-Anne*) or surname (*Parry-Jones*). And personal hyphens can make the news. In 2013, it was reported that the New York rapper Jay-Z was henceforth going to spell his name without the hyphen. Tongue-in-cheek, a *Guardian* headline called this 'earth-shattering news', and a 'massively disrespectful move against hyphens'. But the fact remains that the paper did report the change, and gave it a headline. And it wasn't the only paper to do so.

Cultural issues can arise relating to the presence or absence of a hyphen. Around 1900 in the USA there was a derogatory usage of 'hyphenated Americans' – those who wanted to show their ethnic origin – and who said they were *Irish-American*, *Italian-American*, and so on. The practice was widely attacked by, among many others, President Woodrow Wilson (in an address in support of the League of Nations in 1919): 'Any man who carries a hyphen about with him carries a dagger that he is ready to plunge into the vitals of this Republic whenever he gets ready.' Strong stuff.

Place-names raise issues too. We have to learn which form a community prefers, as part of the spelling. So, we normally see *Newcastle-under-Lyme* alongside *Newcastle upon Tyne*. However, because the conventions are arbitrary or historically obscure, there's a great deal of vacillation. 'Explore Stratford upon Avon' was the headline of the Shakespeare Country tourist website in 2014; and the first paragraph begins: 'Stratford-upon-Avon is a picturesque town ...' Cultural history plays its part. In Quebec, place-names are hyphenated if they are French in origin (often at length, as in *Ste-Marthe-du-Cap-de-la-Madeleine*), but not if English.

The modern trend is to simplify names, and not to introduce hyphens, periods, and apostrophes. That's the policy of the US Board of Geographical Names, for example. But local feeling can force exceptions, and in some places there have been successful proposals to change a name by adding a hyphen. In January 2014, the cities of East Carbon and Sunnyside in Utah merged, resulting in East Carbon-Sunnyside. Not everybody liked it (the council vote was 7–4 in favour), so the decision was viewed as temporary. Any proposals for punctuational change in a place-name lead to heated public meetings and petitions. But hyphen-heat is nothing compared with the heat generated when people decide to mess around with the apostrophe, or decide to do something about it.

Hyphen-treasures

"WELL, REALLY, MY DEAR!"

Mrs. R. "CHRISTOPHER DARLING, I NEVER *CAN* REMEMBER WHETHER 'SODA-WATER' IS WRITTEN AS ONE WORD OR TWO JOINED TOGETHER BY A SYPHON ?!"

Divided opinions about hyphens go back a long time. Here's *Punch* (27 December 1856) objecting to what it calls a 'Germanism in Journalism':

> We very much wish that our contemporaries, in alluding to the pictures about to be exhibited at Manchester, would cease to denominate them as Art-Treasures. Why not call them Treasures of Art? Suppose we were to talk of Imagination-Works, meaning works of Imagination, should we not be deemed to talk very affected stuff? You might as well say Science-Discovery as Art-Treasure: or describe a learned or virtuous person as a learning-character, or a

virtue-man. A joke, on the same principle, might be termed a wit-speech, or a fun-saying. It is all very well to say mince-pie and plum-pudding: these are pleasant compounds, and not hashes of abstract and concrete, disagreeable to the sense of fitness. What, however, makes Art-Treasures a particularly disagreeable word is that it is a vile Germanism; and the same objection applies to all the various phrases consisting of "Art" skewered to some other word with a hyphen. Let us hear no more of art-coffee-pots, art-cream-jugs, art-fenders, art-fire-irons, art-cups, and art-saucers, art-sugar-tongs, and art-spoons: in short, no more art-bosh, art-humbug, and art-twaddle. Stick to the QUEEN's English, and there stop. Corrupt it not by adulteration with German slang; do not teach the freeborn British Public to adopt the idioms, or rather idiotisms, of the language of despots and slaves.

28

Apostrophes: the past

Agonizing over apostrophes can land you in court. This was one of the outcomes of the amazing journey undertaken by American writer Jeff Deck and his bookseller friend Benjamin D Herson in 2007. They decided to 'change the world, one typo correction at a time', and created the Typo Eradication Advancement League (TEAL) to take the crusade forward. Armed with markers, chalk, and correction fluid, they went all over the USA, finding errors in public signage and correcting them. Missing, unnecessary, or misplaced apostrophes were one of the commonest targets. The journey took them a year, and they wrote it up in a delightful book, *The Great Typo Hunt* (2010). The headline on the inside jacket reads: 'The signs of the times are missing apostrophes.'

In Arizona, they went a correcting step too far. They visited the Grand Canyon, where they found in a viewing tower a chalkboard sign that included the word *womens'*. They corrected it to *women's*. Two months later, their trip complete, they received a summons from the National Park Service, charging them with defacing federal property and vandalizing a historical sign. It turned out that the sign had been hand-painted by the architect, Mary Colter, who had been commissioned to develop the Canyon site in the 1930s.

If Jeff and Benjamin had realized the significance of the sign, they of course wouldn't have touched it. Their aim was to correct modern errors, not to rewrite history. But ignorance is no defence, and in court they pleaded guilty. They paid $3035 in restitution and received a year of probation, during which time they were forbidden to enter all National Parks and were banned from typo correcting. They were lucky. Another outcome would have been six months in jail.

There's no TEAL in Britain, but there is an Apostrophe Protection Society, started by journalist John Richards in 2001 'with the specific aim of preserving the correct use of this currently much abused punctuation mark'. Its tone is moderate, unlike the haranguing voices of those who threaten to break the windows of any greengrocer seen to be advertising *potato's*:

> We are aware of the way the English language is evolving during use, and do not intend any direct criticism of those who have made mistakes, but are just reminding all writers of English text, whether on notices or in documents of any type, of the correct usage of the apostrophe should you wish to put right mistakes you may have inadvertently made.

It's an appeal that many have listened to. The website had received over 1.7 million hits by early 2014.

Clearly there is a standard use of the apostrophe that has to be respected if people want to avoid the criticism of being uneducated, careless, or illiterate. This is a climate that has affected the whole of orthography (including spelling) since the eighteenth century, when a notion of 'Standard English' finally emerged into the light after some 400 years of development. People became aware that they needed to use this variety of written English if they wanted to be thought educated and socially acceptable, and schoolteachers began to insist upon it. Standard (or 'correct') punctuation, along with spelling, became one of its defining features.

William Cobbett was one who singled out the apostrophe

as a marker of social acceptability. In Letter 14 to his son (in *A Grammar of the English Language*, 1829) he calls it a 'mark of elision', illustrates it by *don't*, *tho'* and *lov'd*, and offers this advice:

> it is used properly enough in *poetry*; but, I beg you never to use it in prose in one single instance during your whole life. It ought to be called the mark, not of *elision*, but of *laziness* and *vulgarity*. It is necessary as the mark of the possessive case of nouns ... That is its use, and any other employment of it is an abuse.

While the perceived misuse of any punctuation mark would come in for criticism, the apostrophe does seem to have attracted more vituperation than any other, especially since the mid-twentieth century. And the question that remains unasked, in all the accounts of punctuation that I have read, is: why?

A clue lies in the time-scale of its arrival in English. The apostrophe arrived very late, compared with most other marks, in the closing decades of the sixteenth century, and took a long time to develop its present range of standard usage. Grammarians and printers were still trying to work out what the relevant rules were even at the end of the nineteenth century. They weren't entirely successful, leaving a number of unresolved issues over usage that generated further variation and associated controversy.

English did without apostrophes for almost a thousand years. The meanings conveyed by this mark were handled in other ways. Anglo-Saxon scribes would show an omitted letter by a horizontal mark over a letter (there's an example on p. 12). Possession was expressed through an inflectional ending on a noun (the genitive), most often *-es* (*scip* = ship; *scipes* = ship's), commonly spelled *-ys* or *-is* in the fifteenth century. Its pronunciation as a separate syllable died out, and the *es* spelling eventually simplified to *s*, hence the modern form. All of this happened long before the apostrophe arrived in English – which is why it's not very accurate to say, as some present-day pundits do, that the mark was originally used to show the omission of genitive *e*.

Nor, incidentally, is there any truth in the story that the modern *'s* is a shortening of an older form *his*. A construction of the type *the kyng hys sonne* was indeed common in the sixteenth and seventeenth centuries, and can be traced back to early Middle English. But its origin lies in the way *his* was pronounced without the *h* when it was unstressed (as it still is today in such contexts as *I saw his mother in town*). The pronunciation of *prince his son* was thus the same as *princes son* (= prince's son), so the two usages became confused. Over time, the *his* construction began to influence other nouns: we find it being used after women as well as men, as in *my moder ys sake* and later *Mrs. Francis her mariage*, and then with plurals, as in *you should translate Chillingworth and Canterbury their books*. We can still encounter the old use today, such as *for Jesus Christ his sake* in *The Book of Common Prayer*. The emergence of the apostrophe has nothing to do with the history of this syntactic construction.

The apostrophe's origins lie in Europe, where early sixteenth-century printers introduced it (based on Greek practice) to show the omission of a letter (usually, showing the elision of a vowel in speech). Its earliest appearance in England is in a book printed by John Day in 1559: William Cunningham's *The Cosmographical Glasse*. It was definitely used as a sign of omission there, not possession: we see *the partes of th' earth* but *moones age*. Ben Jonson, in his *English Grammar* (early 1600s), devotes the entire first chapter of his section on syntax to the apostrophus, 'the rejecting of a vowel from the beginning or ending of a word', as seen in *heav'n* or *desir'st*. He is very keen that apostrophes should be used, complaining that 'many times, through the negligence of writers and printers, [it] is quite omitted'.

It wasn't only negligence. There was a genuine uncertainty over how this new punctuation mark was to be used. Sometimes there would be an omission with no apostrophe at all: *Will you ha the truth on't*, says the Clown in *Hamlet* (in the First Folio edition) – not *ha'*. And a colloquial form of *he* turns up as *a* as well as *'a* and *a'*. We see it used to represent single letters (*th'* for *the*), two letters (*'em* for *them*), and even whole words (*'faith* for *in faith*, *'sblood* for *God's blood*).

Writers and typesetters – worried about the possible ambiguity in such a sentence as *these are the kings* – then began to use the apostrophe to mark the possessive option, but in a very unsure and erratic way. We see far more examples of possessives lacking an apostrophe than showing one. If the noun was a proper name, there is often one present (*Gonzago's wife*, *Apollo's temple*), but we also see a vacillation even in a single line: *Did Romeo's hand shed Tybalts blood*. If the noun wasn't a name, it would usually be absent, whether animate (*schoole-boyes teares*) or inanimate (*the fields chiefe flower*). But a developing sense that apostrophe = possession is evident, not only in nouns but also in pronouns. We see such spellings as *her's*, *our's*, and *it's*.

The typesetters also found the apostrophe a useful solution to unusual or alien-looking words. When Malvolio finds Olivia's letter in *Twelfth Night*, we read: *these bee her very C's, her V's, and her T's*. The plurals of foreign loanwords also attracted them, especially when they ended in a vowel (*dilemma's*, *stanzo's*), but they were used with native words too, and after consonants as well as vowels (*these pardon mee's*; *hum's, and ha's*). It was the beginning of a long association of the apostrophe with plurality.

And an association with the letter *s*. As both genitives and regular plurals used that letter, it perhaps wasn't surprising to see Elizabethan typesetters developing something of a Pavlovian response: if a word ends in a vowel + *s*, then insert an apostrophe. So we see them appearing with present-tense third-person singulars: *doe's*, *see's*, *ha's*. Even sometimes with consonants: *me think's*. All the confusions that we're familiar with in present-day English are found in these early days. If a noun ends in -*s*, what's to be done? We see them experimenting with various solutions: omission (*Venus doves*), expansion (*Marses fierie steed*), older use (*Mars his heart*), and insertion – but not always in the right place (Calchas in *Troilus and Cressida* lives in *Calcha's house*).

During the seventeenth century a consensus over some of the uses began to emerge. Quite clearly there could be a problem of comprehension if there was no systematic way of distinguishing between possessives with a singular and a plural noun. Context is sometimes a help, as in these two Shakespearean examples:

> the use of following *his* shows that it's a singular when King Henry says:
>> Wilt thou, vpon the high and giddie Mast,
>> Seale vp the Ship-boyes Eyes, and rock his Braines ...
>> (*Henry IV Part 2* 3.1.19)

> the preceding syntax shows it's a plural when Coriolanus says:
>> The smiles of Knaues
>> Tent in my cheekes, and Schoole-boyes Teares take vp
>> The Glasses of my sight ...
>> (*Coriolanus* 3.2.116)

But often context is no help, and the pressure to make a systematic distinction grew during the eighteenth century.

Lindley Murray, following earlier grammarians, recognizes the two conventions, *'s* and *s'*, so we might think that this would solve the problem once and for all. But there remained doubts. Joseph Priestley in his *Rudiments of Grammar* (1761) worries about how to distinguish constructions that sound the same, such as *the princes injuries*, and suggests the best solution is to avoid the problem altogether and write *the injuries of princes*. And C P Mason's *English Grammar* (1876) shows how the idea of elision was still present in people's minds. He accepts that we need an apostrophe in the singular because it 'marks that the vowel of the syllabic suffix has been lost', but he goes on: 'It is therefore an unmeaning process to put the apostrophe after the plural *s* (as *birds'*), because no vowel has been dropped there.'

The situation was made more complicated by the views of spelling reformers, who had become increasingly energetic during the nineteenth century. George Bernard Shaw avoided apostrophes whenever he could, and robustly defended his practice in his 'Notes on the Clarendon Press Rules for Compositors and Readers' (1902):

> The apostrophes in ain't, don't, haven't, etc. look so ugly that the most careful printing cannot make a page of colloquial dialogue as handsome as a page of classical dialogue. Besides, shan't should be sha'n't, if the wretched pedantry of indicating the elision is to be carried out. I have written aint, dont, havnt [*sic*], shant, shouldnt, and wont for twenty years with perfect impunity, using the apostrophe only where its omission would suggest another word: for example, hell for he'll. There is not the faintest reason for persisting in the ugly and silly trick of peppering pages with these uncouth bacilli. I also write thats, whats, lets, for the colloquial forms of that is, what is, let us; and I have not yet been prosecuted.

It's impossible to say how influential Shaw's views were, but they do illustrate the large divide between those who found apostrophes an irritation and those who introduced them in all possible places (*1920's, NCO's,* and so on).

The point to note is that, even as late as 150 years ago, experts were still not in agreement over all uses of the apostrophe. Nouns ending in -*s* continued to be a particular worry: *Keats' poems* or *Keats's poems*. And people didn't know what to do with pronouns: *theirs* or *their's*? *its* or *it's*? After all, it was reasoned, if the apostrophe marks possession, then surely it should be used in pronouns as well as nouns? If we have *the dog's bowl*, then why not *it's bowl*? And if *the dogs' bowl*, why not *the bowl was their's*?

With the grammarians disagreeing, the printers had to take a stand. George Smallfield, for example, in *The Principles of English Punctuation* (1838), is in no doubt:

> The reader is also requested to remember, that, besides *nouns*, there are *pronouns*, which have a possessive case, answering to the genitive case of nouns; but though it is not uncommon to see the possessive case written with an apostrophe, that mark is unnecessary. No one would now write he's or hi's for *his*; but it would not be more incorrect than her's for *hers* – our's for *ours* – your's for *yours* – and their's for *theirs*. The *s*, in all these instances, is the sign of the possessive case, and is alone sufficient. Hence, it is improper to conclude a letter by signing one's-self, Your's.

This view became the norm: no apostrophes for pronouns – much to the confusion of generations of schoolchildren who, having had the rule drummed into them that the apostrophe marks possession, now find a set of examples where it doesn't. (And additionally, an exception within the exceptions, for possessive determiner *one's* was allowed to keep its apostrophe, presumably because of its association with the numeral.)

Uncertainty over its use in the possessive later extended to its use to mark a plural. To begin with, the issue received hardly any recognition. Examples like *potato*'s are never mentioned, and on the whole the plural apostrophe gets a good press. Goold Brown's *Institutes of English Grammar* (1890), for example, accepts it in such cases as *Two a's, three b's, four 9's*, and where it acts as a guide to pronunciation, as in *pro's and con's*, where *pros* might not be recognized, or mispronounced as 'pross'. Henry Fowler was evidently not bothered by it, for he makes no mention of plurality errors in the entry on 'Possessive Puzzles' in his *Dictionary of Modern English Usage* (1926).

But during the twentieth century, attitudes changed. When Ernest Gowers revised Fowler's *Dictionary* for a second edition in 1965, he added a section to Possessive Puzzles. He allows an apostrophe in *dot your i's and cross your t's*, but he denies it in such cases as *one million whys, the 1930s*, and *N.C.O.s*, commenting:

> To insert an apostrophe in the plural of an ordinary noun is a fatuous vulgarism which, according to a correspondent of *The Times*, is infecting display writing.

He quotes *tea's, shirt's, alterations's,* and other examples from shops and signs. His opinion was influential; the newspapers continued to publish letters from their readers (language issues always guarantee a good letter-bag); and by the end of the century people were pillorying the usage everywhere. According to *OED* citations, the first person to associate it with greengrocers' signs was Keith Waterhouse in *English Our English* (1991), and the label *greengrocer's apostrophe* has its first recorded use the following year. It caught on, and sparked something of a craze to find the worst misuses. A letter to *The Independent* (14 February 1993) said simply:

> The best greengrocer's apostrophe I've ever seen is *asparagu's*.

But greengrocers weren't the only businesses to be caught up in apostrophic controversy.

29

Apostrophes: the present (and future)

The same uncertainties that have caused concern among individual users of English have also affected businesses. Here, the main issue is in relation to the possessive, where the variation seen since the seventeenth century is writ large – literally. Pub-signs display *The Bull's Head* and *The Bulls Head*. Shop fronts show *Gents' Hairdressers* and *Gents Hairdressers*. Stores have signs pointing to *Women's Clothing* and *Womens Clothing*. Signposts point you towards the *Magistrates/Magistrates' Court*. In London, the Piccadilly Line takes you to *Earl's Court* and then *Barons Court*.

As you walk around London, you see *Harrods, Selfridges, Boots, Barclays, Lloyds,* and *Starbucks,* but *McDonald's, Harry Ramsden's, T.G.I. Friday's,* and (before 2012) *Waterstone's.* Go into a bookshop and you can buy a copy of *Gulliver's Travels* or *Finnegans Wake.* But if you go to the Irish pub in Edinburgh or the Irish restaurant in New York, you would be visiting *Finnegan's Wake.* It's difficult to generalize about what has led to these various outcomes; the story behind each name is individual. But some trends can be observed, as we see if we explore a couple of the histories.

Charles Henry Harrod opened his shop in Knightsbridge in 1849. A sign at the front of the building in 1874 said *Harrod's Stores.* The apostrophe was still being used twenty years later: an advertisement in 1895 for a sewing-machine tells readers that it can be bought from the first floor of *Harrod's*

Stores, Brompton. But as the century ended, variation crept in. Manufacturer marks on metalware products made for the firm show a mixture of *Harrod's* and *Harrods*. Two catalogues have *Harrods'*. By the early 1900s, the apostrophe had largely disappeared. An advertisement in *The Times* for 9 December 1907 says: *15 acres of Christmas gifts at Harrods*. The word *Stores* was officially dropped in 1920, and there is no apostrophe after that date. Letters to the press worrying about the change gradually died away.

Lloyds is an even more interesting case. In 1765 the company was set up by four people: two named Lloyd and two named Taylor. The Taylors eventually left the business, so Lloyds & Co became the norm. As there were two people, the plural form was correct. In 1865 the firm became Lloyds' Banking Company. However, Lloyds was the legal name in the 1889 Certificate of Incorporation, and the company would have had to enter into a fresh process of registration if they wanted to change it – something they didn't want to do. Why did they decide to drop the apostrophe when the name shortened? Professor of English Cedric Barfoot wrote to the Lloyds archivist in 1990 to find out, and reported his reply in an article ('Trouble with the apostrophe: or, you know what hairdresser's are like'):

> The decision to drop the apostrophe was no doubt taken, after some agonising, in 1889 because nobody was getting *Lloyds'* right. People automatically assumed (as they still do) that the firm originated as *Lloyd's*, and legal documents drawn up under the name of *Lloyd's Bank* were no doubt putting us in some difficulty. The only way to avoid expensive and lengthy unscrambling of errors has been to eradicate their cause.

Might it be reintroduced? The archivist thought not, mainly

because *Lloyd's* now refers to the shipping and insurance company, and this would be to add further confusion. (Notwithstanding, many city journalists do make the distinction, continuing to use *Lloyds'* for the bank.) He concluded:

> the reason for there being no apostrophe in our legal name is that there is no easy place to put it: if we were *Lloyds' Bank* (as some would say we should be) no-one would get it right; if we were *Lloyd's Bank*, we would be insensitive to our roots, and invite confusion with other interests.

We can see in these cases how several issues intertwine in deciding what to do with an apostrophe: notions of tradition, ownership, client relationship, public identity, legal standing, cost, and time. The death of an owner can affect the matter. While Jesse Boot was alive, there was a natural reason to refer to the company as *Boot's*. It asserted his position. The apostrophe was felt to be less needed after his death. And if a company is taken over, as often happens, there is even less need to remind the new owners of how things used to be – hence the case of *Waterstone's*, taken over once again in 2011, and this time losing its apostrophe as part of a rebranding exercise.

The *Waterstones* decision sparked huge publicity, most of it negative from those who felt that this was yet another nail in the apostrophe's coffin. The new chief executive defended the change on both semantic and pragmatic grounds. His semantic argument wasn't so convincing: dropping the apostrophe suggests plurality, he said, there being lots of the stores. This isn't a strong reason, for apostrophes can disappear regardless of how many stores are involved (there are not lots of Harrods). His pragmatic arguments were more powerful, citing motivation from the simplified punctuation found on the Internet, and referring to the modern trend to make public print less cluttered in appearance.

The strongest pragmatic reason is always identity. Owners can call their businesses whatever they like, as long as there's no conflict with already-existing businesses, and the decision will be based on factors to do with corporate identity, reflecting the range of considerations we have seen operating in such cases as Lloyds. Historical arguments cease to be relevant in a new commercial climate. It's no good people saying 'Waterstone's was originally short for Waterstone's Bookshop' if the company thinks a more succinct name will have greater impact. Historical arguments date as rapidly as the social changes that distance us from them.

Because of their public prominence, business naming decisions do reinforce a climate of change, so those who feel their life depends on the use of the apostrophe are right to feel threatened. But this climate isn't recent, as some have suggested (usually citing the Internet): it has been evolving throughout the past century, and can be seen in other naming contexts, especially in place-names.

In 1890 the US Board on Geographic Names made a far-reaching decision, which is still in force:

> Apostrophes suggesting possession or association are not to be used within the body of a proper geographic name.

Their reasoning was semantic.

> The word or words that form a geographic name ... change from words having specific dictionary meaning to fixed labels used to refer to geographic entities. The need to imply possession or association no longer exists.

It's thought that a quarter of a million apostrophes were deleted from US names as a consequence (*Harpers Ferry*, *Pikes Peak*, and so on). The apostrophe stayed if the name had nothing to do with possession, such as *O'Fallon* in Illinois.

Administrative names were also exceptions in the official US repository, the Geographic Names Information System, such as schools, churches, cemeteries, hospitals, airports, and shopping centres. Such names, the Board concluded, 'are best left to the organization that administers them'.

That makes sense. As with Waterstones, semantic reasoning alone never convinces. Underneath every semantic argument is a pragmatic argument crying to get out. And it's the pragmatic factors that count for most. Place-names in particular are governed by tradition: along with surnames and dialect words, they form the autobiography of a community. We are talking identity again, not intelligibility, even though there may be some cases where it isn't clear whether the name refers to a singular or a plural (was it *Pike* or *Pikes* after whom the peak was named?). And local protests can force a change – though not very often. The US Board gets around thirty applications for the use of an apostrophe each year, but only five 'possessive' names have been recognized: Martha's Vineyard, Massachusetts (1933), Ike's Point, New Jersey (1944), John E's Pond, Rhode Island (1963), Carlos Elmer's Joshua View, Arizona (1995), and Clark's Mountain, Oregon (2002).

Variations in the punctuation of public naming practices reinforce the climate of uncertainty that surrounds everyday usage, and this fosters inconsistency. If there's a clear semantic or pragmatic reason for an apostrophe, the usage will attract no attention. When we need to capture a contrast in meaning, to avoid ambiguity (such as *I love my uncles visits*), there's no argument: the apostrophe proves to be a useful device, allowing us to succinctly say what would otherwise be wordy (*the visits of my uncle/uncles*). And when we need to mark an identity, there's no argument: nobody will dare to tell big *Dermot O'Connell* that his apostrophe is unnecessary.

Our problem comes only when questions of ambiguity or identity do *not* arise. We don't misunderstand the Shakespeare examples in Chapter 28, even though they have no apostrophes, because the linguistic context tells us clearly what is meant. And we don't get confused if signs pointing to the London railway station sometimes say *King's Cross* and sometimes *Kings Cross*. (The website <www.kingsx.co.uk> has (in 2014) a big heading: *King's Cross Online*; immediately underneath is the heading *Welcome to Kings Cross Online*.) Cases like these make us feel that apostrophes are unnecessary: inserting or omitting them makes no difference to our ability to understand a meaning or to perceive an identity. And because these are in the vast majority, we find ourselves faced with the variation everywhere we go. This is what leads to people wanting to do something, such as form an Apostrophe Protection Society or go on a typo hunt around America.

What is it that makes some people react so strongly to apostrophes, while others don't? Educational background is certainly part of it. If we have had apostrophes beaten into us in school, then we will defend them to the death. As one listener wrote to me, after I talked about punctuation in a programme for my Radio 4 *English Now* series in the 1980s: 'I suffered for my apostrophes, which is why I get upset when I see people misusing them.' Social and cultural background is a part of it too: if we were brought up at home in an apostrophic atmosphere, we will have assimilated our elders' linguistic values – values that reflect the need to respect the conventions that society recognizes as Standard English. If we experienced a more relaxed personal punctuational history, we are less likely to feel strongly about these things, and will feel puzzled, confused, or angry when others harangue us for our supposed laxity.

That is why the Internet is at the centre of so many

punctuation arguments these days. We are in the middle of a transitional period in which our experience of the written language is undergoing a radical shift. The Internet now contains more written language than in all the libraries of the world combined, and the screen (fixed or mobile) is the place where young people most often experience it. The apostrophe is but one of the features that provide us with a different linguistic experience when we read and write online, or send and receive text messages by phone, but changes in its usage were among the first features to be noticed. As with the hyphen, omission was fostered by aesthetics, ergonomics, and fashion: it looked better, made typing easier, and everybody else was doing it.

The Internet didn't start these trends but it certainly reinforced them and speeded them up. And the constraints of the technology particularly affected the apostrophe, as this was one of the symbols that was excluded from the domain name system that provides us with our Internet addresses. The apostrophic identity of *McDonald's* restaurants is clear; but online we have to use such addresses as <www.mcdonalds.co.uk>. Multiply this example by all the names where apostrophes traditionally form part of an identity, and it's easy to see how online usage as a whole could one day be more generally affected, and eventually transfer into offline situations.

Media headlines about the Internet causing the 'death of the apostrophe' are premature. Electronic communication hasn't been around long enough for us to see what kind of long-term linguistic impact it will have. At the moment there are plenty of apostrophes online, their frequency depending on the genre of Internet activity we're looking at. They are infrequent in short messaging and instant messaging, for example, but still strongly present in blogs and websites. Their use in emails is very much determined by individual differences. Someone who begins an email to me with 'Dear

Professor' is more likely to use apostrophes than someone who greets me with a 'Hi Dave'.

Teachers have to cope with all this. They have to teach their students how to *manage* the apostrophe, which these days means guiding them towards an informed awareness of the stylistic differences that exist. At one extreme, we have extremely informal styles of communication where non-standard English is routine and writers rarely use an apostrophe – and only when it's absolutely essential to make a meaning clear. At the other extreme we have formal and informal styles of communication where Standard English is obligatory and the use of the apostrophe is motivated by the traditional rules governing letter omission (*haven't*), possession (*boy's/boys'*), and the avoidance of awkward juxtaposition (*dot the i's*), and sanctioned by the recommendations of examining boards. In between, we have the areas where educated people, perfectly capable of using apostrophes, choose to drop them for professional reasons, such as achieving a 'clean' look in a brand-name or a street name. Why they do so makes for an interesting teacher–student discussion.

This is all part of the aim to make students masters of punctuation (as I'll discuss further in the Appendix), by making them aware of what is going on, so that they can make an informed decision about when it is essential to use the apostrophe (if they want to avoid social criticism or get poor marks) and when it is optional. Any course of study should also make them aware of special uses of the apostrophe. A few fixed phrases require it, such as *will-o'-the-wisp* and *ne'er-do-well*, or allow it as a popular option, as in *rock 'n' roll* and *fish 'n' chips*. Distinctive pronunciations give rise to it, such as colloquial forms (*goin'*, *'cos*, *Cap'n*) or poetic variants to satisfy the metre of a line (*o'er*, *e'er*, *'gainst*). There are unique cases: the nautical pronunciation of *forecastle* resulted in *fo'c'sle* or the unique triptych *fo'c's'le*; and there is nothing else in English quite like *o'clock*. An abbreviated word prompts an apostrophe until it becomes established, as in *'flu*, *'phone*, *'bus*, and *'cello*, all common in Victorian times. *Hallow-e'en* has morphed into *Halloween*. Usage is divided over whether to use an apostrophe for years: *'06* for *2006*. Purely graphic shortenings can be seen in tables and other locations where space is at a premium, such as *Ass'n* for *Association*.

No other punctuation term has generated so much of a vocabulary as this one. The online *Urban Dictionary* provides a representative collection at *apostrophe*, which it defines as follows:

> Particularly useful piece of English punctuation for making yourself look stupid. You can do this in three main ways: 1. Putting an apostrophe in when it's completely unnecessary. 2. Leaving it out when it's needed. 3. Putting it in the wrong place.

This is accompanied by entries describing various acts of misuse: *apostrophe abuse*, *apostrophe catastrophe*, *apostrophe atrocity*, *apostrophe crime*, and *apostrophe-fuck*. Associated conditions include *apostrophapathy* ('the state of being of someone who just doesn't care about apostrophes'), *apostrophatarded* ('unable to use apostrophes correctly'), *apostrophe paranoia* ('condition suffered by English teachers and others who see missing and misplaced apostrophes [in places where they are actually correct]'), *apostrophobia* ('fear of the misuse of apostrophes'), *apostrophitis* ('the epidemic tendency to insert apostrophes where they do not belong'), *apostrophury* ('feeling that is evoked in grammarians and other sensible people when they see apostrophes misused'), and the politically correct *apostrophically challenged* ('the inability to make proper use of the apostrophe'). I missed *apostrophilia* ('love of apostrophes'), but otherwise this seems a pretty comprehensive list. *Urban Dictionary* also recommends *apostrophectomy* ('the removal of superfluous apostrophes').

After all this, it was a relief to read about *Apostrophy* – a New Jersey rock band formed in 2005.

30

Marks of inclusion (or exclusion): round brackets

The hierarchy of levels introduced in Chapter 14 is the organizing principle of the punctuation system. It has taken us from the most general considerations of layout and paragraphing down to the detailed level of hyphens and apostrophes. But there is one kind of punctuation that was not included in this treatment, because it operates outside the hierarchy – or, more precisely, in parallel with it. Its function, like most other marks, is to separate, but it is different from them in that it works in pairs, to show one unit being included within another. (Or, from a different perspective, to show that a unit is being excluded from the surrounding text.) There are two main types: *round brackets* (also called *parentheses*) and *quotation marks* (Chapter 31).

Parentheses is an awkward term, as it refers both to the mark and to the content within the mark: parentheses contain parentheses. Printers use a shortened form: *parens*. In everyday use, the popular term is *round brackets* – in British English often shortened to *brackets*. *Curved brackets* is a less-used alternative, as is the Latin term *lunulae* ('little moons'). Some sort of adjectival qualification is needed, though, in view of the occurrence of the other types of bracket described below, and in view of the fact that, when American English uses *brackets* on its own, the word usually refers to square brackets.

The main value of round brackets is that they allow anything to be included within anything. Here are some of the things that can happen (all taken from earlier chapters of this book):

- a sentence within a paragraph
  (Spoiler alert.)
- a sentence within a sentence
  This anticipates the important role given to
  semantics in the twentieth century (see Chapter 11).
- a clause within a sentence
  The extract also shows the presence of other forms of
  punctuation (which I'll discuss in the next chapter).
- a phrase within a clause
  the result can be ambiguity or unintelligibility (from
  a semantic point of view)
- a word within a phrase
  Book 3 of his (Latin) work is ...
  Dr Johnson's *Dictionary* (1755) ...
- a prefix or suffix within a word
  to our addressee(s)

Clearly, round brackets offer writers the chance to 'say two things at once'. It would be possible to write, in the last example, 'to our addressee or addressees', or, in the previous example, 'Book 3 of his work, which was written in Latin ...'. The brackets allow increased compactness of expression, and are thus likely to be frequent in genres (such as academic prose and poetry) where writers are articulating meaning of some complexity.

The text they contain is usually short. It's possible for a parenthetic remark to continue for more than a line, or even to contain more than one sentence, but this can make a text more difficult to process, as the reader has to keep the main sentence structure and meaning in mind while coping with the parenthetic content:

The importance of having the equipment checked by two
independent companies (as recommended by the 2012
UK government report on *Services to Industry* and since
confirmed by further reports in France and Canada – see
the paper by Richardson in this volume) is still not always
recognized.

In such cases, the 'magic number seven' principle (Chapter
24) operates again. Our working memory finds it difficult to
cope when put under such pressure. There's no grammatical obligation to keep the parenthetic content short, but the
longer it gets, the more we may find ourselves having to read
the sentence twice (at least!) to grasp its meaning.

Similarly, the use of round brackets within round brackets
is something writers generally avoid. There's no problem if
the nested item is a single word or date, but as soon as the
content lengthens, the reader is presented with an undesir-
able processing load:

(as discussed by Jones (1990) in his influential essay)
(as discussed by Jones (in an influential essay first
published in 1990) and other physicists)

Two levels of nesting are rare, and usually criticized as bad
style:

(as discussed by Jones (in an influential essay (now
available online) first published in 1990) and other
physicists)

Pragmatic factors also intervene. Some people hate the look
of adjacent parentheses:

(as discussed by Jones (2010))

Square brackets (see below) are sometimes used to address

this problem. They do reduce any semantic confusion, but the aesthetic considerations remain:

(as discussed by Jones [in an influential essay first published in 1990] and other physicists)

(as discussed by Jones [2010])

Round brackets are not the only kind of correlative punctuation marks. Commas and dashes can also be used in pairs, as can quotation marks, to show an included unit. As a result, we have a choice of semantic effects, which can be explored by comparing the use of the four forms in the same sentence:

The train, arriving late as usual, was full of tourists.
The train – arriving late as usual – was full of tourists.
The train (arriving late as usual) was full of tourists.
The train 'arriving late as usual' was full of tourists.

The least obtrusive mark, and semantically the most neutral choice, is the comma: this enables a writer to remark on the train being late without any further implication. The other three choices each add something extra.

- The dashes, as already discussed in Chapter 17, suggest an informal or dramatic spontaneity that isn't present in the other options. We can readily imagine the remark being spoken in a tone of voice that would express the speaker's attitude (of irritation, frustration …).
- The round brackets convey no emotional content, simply suggesting that the remark is of secondary importance – an explanatory or amplificatory aside – which might be omitted without the general tenor of the passage being seriously affected. In speech, the parenthetic remark is typically less prominent – spoken with lowered pitch and reduced loudness. The punctuation is drawing the

reader's attention to the fullness of the train, not the lateness.

- The quotation marks, as their name suggests, indicate that the remark is an allusion to some other text, spoken or written. The result is extra prominence: the sentence is now more about the lateness of the train than its fullness.

Usage has changed over the centuries. In Shakespeare's day, round brackets had a wide range of functions (including those now expressed by the dash), most of which are no longer used. We find them, for example, enclosing a term of address, an interjection, a subordinate clause, or a comment aimed at the listener (all examples from the First Folio):

We are not (Sir) nor are we like to be

But (ah) I will not, yet I loue thee well

Enter Ferdinand (bearing a log)

The one, I haue almost forgot (your pardon:)

Modern editions would either omit the brackets or replace them by commas or dashes.

Modern uses of round brackets are also anticipated in the First Folio, as when they are used to clarify the semantic structure of a passage. Look at this extract from *Two Gentlemen of Verona* (1.1.96):

I (a lost-Mutton) gaue your Letter to her (a lac'd-Mutton) and she (a lac'd-Mutton) gaue mee (a lost-Mutton) nothing for my labour.

This is much clearer than the repeated use of commas (which is how the Penguin edition of the play prints it):

I, a lost mutton, gave your letter to her, a laced mutton; and she, a laced mutton, gave me, a lost mutton, nothing for my labour.

By contrast, the Arden edition of the play keeps the brackets.

In certain circumstances, the set of correlative choices reduces to two. This happens when the item to be included is a sentence.

The train (I call it a train even though it had only one carriage) was full of tourists.

Commas are now impossible, because they are never used to end independent sentences. The conflict of functions would make for a challenging sequence:

The train, I call it a train even though it had only one carriage, was full of tourists.

Care also has to be taken when round brackets are accompanied by other punctuation marks. Here, usage has changed over the centuries. In the First Folio we see cases like '(your pardon:)' above, where the colon is included before the final bracket. Today, the convention is to place any following punctuation outside:

I managed to catch the train (the direct one), which meant I got to my interview on time.

I managed to catch the train (the direct one).

A common mistake in immature writing is to put the mark inside – or, if the parenthesis contains a sentence expressing a statement, to overpunctuate:

I decided to go by bus (the train was very expensive.).

It's possible to use question marks and exclamations before the final parenthesis, but this presents pragmatic problems:

I decided to go by bus (never by train!).

I decided to go by bus (will John approve?).

Two marks are necessary, because they perform different functions. But not everyone likes the look of such sequences, especially when the main sentence requires the same mark as the one within the parentheses:

I decided to go by bus (never by train!)!

Could I go by bus (is there a direct bus?)?

Formal styles of writing tend to avoid them.

Round brackets today also have a limited set of specialized functions, enabling us to succinctly identify examples, references, and cross-references, as in the citations to plays throughout this book; numbers or letters in a list, as in (*a*), (*b*), (*c*); and alternative forms of a word, as in *O*(*h*). They also, of course, have a range of technical functions, especially in mathematics and programming, and individual conventions will be encountered in reference publishing. A dictionary or index, for example, may use round brackets to identify a particular kind of information:

overcome 3.19; (~ *with*) 16.69
overhang (verb) 3.18

We should also note the unusual case of an unpaired usage, when lower-case letters are used to identify items in a list:

a)
b)
c)

The need to differentiate kinds of included information led to the development, chiefly from the eighteenth century, of other kinds of bracket. Most of the modern uses are technical. Mathematics and programming, in particular, couldn't do without them. Nor could phonetics, as different kinds of bracket are used to distinguish units in speech and writing: the sound [t] in square brackets, the phoneme /t/ in slashes, the grapheme <t> in angle brackets. But in everyday writing, brackets other than parentheses are uncommon.

- [ ] *Square brackets*, also called *crotchets*, or simply (especially in the US) *brackets*, are chiefly encountered when a writer wants to modify a quotation (omitting or adding content) or to make a clarification. I've used them several times in this book:

  omission: 'The important point […] is that nobody is excluded.'

  addition: '[some authors] point their Matter either very loosely or not at all'

  gloss: 'a shippe in Tamyse [Thames]'

  clarification: 'Julie [his editor, Julius Schwarz]'

  expansion (here, of an abbreviation in a manuscript): 'mo[re] correct'

  And I mustn't forget '[*sic*]', a Latin word meaning 'thus' – the conventional way of drawing attention to an authorial error or idiosyncrasy in a quotation or a piece of reported speech, as in 'havnt [*sic*]'. It's a convenient means of showing that an error is not the writer's, but is found in the original text.

- { } The *brace* was introduced in the seventeenth century

as a way of vertically linking units (such as lines, numbers, and musical staves). The word is from French, referring to the width between the two arms. I don't use it at all in this book (apart from in this chapter), and I can't think of any reason why I should. They're typically found in technical or instructional writing to specify a limited set of options:

a series of numbers: '{1, 3, 5, 7, 9}'

a set of choices: 'Choose an appropriate size {small, medium, large}'

a combination of notes: 'the chord {a, c, e}'

In informal handwriting, it's a useful option when the writer wants to highlight a group of lines. Terminology again varies: they've been called *curly brackets* and *squiggly brackets*.

• < > *Angle brackets* or *chevrons* are rare in traditional writing, but are increasingly visible as a result of electronically-mediated communication, where they enclose HTML commands (such as <i> for italics), and also act as a way of unambiguously identifying a URL or an email address without interference from any surrounding punctuation. Here's an example from earlier in this book:

The website <www.kingsx.co.uk> has a big heading ...

Literary editors also make use of angle brackets when transcribing a manuscript that includes an illegible or lost section. Anything within these brackets is a conjecture:

several of the people <argued> against the decree

Any of these correlative marks can be used, in pairs or singly, for artistic purposes. All have been used in electronic communication as a resource for creating emoticons. And there are even more unusual cases in poetry, where the observation that parentheses include content of secondary importance needs to be turned on its head. In a poem, what is within the parentheses is always significant – often more so than in the surrounding text.

Interlude: The poet of parentheses

 E E Cummings has been called 'the poet of parentheses', from the way he manipulates round brackets in an extraordinary number of creative ways, breaking the rules of everyday usage, and making them work along with spacing and other punctuation marks to produce pictorial poems. Several of his poems use multiple examples of parentheses, but in 'mortals)' the device is used just once, to great effect. Imagine a pair of circus trapeze artists as you read it.

mortals)

climbi
  ng i
  nto eachness begi
  n
dizzily
  swingthings
of speeds of
trapeze gush somersaults
open ing
  hes shes
&meet&
  swoop
    fully is are ex
        quisite theys of re
turn
  a
  n
  d
fall which now drop who all dreamlike

(im

The opening line has no left-facing parenthesis, and it's not immediately clear why. The meaning of the text is clear enough: the grammar tells us that the acrobats are mortals who climb into each other. We then see them climbing to their launch height – somewhat uncertainly, judging by the broken words. Their movement towards each other gathers speed, losing word spaces along the way (*&meet&*). A drifting sequence of lines of gradually increased length reflects their swooping motion, and leads to a point of *re turn*, the split word forcing us to move along with the acrobats. We feel their downward fall in the vertical arrangement of *a n d*. The final line, with its opening bracket, leaves the poem literally hanging in the air. It requires a resolution, and we find it by looking back up to the opening line, where that closing bracket is now explained, and we begin the reading process all over again, moving again with the acrobats.

The inverted parentheses thus provide a frame for the poem, bringing its end into graphological contact with its beginning. The effect is semantic as well as pictorially symbolic. Cummings wrote in a letter (31 October 1958) that the aerialists are 'transformed from "mortals" into "im"mortals because they risked their lives to create something beautiful'. And he adds: 'Finally they all disappear into the place from which they appeared.' The poem's punctuation, and especially the parentheses, shows it all.

31

Marks of inclusion: 'quotation marks'

Quotation marks are the other convention that falls outside the punctuation hierarchy. Like round brackets, they can be used to include text of any size, from a part of a word to a series of paragraphs. And like round brackets, there's a certain amount of terminological uncertainty. A traditional British usage is to call them *inverted commas*, a term that dates from the eighteenth century. But *quotation marks* (also first used in the eighteenth century) has come to be more frequently used, along with *quote marks* and simply *quotes*. In using these, though, we need to bear in mind that the marks do a great deal more than simply 'quote'. *Speech marks*, similarly – the term of choice in the present-day British language curriculum – tell only a part of the story.

Take these examples, all from the previous chapter. Only one of them is a genuine quotation:

- they identify a gloss: *'lunulae* ("little moons")'
- they highlight a commonly used phrase: 'parentheses offer writers the chance to "say two things at once".'
- they identify a previous reference: 'the "magic number seven" principle'
- they enclose a set of examples (as in the present list)
- they enclose an actual quotation: 'The train "arriving late as usual" was full of tourists.'

This list also illustrates the unique characteristic of this punctuation mark: it appears in two guises – single (' ') and double (" "). The shape of the latter has motivated a common children's description: *sixty-sixes* and *ninety-nines*.

The double mark is the earlier, going back to the *diple* (p. 15), which was placed in the margin to show a quotation, or a piece of text of special significance. Over the centuries, this evolved into a pair of semi-circular marks placed opposite the line(s) to which attention was being drawn. They were located only outside the line(s) to begin with, but by the end of the sixteenth century we see them within, and raised above the following line of type. A typical example is seen in Shakespeare's First Folio, when Belarius reflects on a popular sentiment (*Cymbeline*, 4.2.26):

> "Cowards father Cowards, & Base things Syre Bace;
> "Nature hath Meale, and Bran; Contempt, and Grace.

Printers thought of them as a special use of commas, calling them *turned* or *inverted* commas. This was an accurate enough name to begin with, as (in examples like the one from *Cymbeline*) only the opening of the quoted text was marked. But it became semi-accurate once writers and printers realized they needed to show the place where a quotation ended, because the closing double commas are not inverted. The use of closing commas was a practice that emerged during the eighteenth century, when the popularity of the novel grew, and conversational turns among the various characters had to be clearly indicated. The literary fashion was for direct speech. Authors needed a 'mark of silence', and this was met by using the double mark but reversing its direction. There was a logic behind the change: if inverted commas introduced speech, then un-inverted commas would end it.

The use of double marks appealed to writers in the eighteenth century, when heavy punctuation was favoured, and it is recommended by Lindley Murray in his influential grammar. The early nineteenth-century printers, such as George Smallfield and John Wilson, all recognize double marks as the norm, and reserve single for a quotation within a quotation. But in the later part of the century, Horace Hart, in his *Rules* for Oxford University Press, reversed the practice, recommending single quotes for the first quotation and double for the second. The English-printing world has been divided ever since. Double quotes are the norm in the USA, single in the UK, with other countries pulled one way or the other, according to publishing house and genre. A country's newspapers, for example, might use a different style from its textbooks.

The move from double to single was made on pragmatic grounds, in an age when heavy punctuation was falling from favour. Single marks were felt to be simpler, more elegant, less cluttered. During the twentieth century, they were thought to conform more to the general trend to simplify the appearance of punctuation. Ergonomic arguments supported the aesthetic ones: on a keyboard, double marks were a mite more awkward, as they required the use of the shift key. Economic arguments were put forward too: single quotes saved space, and thus paper. But none of these arguments was sufficiently persuasive to dislodge the practice from those countries and publishers that favoured it. And in any case the proponents of double marks had a supporting argument of their own, of a semantic kind: double marks avoided any confusion with the apostrophe:

'I've put food next to all the dogs' bowls'

"I've put food next to all the dogs' bowls"

The problem is greater when vertical (or 'dumb') marks are used instead of typographic (or 'curly') marks, as then all three – opening quote, closing quote, and apostrophe – look identical. Perhaps that is why people began to call curly marks *smart quotes*. They provide a semantically intelligent solution.

The printers had to solve several problems arising out of the use of quotation marks. What to do, for example, if a quotation extends over several paragraphs? Some writers inserted a mark at the beginning and end of each paragraph. The practice now is to have opening marks at the beginning of each paragraph, but a closing mark only at the end of the whole quotation. The reasoning is that, if there were a closing mark at the end of each paragraph, it could mislead the reader into thinking either that the quotation has come to an end (when it hasn't) or that the next paragraph is a totally different quotation (when it isn't).

And where should quotation marks be placed in relation to other punctuation marks? Hart sees no problem if there is a good semantic reason, as in:

(a) 'Why does he use the word "poison"?'

(b) Alas, how few of them can say, 'I have striven to the very utmost'!

(c) But I boldly cried out, 'Woe unto this city!'

In (a) and (b), the question mark and exclamation relate to the sentence as a whole, not the quoted element; in (c) the exclamation relates just to the direct speech. In all such cases the marks needs to be placed, as Hart put it, 'according to the sense'. And in all these cases double-marking should be avoided when the quotation is a sentence, even though grammatical logic might dictate otherwise.

Alas, how few of them can say, 'I have striven to the very utmost.'!

But I boldly cried out, 'Woe unto this city!'.

This is a pragmatic principle: minimizing visual clutter.

It took the printers and stylists several decades to work their way through the issues raised by quotation marks. Even today usage is by no means universal. What to do, for example, when both the main sentence and the quotation have the same grammatical status? In the following example, both are statements. Should the period go inside or outside the closing quote mark?

(d) We need not 'follow a multitude to do evil.'

(e) We need not 'follow a multitude to do evil'.

Hart comments:

the almost universal custom at the present time is for the printer to include the punctuation mark within the quotation marks at the end of an extract, *whether it forms part of the original extract or not.*

This he thinks is 'bad practice', and he recommends that the mark (whatever it might be – period, colon, comma …) be placed *outside* the quote mark, as in (e) above. But he adds a caveat: 'unless the author wishes to have it otherwise'. His advice fell on deaf ears in the USA, and thus we see both (d) and (e) in use today, wherever in a sentence a quotation appears:

I wanted to recite 'To be or not to be', but my mind went blank. [British English]

I wanted to recite 'To be or not to be,' but my mind went blank. [American English]

But the British practice is not entirely uniform, for – apart from the uncertainty over authors' wishes – we find the marks *inside* the closing quotes in cases of direct speech after a reporting clause:

> Mary said, 'You're right.'
> 'You're right,' Mary said.

This is a rare case where it's permissible to end a sentence with a comma. The point needs to be carefully taught to young learners, who otherwise might think it perfectly acceptable to write:

> 'You're right.' Mary said. *or* 'You're right.', Mary said.

They would have grammatical logic on their side, if they did this, but punctuation conventions are rarely a matter of logic. Far more often, it comes down to pragmatic considerations of tradition, identity, and taste. And whichever set of practices you use, there is a further pragmatic rule: be consistent.

The same principle applies to the other uses of inverted commas, where their function is not to quote at all. I gave some examples at the beginning of this chapter, but there are many more, with a range of functions that is hinted at by the various labels that have been used for them: *scare quotes, sneer quotes, shudder quotes, cute quotes*. All the terms point in the same direction: a word or phrase is being used differently from its normal use, and the marks tell the reader that they can't take it for granted, but must look for a special meaning in the mind of the writer.

> That is a 'solution'.

> Who knows how many cases have been 'cured'?

It's clear that the writers are disassociating themselves from the words in some way, but in what way, exactly? Are they being ironic, sarcastic, emphatic, distancing, sceptical, apologetic, critical, drawing attention …? We need to look carefully at the context. It could even be that the word is a genuine quotation, as in newspaper headlines and reports (though it's not always clear from whom):

Crisis demands 'strong' response [newspaper headline]

He has referred to 'bullying' tactics.

There's a particular problem if they are used in advertising for emphasis, as they inevitably convey a sceptical meaning:

Great 'reductions'

'New' models

Sales executives beware! Style-guide advice is to use scare quotes as little as possible, as they are often ambiguous. But they remain popular, and – uniquely for a punctuation mark – can also appear while speaking in the form of *air quotes* (or *finger quotes*), when the first two fingers of each hand are raised and waggled while the focused word is being said (usually in a distinctive tone of voice and preceded by a short pause). As this only works if the listener is looking at you, air quotes are of limited use. Saying the words 'quote unquote' provides an alternative.

After this, it's a relief to find straightforward cases of the marks being used unambiguously in serious settings, such as:

- titles of short works, such as poems, songs, short stories, article titles, chapter headings, and TV episodes:

    Three years later Eliot wrote 'The Waste Land'

- linguistic glosses and translations:

We see the same etymology in Welsh *llan* 'church'

- citation forms:

  'color' is an American spelling

- proverbial and aphoristic expressions:

  I think it's a case of 'Least said, soonest mended'

- a nickname within a real name:

  Joe 'King' Oliver

But even in these cases, there can be usage variation. How long does a story have to be before its title warrants the more imposing italics? Some people refer to Wordsworth's 'Prelude', some to his *Prelude*. And should it be 'color' or *color*? Publishing houses take different views about such matters.

There has always been an element of daring in the use of quotation marks. In the early days, writers and typesetters experimented with them, exploring their expressive potential along with other typographic features. Direct speech was sometimes printed in italics, with or without the marks. Double marks were sometimes used for direct speech and single marks for reported speech:

He said "I am satisfied".

He said that 'he was satisfied'.

And there were alternating usages to show a change of speaker:

"Are you ready?"
'I am.'
"Have you got the case?"
'Of course.'

In mainland Europe, quotation marks of either kind were widely avoided, with a new speaker shown by a new line and a dash – and this practice was sometimes followed by writers in English, such as James Joyce in *Ulysses*. Joyce disliked their cluttered appearance, especially when doubled. He called them 'perverted commas'.

Idiosyncratic uses are common in literature. T S Eliot, for example, uses them for questions in 'The Waste Land', but not for responses:

> 'What is that noise?'
> The wind under the door.
> 'What is that noise now? What is the wind doing?'
> Nothing again nothing.

They're usually omitted when a writer is reporting what a character is thinking. And several novelists avoid them altogether (p. 92). In fact, there are a number of genres today when direct speech is used without quotation marks. We don't see them in dramatic dialogue, for example (see the illustration on p. 140). Nor do we see them in verbatim reports, such as court proceedings or parliamentary debates, where a colon introduces the speech (as shown on p. 133). And in formal writing, if the quotation becomes lengthy, the advice is to display the quote as a separate paragraph, indented, and often with white space above and below (a *block quotation*), as can be seen many times in this book (see the quotation from Hart above). Here again, though, there is fuzziness, for how long is 'lengthy'? More than two lines? More than three? That's another pragmatic question: lengthiness is in the eye of the publisher.

Most people would accept that quotation marks shouldn't be used so much that a page begins to look fussy or cluttered. And some writers – such as Cormac McCarthy and NoViolet

Bulawayo – take this principle to extremes, avoiding them altogether.

But if you want to cut down on quotation marks, what are your alternatives?

Interlude: A fashionable vulgarism

Suspicion about scare quotes goes back a long way. In 1859, in its issue of 4 June, Mr Punch attacked what he called a 'fashionable vulgarism':

> The following is an example of a style of fashionable announcement lately grown customary:--
>
> "LADY PAKINGTON 'received' last evening, at the official residence of the First Lord of the Admiralty."
>
> Observe that "receive" is printed between inverted commas. Why? The question may be answered by a quotation from the poetry of the lower orders:--
>
> "JOSEPH BUGGINS 'guv' a party"
>
> The inverted commas in the foregoing line serve to mark the word "guv" as the vulgar preterite tense of the verb "to give." In the same way, perhaps, those which enclose the term "received" are meant to stigmatise it as a verb active, which ought to govern an accusative case expressed, but which only does govern an accusative case understood; that accusative case to be conjectured from its obviousness, in a spirit of candour. We know that LADY PAKINGTON received company. There are ladies who receive stolen goods – for example. These considerations should prevent a refined journalist from putting the word "received" in inverted commas after the name of a lady.

32

Graphics and *italics*

The previous chapter completes the account of the traditional set of punctuation marks, but the story of punctuation is not yet over. Several minor marks have to be noted, along with proposals for new marks. I also need to reflect on the fascinating things people do with punctuation, from the usefully ingenious to the weirdly eccentric. And there's an important overlap with other features of orthography that needs to be explored.

To begin with the overlap. In addition to punctuation, the orthographic system of a language includes spelling, capitalization, layout, and typography, and these should never be seen in isolation from each other. Punctuation interacts with each. Hyphens and apostrophes have a role to play in spelling. Initial capitals complement periods in identifying sentences. Strings of CAPITALS provide an alternative to other ways of showing emphasis. Sequences of initial capitals can express Very Special Points. Spacing is a critical feature in paragraph identity. And typographic features offer alternative solutions to some of the semantic and pragmatic problems recounted in earlier chapters.

The previous chapter illustrated one such problem: how do we reduce the burden placed on quotation marks, which have such a wide range of functions that usage is often ambiguous. My example was 'Great "reductions",' where the scare quotes convey a scepticism that diverts the reader from the writer's aim, which was simply to emphasize and focus attention. Replacing the marks by a distinctive typeface provides a solution. There are several possibilities:

italics: Great *reductions*

bold: Great **reductions**

underlining: Great <u>reductions</u>

small capitals: Great REDUCTIONS

full capitals: Great REDUCTIONS

combinations of the above: Great ***<u>reductions</u>***, Great *REDUCTIONS* ...

And, of course, colour, type size, font changes, and the creative positioning of the words and letters add many further options. In the nineteenth century, these would all be exploited: typographical variety was the norm. A concert poster or book announcement, for example, would have every line in a different setting, as illustrated on p. 320 by the title page of *The Yorkshire Garland* (1825). This kind of typesetting is rare today. Graphic designers prefer simplicity, and amateur website designers – awed by the dozens of graphic options made available online – are warned to be sparing in their selection of typefaces.

All of these options are part of our everyday encounter with the professional graphic world, online and offline; but when it comes to everyday writing at home or in school, what we do is much reduced. Handwriting routinely allows only underlining (straight and wriggly) and capitalization (of various sizes), though of course with special effort we can add colour and other features if we think it appropriate. These were also the only features available in old-style typewriting

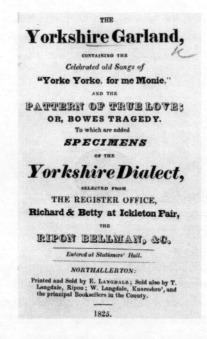

THE
Yorkshire Garland,
CONTAINING THE
Celebrated old Songs of
"Yorke Yorke, for me Monie,"
AND THE
PATTERN OF TRUE LOVE;
OR, BOWES TRAGEDY.
To which are added
SPECIMENS
OF THE
Yorkshire Dialect,
SELECTED FROM
THE REGISTER OFFICE,
Richard & Betty at Ickleton Fair,
THE
RIPON BELLMAN, &C.
_____
Entered at Stationers' Hall.
_____
NORTHALLERTON:
Printed and Sold by E. LANGDALE; Sold also by T.
Langdale, Ripon; W. Langdale, Knaresbro', and
the principal Booksellers in the County.

1825.

– with the additional constraint that wriggly underlining was impossible and capitals were of a single size. Writing on screen in theory offers all typographic possibilities, but most writers don't use more than the easy options provided by their keyboards, where underlining and capitalization are supplemented by italics and boldface. These four features are part of daily life for Internet users, though, so it's important that people become aware of the conventions and pitfalls surrounding their use. In particular, the function of *italics* (or *italic*, in traditional British terminology) overlaps with that of quotation marks, and requires separate consideration.

The use of italics originates in a medieval handwriting style, and has in its long history developed a remarkable range of functions, not all of which are easy to formulate as rules. Practice has altered over the centuries, with printers and publishers adding one change here, another change there, and making decisions about usage on the basis of reasoning that has long since been forgotten. A publisher's style guide will tell us, for example, that titles of books are to be in italics – but not the titles of sacred texts, such as the Bible or the books it contains. The names of newspapers seem to vary capriciously: we see the *Daily Express* and the *Daily Telegraph*, but *The Times* and *The Economist*. 'As a rule, print the definite article in roman', says Horace Hart in his *Rules* for Oxford University Press, but he allows the exceptions on the grounds that 'those publications prefer to have it so'. When pragmatic considerations outweigh semantic ones, the stage is set for widespread uncertainty.

The basic function of italics is clear enough: to make a word or phrase stand out from the surrounding text, either for emphasis or to distinguish it from other words with which it might be confused.

- emphasizing: 'there was a *third* man' [carrying Harry Lime across the street]
- distinguishing: '*adjective* is a noun' [totally confusing without the italics]

But this apparently simple principle goes in a bewildering number of directions.

It is unproblematic in cases like these:

- citing a linguistic form: 'the past tense of *go* is *went*'
- first mention of a technical term: 'This is known as a *stamen*. The stamen has to be …'
- identifying an individual letter or number: 'draw a line between *a* and *b*', 'Her name is Catherine with a *C*', 'he needed a *3* to win'.
- naming a vehicle, such as a ship, train, or spacecraft:

> '*Voyager* has reached the outer planets', 'he served on
> HMS *Renown*' [the prefix is not italicized, because it isn't
> part of the ship's name]

- giving a technical Latin name to plants or animals: 'a
  fine display of *primula vulgaris*' [primroses]
- giving directions in a dramatic or musical performance:
  '*Enter Hamlet*', '*ff*' [fortissimo]

There are also several technical contexts where it is standard
practice to use italics, such as in algebra ('$x + y$'), physics
('the constant c'), medicine ('symptoms of *E. coli*'), and law
('as seen in *Smith* v *Brown* 1930'). Even here, though, there
may be divided usage: we will find both '*Smith* v *Brown*' and
'*Smith v Brown*'.

Uncertainty over usage is more of a problem in the two
most frequently encountered cases of italics: work-titles and
loanwords. In each case, the principle seems straightforward
on first sight, but presents problems in application. Take
titles. The basic idea is that the title of a large work should
be in italics, and sections of a work in quotation marks. So
we find:

> Chapter 13 of his *English Grammar* is headed simply
> 'Coordination'.

Titles of books, journals, newspapers, operas, plays, films,
computer games, and other major works all have italics in
traditional publishing. But what counts as a major work on
radio and television? If the programme is a series, then it
would seem to work like a book, so I'd expect to see *The
Simpsons* and *The Archers*, with individually named episodes
in quotation marks. That allows us to say, should we need to:

> 'The New Moon' is an episode of *The New Moon*.

But should the title of a one-off ten-minute programme be in italics? Is that a 'major work'? And in literature, if titles of novels are italicized and titles of short stories are in quotation marks, what do we do with novellas? And does the name of a comic strip warrant italics?

The principle is also affected by perspective. Titles of large works can form part of a hierarchy, and lose their 'largeness' when seen in the context of something larger. This next example follows the expected pattern:

The first section of *The Waste Land* is headed 'The burial of the dead'.

But what do we do if we go a level up? Should it be (a) or (b)?

(a) In T S Eliot's *Collected Poems*, we find *The Waste Land*.

(b) In T S Eliot's *Collected Poems*, we find 'The Waste Land'.

Further context can push us in the direction of (c) rather than the apparently inconsistent (d):

(c) In T S Eliot's *Collected Poems*, we find 'The Waste Land' and 'Eyes that last I saw in tears'.

(d) In T S Eliot's *Collected Poems*, we find *The Waste Land* and 'Eyes that last I saw in tears'.

A similar uncertainty applies in the case of loanwords. Here the principle is to use italics if a borrowed word is new, arcane, or 'looks foreign'. So we would expect to find accented words italicized, such as *vis-à-vis* and *élan*. But how long does a loanword have to be in English before it stops 'looking foreign'?

déjà vu, *deja vu*, déjà vu, deja vu

There is no rule about the time it takes to anglicize a word. The more widely it is used, the sooner the italics will be dropped. We rarely see italics these days in such words as:

guru, fatwa, terminus, status quo, tai chi, cul-de-sac

But in recent days newspapers have presented me with:

doyen, conversatione, wunderkind, oeuvre, nom de plume

Longer phrases (*terminus ad quem, je ne sais quoi, deus ex machina*) tend to retain the italics, especially if there is a possible pronunciation confusion (*double entendre, agent provocateur*). Learnèd and specialized terms (*schadenfreude, weltanschauung*) will take longer to lose them, but even here it all depends on familiarity. Readers of a psychology journal might not expect to see *gestalt* italicized, but if the term turns up in an art journal it probably would be. Those who know the worlds of *batik* and *singspiel* well may find the terms so familiar that they no longer use italics, whereas outsiders would still find them strange. This is a domain full of 'probablys', 'mays', and 'mights'.

Fashions have changed greatly over the centuries, and are still changing. We no longer use italics to show direct speech, as was common practice in the sixteenth century. Nor do we use them for proper names, as seen in Shakespeare's First Folio:

Renew, renew, the fierce *Polidamus*
Hath beate downe *Menon*: bastard *Margarelon*
Hath *Doreus* prisoner. (*Troilus and Cressida*, 5.5.6)

Commonly used Latin abbreviations (such as *i.e.*, *op. cit.*, *ibid.*, *viz.*, *e.g.*) were usually printed in italics in the nineteenth century, but Horace Hart recommended romanizing them, apart from *c* (= circa), and we rarely see them italicized today.

Italics gave the printers several headaches in relation to punctuation. What should they do if writers wanted to cite a book title within a piece of text that is already in italics, as in a stage direction? Some sort of distinction needs to be made, to avoid ambiguity or unintentional humour:

> *Smith enters the room carrying David Copperfield.*

They decided to reverse the process, putting the title in roman type – though not everyone found the aesthetic result palatable, preferring quotation marks instead:

> *Smith enters the room carrying* David Copperfield.
> *Smith enters the room carrying* 'David Copperfield'.

And what should they do if writers italicized a noun, but wanted to pluralize it or give it a possessive? Should the *-s* be in italics too?

> (a) the *Renown's* engines *or* the *Renown*'s engines?

> (b) the *Renowns* of this period *or* the *Renown*s of this period?

Semantic reasoning suggests the second, as the inflection is not a part of the name. Pragmatic reasoning (avoiding an awkward juxtaposition of fonts) suggests the first. Both will be seen. And a similar question was raised by accompanying punctuation marks, in cases such as these:

> (*Troilus and Cressida*, 5.5.6)

> *doyen, conversatione, wunderkind, oeuvre, nom de plume*

The commas and parentheses are in roman type, which is recommended practice – again, on semantic grounds, as the punctuation is part of the discourse, not the individual words. But the alternatives will nonetheless be seen, especially online, where many writers see no point in spending time and energy making a typeface change that is unlikely to be noticed. And in handwriting, of course, the distinction disappears behind the idiosyncrasies of personal hands.

Different graphic mediums present writers with different options, not all of which are mutually translatable. Italics are difficult to replicate in handwriting, and so alternative means must be found to capture their linguistic functions – usually by means of a straight underline. But handwriting does things that traditional and online printing does not routinely allow, such as multiple underlining in cases of emphasis. Similarly, it is not always possible to equate the typographic features of traditional and electronic printing: hyphenation practices differ, for example, and the kinds of distinction beloved of printers (such as em vs en dashes and small vs large capitals) are generally absent online.

The Internet is a major factor in present-day change. Italic script is slightly less easy to read than roman, and slows reading speed, so long stretches of text in italics tend to be avoided other than in special circumstances (such as an extended stage direction in a play script). But even short pieces of text can be affected on the computer screen, where resolution is lower. Boldface or colour is more visible, so we often see these features replacing items that in traditional publishing would be in italics. And we also see the italic convention dispensed with altogether. 'HMS Renown' and 'primula vulgaris' are likely to appear online with no italics at all. The electronic world is making us rethink several traditional practices in relation to punctuation, and offering fresh opportunities.

33

Punctuating the Internet

A brave new world that has no punctuation in it? That is the myth which developed in the early days of electronic communication, when people saw emails and chatroom exchanges lacking standard punctuation – and sometimes with no punctuation at all. But it has turned out to be only a fraction of the story.

To begin with, alongside punctuation minimalism, there is punctuation maximalism, where we see more marks than would be found in traditional handwriting or printing. The trend is facilitated by keyboard technology: simply by holding a key (other than a letter or numeral) down, we can generate an indefinite string of symbols, thus allowing exchanges such as:

> will we see you at the party???????
> yes!!!!!!!!!!!!!!!!!!

This is not the first time repeated symbols have been used in English – they were always an option in informal letter-writing – but they have never been used so extensively. And the practice extends idiosyncratically to symbols that were never used in sequence before, such as > > > > > > > > and (((((((((((. The meaning of such sequences only becomes clear by looking at the context – and not always then.

The minimalist trend has its predecessors too, as we saw in earlier chapters with such writers as Cormac McCarthy

(Chapter 11), and of course the earliest English writing was most minimalist of all, with its almost total lack of punctuation marking. What Internet users have done, largely by instinct, is make a connection with writing in its most primitive state. They've been able to do it because, for the first time since the Middle Ages, they have available a medium which allows writing to appear in the public domain without the intervention of the cadre of professionals whose job it is to maintain consistency in Standard English – editors, copy-editors, and proof-readers. When writing a blog online, nobody is looking over your shoulder.

For punctuation, the scenario is unprecedented and can be unnerving, as Constance Hale and Jessie Scanlon observe in their influential *Wired Style* (1999):

> If you're writing on or about the Net, prepare for a clash of cultures – between copy editors and coders. The first live by the book, faithful to every mechanical rule; the second live by the keyboard, wildly appropriating every punctuation symbol in ASCII. Online, publishing meets programming – and punctuation leads a double life.

The situation is no longer as dramatic as Hale and Scanlon suggest. They were writing in the late 90s, when the Internet was still a novelty to most people, and all kinds of weird practices were being experimented with as users struggled to come to terms with what the technology was allowing them to do. Things have settled down a lot since then. Apart from anything else, the online demographic has risen sharply. It's no longer solely a young person's medium. And as the average age of users rises, so conservative linguistic practices become more evident.

The arrival of the Internet is not the end of punctuation as we know it. Rather, as Hale and Scanlon suggest, we live in two punctuation worlds now – one standard, the other nonstandard. The situation parallels what we see in the more general linguistic scenario that sociolinguists call *diglossia* (the simultaneous use in a society of a language that has two contrasting varieties, such as Classical Arabic and colloquial Arabic) – only here we would need to call it *digraphia*. In the offline world, Standard English punctuation is still alive and well; in the online world, nonstandard punctuation is alive and well. But the situation is mixed, for only certain genres of online writing display the wildness Hale and Scanlon observed. Quite a few online sites – most of the Web, and many bloggers and social networkers – remain faithful to traditional punctuation norms.

The essential first step, in the modern management of punctuation, is to understand what's going on in those genres where nonstandard punctuation is the default practice. For a young learner (and for older users too) the challenge is not to mix the two worlds up. The media panic is that new punctuation habits learned in the online nonstandard world will transfer to the offline standard one. For teachers, the challenge is to draw their students' attention to the stylistic differences between standard and nonstandard usage. And for this to happen, a grasp of what is taking place online is a necessary first step.

The foundation of this understanding comes from the perspectives I introduced earlier in this book. The distinction between semantics and pragmatics is crucial. As my earlier chapters illustrated, punctuation is only occasionally semantically necessary: there are very few occasions – *pace* St Augustine and Lynne Truss – when a punctuation mark is essential to expressing a meaning. *Eats, Shoots & Leaves* works well as a joke precisely because it is so rare. And examples such as *its* and *it's* are persuasive only when viewed in isolation

– something that never happens in real life. There can never really be confusion between *it's* and *its*, because they never occur in the same part of a sentence – one being a possessive pronoun, used before a noun (as in *the tree has shed its leaves*) and the other being a subject+verb (as in *it's very interesting*).

There are few semantic grounds for valuing punctuation. But there are unassailable pragmatic grounds. Punctuation is, firstly, a recognized feature of Standard English. It isn't the most important feature: that accolade belongs to spelling, because *every* word has to be spelled acceptably, whereas punctuation by its nature is sporadic. It is, however, far more noticeable than nonstandard grammatical constructions (*ain't, I was sat, haven't got nothing*, etc) as these turn up relatively infrequently compared to punctuation marks. As a result, if writers punctuate badly in settings where standard English is expected, and make a mistake in such words as *its*, the errors are likely to be noticed, and the perpetrator judged accordingly.

But punctuation is important for more than just reasons of social expectation and acceptability. It has proved to be valuable in aiding swift comprehension, especially as texts have become longer, more complex, and more varied over the centuries. It helps writers to organize their thoughts on the page, and it helps readers to process continuous text with a minimum of discomfort. While it's possible to read a piece of text without any punctuation at all and still understand it without ambiguity – as we saw at the very beginning of this book – such a task is undeniably more difficult. You can prove this to yourself quite easily, replicating the kind of study done in readability research. Take a paragraph; omit all punctuation; and monitor yourself (or someone else) reading it. Then do the same with the punctuated text. There will be more pauses and false starts in the unpunctuated text. Your eye-movements will dart about, as you look ahead for cues that would normally be found in the punctuation. You will understand the text well enough, but it's likely to have been an uncomfortable experience, and later you will have greater difficulty remembering what it was about.

This kind of exercise is illuminating only if the texts are of some length. Omitting punctuation in a short text presents few if any problems. After all, we see this every day of our lives in street signs, notices, posters, and many other settings. There's no punctuation after the words GIVE WAY or STOP WHEN LIGHTS ARE RED. And most titles of books aren't punctuated, even if they are long, such as *The Man Who Mistook His Wife for a Hat* or *The High Rise Glorious Skittle Skat Roarious Sky Pie Angel Food Cake*. So we might expect online users to be most ready to dispense with standard punctuation in genres where messages are short, such as texting, Twitter, instant messaging, brief emails, and chatroom or forum exchanges. Which is exactly what we find.

But dispensing with standard punctuation doesn't mean using no punctuation at all, even though this does sometimes happen. There's usually some sort of punctuation present. And quite intricate uses have developed, a few of which I've mentioned in earlier chapters, such as the use of ellipsis dots (...) to show incompleteness on Twitter, or the omission of a final period or the use of an exclamation mark to convey warmth and rapport. URL domain names have their own punctuation 'grammar'. They disallow spaces between words: a sequence needs to be linked using hyphens (*www.this-is-my-site.com*). Dots can only appear as component separators. Domain names are also case-insensitive: *this-is-my-site* and *THIS-IS-MY-SITE* would point to the same place. A further option, avoiding hyphens, is to use camel-case, as in *ThisIsMySite*.

The *asterisk* is another mark that has developed a little system of its own. In traditional publishing, it started life as a footnote marker, then came to be used as a mark of letter omission, as noted by Lindley Murray, and as a section separator in novels. In the nineteenth century it competed with the long dash as a way of hiding a sensitive word, or a part of a word (d***, d**n) – a practice that had become so common, by the end of the fastidious Victorian era, that it attracted the attention of Mr Punch, who in his issue of 15 December 1909 commented on 'an improvement in trade':

> The type-founders are now working overtime making asterisks in order to cope with the huge demand which has sprung up since the action of the Libraries in regard to a certain type of fiction.

If he were still around today, he would doubtless have had much more to say about the proliferation of asterisks in Internet settings, where they can mark a semantic comment (*sigh*) or emphasis ('there was a *third* man'). In fact, asterisk semantics is even more subtle, as it allows two degrees of intensity:

> I said *don't do it*
> I said *don't* *do* *it*

And he would doubtless have been even more scathing about the terminological profusion that surrounds the symbol: *star, splat, wildcard, dingle, spider, aster, twinkle* …

The other really noticeable Internet mark is the *slash* – another term that attracts alternative names, such as *slant, solidus, virgule, diagonal,* and *oblique*. The mark is widely used in offline contexts, such as:

- a substitute for *or*: 'he/she', 'hot/cold'

- a substitute for *and*: 'the Smith/Brown review', '2005/6'
- a mark of abbreviation: 'w/o' [=without], 'c/o' [care of]
- a separator in dates: '1/1/16' [=1 January 2016]

In more specialized contexts we see it, for example:

- in literature, marking a line-break in a poem or play: 'Double, double toil and trouble: / Fire, burn; and cauldron, bubble'
- in mathematics, showing a fraction or division: 1/3
- in linguistics, showing a sound-unit to be a phoneme: /t/
- in transcribing a conversation, to show where one person's speech overlaps with another:

  A So I really think he should / try a different
  B He ought to, you know

Usually, slashes have no spaces on either side; but some style guides recommend them to aid visual clarity, especially when separating compound words or a long sequence of items:

New York/Los Angeles
New York / Los Angeles
the verbs *ask/say/reply/declare/suggest* form a class …
the verbs *ask / say / reply / declare / suggest* form a class …

That's the situation in the offline world. What's happening online?

The Internet has added something new: there are now two kinds of slash – forward and (since the 1980s) backward (*backslash*). The latter arose within various programming languages, and is most often encountered in everyday computer use as a component separator in a Windows file path (*C:\ File\DC*). It has had relatively little use outside technical contexts, though it's sometimes seen in chat exchanges or online games, where it marks an emotion, action, or reaction, such as *faints* or *join*. Forward slashes are far more common in these functions, though – so much so that when someone is reading a command or address aloud, the adjective *forward* is often omitted, and we hear a string such as 'original pronunciation dot com slash analysis'.

Forward slashes are universal in URL addresses, the norm for commands in games, and present in the file paths on Mac and Unix systems. The *vertical bar* (or *pipe*, |), part of the standard keyboard, adds a further option as a separator.

Several other orthographic conventions have emerged on the Internet, some of which have their origins in traditional publishing. For example:

- S P A C I N G shows that something is 'loud and clear'
- CAPITALS convey a 'shouting' tone of voice
- _underbars_ (or _underscores_), mark emphasis and general highlighting, and offer an alternative to italics or colour in titles : _The English Language_
- <angle brackets> add a semantic commentary on what has just been said: <gasp>, <sigh>

Usage varies among Internet genres, online groups, and individual users. But everyone who emails uses the @ sign – the locator symbol chosen by Ray Tomlinson in 1971 because it was a symbol that wasn't being used in names or in computer programming, and yet was already familiar from commercial settings. As a symbol with independent meaning (= 'at'), it lives on the edge of the punctuation system, but its function is similar: it both links (two elements in an address) and separates. And this is the reason any book on punctuation should mention other symbols that perform these roles.

Several of these were noticed by the early grammarians, such as Lindley Murray, who compiled a list of 'other characters' at the end of his chapter on punctuation. I've dealt with most of them in earlier chapters, but four items in his list have not yet been described. Terminology has since proliferated (especially online), and functions have sometimes changed, but the symbols are constant:

- the *caret* (^) – marking an omission (from Latin *caret*, 'it lacks'), but now with technical usage in mathematics and programming; alternative names include *hat* and *uparrow*
- an *obelisk* (†) – alerting the reader to a footnote or marginal comment – also called an *obelus* or *dagger* and (in cases where a page has many footnotes) repeated as a double (†† or ‡) or even triple sign; today more commonly used along with a name to show death or extinction, or along with a word to show that it is obsolete
- parallels (||) – another way of alerting the reader to a footnote or marginal comment
- an *index* or *hand* (☞) – pointing out something that requires special attention, and also called by such names as a *fist* (by printers), *manicule* (Latin: 'little hand'), *index*, *pointer*, or *pointing finger*; a feature of early manuscripts, it was very popular in nineteenth-century signs and advertisements, but is rarely seen today

If Murray were writing now, he would have to add this one:

- # – a symbol with a long history of specialized uses (a sharp in music, a checkmate in chess, a space in proofreading …), as well as the routine way of showing a numeral (#3, Symphony #1) in American English; it has come into its own on Twitter, where it is used to mark keywords or topics in a tweet (a *hashtag*); its many labels include *hash* (especially in British English), *pound*

> (especially in the US, but not in Britain for obvious
> financial reasons), *gate, mesh, sharp, crunch, hex, flash,* and
> *octothorpe*

This by no means exhausts the punctuational novelty we
find on the Internet. Users have always sensed the tension
between a medium that is conversational in character yet
mostly graphic in operation. The lack of the features of
normal face-to-face conversational interaction – pitch, loudness, speed, rhythm, tone of voice, facial expression, gesture
– was the motivation for the *emoticon* (or *smiley*), in which
punctuation marks obtained a new lease of life, combined in
ingenious ways with letters and numerals to replicate facial
expressions and bodily movements. Some emoticons are
semantic entities in their own right (a dancing figure, a hug,
a kiss), replacing whole utterances:

> so I'll see you tomorrow
> :))

But some operate just like punctuation, appearing at the end
of sentences as a kind of 'period with presence', informally
reinforcing or manipulating the interpretation of what has
just been said and offering a clarification in cases of potential
ambiguity.

> I don't think I'll be able to go :(
> John's a real idiot to say that :) [i.e. I'm actually happy he
> said that]

Emoticons have attracted a level of interest that far
exceeds their communicative significance. They were never
used as often as first impressions suggested. Studies of
Internet genres repeatedly showed their occurrence in only
a minority of online interactions – usually around 10–20 per

cent. Some genres (such as instant messaging) used them more than others (such as blogging), but none displayed the extraordinary diversity listed in the flurry of potboiler netspeak dictionaries that were published in the 1990s, in which innovators seemed to be competing to create the weirdest and coolest emoticons.

Mickey Mouse 8(:-)
Homer Simpson (_8(|)

The genre moved well beyond everyday communication into creative graphics reflecting contemporary crazes. Vampires?

:-[

But that's just your bog-standard vampire. An entire family emerged:

%-[a confused vampire

/:-[a vampire with a beret

:-E a buck-toothed vampire

:-F a buck-toothed vampire with one tooth missing

etc

This is an art form, not communication. And it was rare indeed to see one of these creations appearing in real online interactions. Just a handful of basic emoticons turned up routinely, such as the smile, the frown, the wink, and the surprise, sometimes with intensification:

:) :(;) :0 – sometimes with the nose added :-)

:) :)) :)))

Age was a factor: the younger the person, the more likely messages would use emoticons. Gender was a factor too: girls used them more than boys.

But all of this is becoming history now. Software developments have substituted colourful icons for the original symbol clusters. My computer offers me the choice of nearly 200 ready-made emoticons. Fashions also change. There was a flurry of publicity about Japanese emoji in 2015. Yet, when I visited a school that year, where the class collected a corpus of online interactions, I saw no emoticons at all – and no texting abbreviations either. When I asked why not, I was told they weren't cool any more. And one student commented: 'I stopped using them when my parents started.'

One reason for the falling-off is probably that emoticons didn't live up to expectations. They were thought to be a way of making the meaning and intention of messages clearer, but in practice they were just as ambiguous as unsmileyed text. Any individual emoticon allows several readings. How would you interpret :)? Happiness, joke, sympathy, good mood, delight, amusement, complacency, sarcasm …? The only way is to look at the verbal context, and to take into account what you know about the sender and the present communicative situation. It's a common experience that a smile can go down the wrong way. 'Wipe that smile off your face.' And users were uncomfortable with emoticon inflation – the pressure to keep using them in a message, to avoid giving the impression that a sentence which lacked one had a different intention behind it. I've had emails in which every paragraph ended in the same emoticon. When that happens, they begin to lose their value. Someone who's always smiling isn't smiling.

A moderate use of a few emoticons will probably remain a feature of online interaction. They are a modern instance of the need for new orthographic devices to clarify written meaning. Long before the Internet arrived, there was the percontation point (p. 194), and more recently the interrobang. The American satirist Andrew Bierce wrote a language-reform essay called 'For brevity and clarity' in which he recommended the use of what he called a 'snigger point, or note of cachinnation [loud laughter]' to show a smiling mouth. That was in 1887. Today, the concern has been to find an unambiguous way of identifying irony or sarcasm, in view of the way many messages fail to have their ironic content perceived by the reader. Some try using exclamation marks to get round the problem, but these are ambiguous. Some use a (static or dynamic) winking emoticon ;-) but that's ambiguous too. This has motivated various suggestions for a semantically specific symbol, which can only mean sarcasm, such as the inverted exclamation mark, a reversed question mark (similar to the percontation mark), a zigzag exclamation mark, a dot inside a single spiral line (the *SarcMark*), and a period before a tilde (the *snark mark*, .~).

There are many other possibilities waiting to be discovered – or rediscovered, for many earlier proposals have sunk without trace. An exclamation mark or question mark with a comma underneath, to be used mid-sentence? Tried out in Canada in the 1990s. Double colons? Used by fantasy writer Piers Anthony to identify one of his characters in his *Kirlian* novels (he called them *quadpoints*). An exclamation mark with a dash through it, to show certitude? Done by French author Hervé Bazin in the 1960s. A combination of two exclamation marks sharing the same dot, to show acclamation? Bazin again. A pair of question marks sharing the same dot, with the right-hand one reversed to face its mate, to show affection? Bazin again. And who knows which of these might not one day go viral, and become a regular part of our punctuation system?

Interlude: Punctuation eccentricity

At the top of any list of punctuation eccentrics, I would firmly place an American businessman, the self-styled Lord Timothy Dexter (1748–1806), who became rich through marrying a wealthy widow and then engaging in a series of naive business adventures that should have failed but somehow succeeded. Of all the stories of his odd behaviour, some no doubt legendary, none is more bizarre than his mock demise. A death obsessive who slept in his coffin, he wanted to know how he would be mourned, so he had his death announced, planned a full-scale funeral, and invited people to a wake – attended, it's said, by over 3000. After his resurrection, so the story goes, he beat his wife for not crying enough!

In 1802 he published a short book about himself, *A Pickle for the Knowing Ones, or Plain Truth in a Homespun Dress*, full of deviant spellings, erratic capitals, and no punctuation. This is not the playful spelling we see in the essays of Artemus Ward, Josh Billings, and other late nineteenth-century writers. This is from someone who left school at the age of eight and worked on a farm. Here are the opening lines (with my translation):

> IME the first Lord in the younited States of A mericary Now of Newburyport it is the voise of the peopel and I cant Help it and so Let it goue Now as I must be Lord there will foller many more Lords pretty soune for it dont hurt A Cat Nor the mouse Nor the son Nor the water Nor the Eare then goue on all is Easey Now bons broaken all is well all in Love Now I be gin to Lay the corner ston and the kee ston with grat Remembrence of my father Jorge Washington the grate herow 17 sentreys past before we found so good a father to his shildren and Now gone to Rest ...

[I'm the first Lord in the United States of America, now of

Newburyport. It is the voice of the people and I can't Help
it and so Let it go. Now as I must be Lord there will follow
many more Lords pretty soon, for it don't hurt a cat nor the
mouse, nor the sun, nor the water, nor the air. Then go on.
All is easy. No bones broken. All is well. All in Love. Now
I begin to lay the cornerstone and the keystone with great
remembrance of my father, George Washington, the great
hero. 17 centuries passed before we found so good a father
to his children, and now gone to rest ...]

When people complained that it was difficult to read, he
added an extra page in the second edition, which begins:

fouder mister printer the Nowing ones complane of my
book the fust edition had no stops I put in A Nuf here and
thay may peper and solt it as they plese

[Further, Mr. Printer, the Knowing Ones complain of my
book the first edition had no stops. I put in enough here
and they may pepper and salt it as they please.]

And he is as good as his word. This is what follows:

34

Pragmatic tolerance

If I had to use one word to summarize the approach to punctuation I have used in this book, it would be *pragmatic*. A pragmatic approach, as I characterized it in Chapter 11, studies the choices we make when we use language, the reasons for those choices, and the effects those choices convey. It is an approach that focuses on explanations rather than prescriptions. Those who adopt this approach believe in confronting the realities of a complex situation rather than simplifying them to the point that they no longer relate to everyday linguistic experience. They believe that by understanding a problem, we are halfway towards solving it. In everyday usage, pragmatic is opposed to dogmatic. There are some things we can be dogmatic about in language, but punctuation is not one of them.

So my approach is in clear contrast to what has been called the 'zero tolerance' approach to punctuation, famously the subtitle of Lynne Truss's best-selling *Eats, Shoots & Leaves*. I've written a riposte to that book already (*The Fight for English*, 2006), so I won't repeat the arguments here. My view comes down to this simple statement: it is not possible to be zero tolerant about a linguistic system that contains so much uncertainty. Every one of the descriptive chapters in the present book encounters genre preferences and personal tastes. I am not talking about the much-maligned greengrocers or those whose punctuation ability is poor because, for whatever reason, the education system has let them down. I am talking about people whom we would all accept to be well-educated, competent users of Standard English.

No two educated people will agree about everything in the world of punctuation. The nineteenth-century pedant Henry Alford proudly claims in *The Queen's English* (§ 124) that when he was editing a particular text he 'destroyed more than a thousand commas, which prevented the text being properly understood'. The text he was referring to was written by someone as scholarly as he was. Indeed, disagreement can be found within one person, as the famous quotation from Oscar Wilde illustrates:

> I was working on the proof of one of my poems all the morning, and took out a comma. In the afternoon I put it back again.

I have lost track of the number of occasions, while writing this book, that I have behaved in exactly the same way. Mark Twain sums it up well, writing in 'The Contributors' Club', the final section of volume 45 of *The Atlantic Monthly* (1880):

> Some people were not born to punctuate; these cannot learn the art. They can learn only a rude fashion of it; they cannot attain to its niceties, for these must be *felt;* they cannot be reasoned out. Cast-iron rules will not answer, here, any way; what is one man's comma is another man's colon. One man can't punctuate another manuscript any more than one person can make the gestures for another person's speech.

I disagree about the first part of this quotation: anyone can learn to punctuate well if taught well – which means understanding the nature of the linguistic system that underlies it, with all its foibles and exceptions. But I whole-heartedly agree with the second part (assuming he would allow me to add 'or woman' at appropriate places).

The individuality of punctuation is something about which literary writers and grammarians agree. Even William Cobbett, in one of the most pedantic works to be written about English in the early nineteenth century, concurs. In Letter 14 of *A Grammar of the English Language* (1829), addressed to his son, he concludes his review of the topic with these words:

> You will now see, that it is quite impossible to give any precise rules for the use of these several points. Much must be left to taste: something must depend upon the weight which we may wish to give to particular words, or phrases; and something on the seriousness, or the levity, of the subject, on which we are writing.

Perhaps that is why we care so much about punctuation: we are aware that its character is shifting and unpredictable, that it doesn't offer the same level of order and correctness that is seen in spelling and grammar, and it disturbs us. We hope to find clear-cut rules and instead find tendencies, trends, and fashions. It seems a mess, so we turn to self-help guides which seem to offer a neat solution but find that they explain only a small part of the punctuation story.

Punctuation has always been a matter of trends. Every chapter in this book shows that it is subject to changes in fashion. No one has ever been able to define a set of rules which will explain all uses of all punctuation marks. Practice varies so much between formal and informal writing, between Britain and America, between page and screen, between publisher and publisher, between author and author, between generation and generation, between men and women. The best we can do is identify norms, plot trends, emphasize the need for personal consistency, and be very cautious indeed about making generalizations. Hardly any rules of punctuation are followed by all of the people all of the time. The pragmatic approach respects this reality, and tries to come to terms with it.

Being pragmatic doesn't mean 'anything goes' – ignoring the rules that do exist. It means respecting all linguistic realities, whether rule-based or not. A corollary is that it also means we should not seek to impose unauthentic rules on the language – insisting, for example, that all cases of *tall, dark(,) and handsome* should / should not have a comma before *and* (p. 250). The teaching of unauthentic rules is actually one of the *causes* of illiteracy, because learners – encountering variation wherever they look, and given no management principles to relate the world they live in to the world of the classroom – can become confused, lose confidence, and end up making the very errors that the rules were intended to eliminate. Uncertainty over apostrophes in *hers, its, ours, yours,* and *theirs* is a classic case in point (p. 282). Having been taught that the apostrophe must be used before *s* when the word expresses possession, they happily generalize the principle to possessive pronouns, only to find that it no longer works (except with *one's*). In which case, can the principle be trusted anywhere? The point is easily anticipated in class, of course, if the weakness in the system is appreciated by the teacher. If it isn't, we lay the foundation for a new generation of punctuation pedants who one day – in cases such as the serial comma – will adopt what they think is a logical solution and insist on everyone else using it.

The reassuring point is that punctuation *is* a system, despite the exceptions and the vagaries of taste. As described in Chapter 13, it is hierarchical in character and offers a fixed number of choices at each level. It is moreover a very small system, compared with grammar – a dozen or so common marks only. This is the point missed by Cobbett in his remark above: even though no two people agree all the time, they do agree some of the time, and it is these areas of agreement that identify the system and provide the basis for any course of study. I can't put a figure on it: I don't know what proportion of the punctuation system is subject to rule as opposed to taste. My feeling is that it is far less than we see in grammar and spelling. Taste affects about half the descriptive observations in this book. But at least the other half is capable of a rule-based account.

Also reassuring is the observation that taste is not always idiosyncratic. A great deal of the variation noted throughout this book is to do with functions rather than forms. Punctuation is not simply a matter of choosing between, say, single or double inverted commas, or between a colon and a semicolon, but of understanding the role that it plays in promoting the effectiveness of a text. For a long time, as we saw in Chapter 7, people thought there were only two functions to punctuation: a guide to pronunciation and a guide to grammar. There are far more, as the descriptive chapters of this book illustrate. There is a ludic function, seen in poetry, informal letters, and many online settings where people are playing with punctuation. There is a psycholinguistic function, facilitating easy processing by writer and reader. There is a sociolinguistic function, contributing to rapport between users. There is a stylistic function, providing genres with some of their orthographic identity.

The importance of genres needs to be appreciated, because they constrain the options available to the writer. Each written genre has its own orthographic style. Advertisements these days use little punctuation, relying on other graphic features to present their content. Certain kinds of legal texts traditionally avoid it altogether, reflecting a view that a case can stand or fall depending on the placement of a comma. Liturgical texts rely on it, especially when there needs to be unison speech from the congregation: if people are praying aloud together, and don't know the prayers by heart, they need frequent and clear punctuation cues to ensure their rhythm and pausing is shared – as the Old English monks knew very well. In every genre, the role of punctuation is holistic: it is the overall look of a text, created partly by many individual punctuation choices, that provides its stylistic identity. And this effect can be observed in any written genre, offline or online – journalism, instructional writing, scientific reporting, text-messaging, blogging … Literature is no exception. Writers like James Joyce, E E Cummings, and Gertrude Stein do bend and break punctuation rules for artistic effect; but bending and breaking rules does not mean arbitrariness and inconsistency. We never see sentences like this:

> ;this" is an! exa)mple ?of an arbitr-ary: and,, inc'onsist.ent
> use of punc(tuation-

There is order in linguistic art, even though it may require some effort to discover it, as we saw with the Cummings poem on p. 305.

To conclude: I agree totally with the aim of the punctuation guides written by G V Carey, Eric Partridge, Lynne Truss, and others, which is to improve our understanding of punctuation and to bring its study into the centre of the educational stage. That is, after all, why I have written the present book. I am as disturbed as those authors were when I see nonstandard punctuation used in settings where we expect standard forms to prevail, as this can affect the user's social credibility or career prospects. The whole point of a standard language is to ensure general intelligibility and acceptability by having everyone follow an agreed and respected set of norms of usage. One of the jobs of education is to teach the written standard, and punctuation is part of that. If students leave school not having learned to punctuate well, then something has gone horribly wrong. My hope is that this book will make this happen less often.

Envoi: Gertrude Stein on punctuation

There are some punctuations that are interesting and there are some punctuations that are not.

I doubt whether anyone has attributed more personality to punctuation marks, or treated them with such loving-hate, as American writer Gertrude Stein. In a 1932 lecture on 'Poetry and grammar', published the following year in *Lectures in America*, she sounds off about punctuation in her characteristic repetitive playful stream-of-consciousness style. Her views are an extreme reaction to the traditional account of punctuation, and I end my book with one of them to illustrate the theme of my final chapter: that at the heart of punctuation there is an unavoidable tension between rules and taste, an intrinsic subjectivity, and a personal commitment that needs to be recognized if the subject is to be truly mastered.

A question is a question, anybody can know that a question is a question and so why add to it the question mark when it is already there when the question is already there in the writing. Therefore I never could bring myself to use a question mark, I always found it positively revolting, and now very few do use it. Exclamation marks have the same difficulty and also quotation marks, they are unnecessary, they are ugly, they spoil the line of the writing or the printing and anyway what is the use, if you do not know that a question is a question what is the use of its being a question. ...

The question mark is alright when it is all alone when it is used as a brand on cattle or when it could be used in decoration but connected with writing it is completely entirely completely uninteresting.

When it is all alone. As on a tavern sign. Which is where I came in.

Teaching punctuation

I see my job as a linguist to talk about the 'what', 'when', 'where', and 'why' of language. Even the 'who' sometimes. I leave the 'how (to teach)' to the professionals. But 'how' inevitably depends on 'what', so I thought it would be useful to bring together the various observations about the teaching of punctuation suggested by the pragmatic approach at various points in this book.

Never isolate punctuation

Punctuation is one part – an important part, but not the only part – of the entire writing system (the *orthography* or *graphology*) of the language, and needs to be seen as part of that system and integrated within it. There are several points of overlap, as seen in Chapter 32, such as capitalization and typography. From a child's point of view, it's the whole graphic picture that is the starting point. Punctuation takes its place towards the bottom of a literacy hierarchy of book, page, illustration, and text.

Orthography, in turn, is part of the language as a whole, so punctuation needs to be seen routinely in relation to other aspects of language structure and use – most obviously grammar, but also pronunciation (in the sense of oral fluency), vocabulary, discourse, and style. Semantics and pragmatics are the foundation topics here, as I've emphasized since Chapter 11, for it's not possible to explain the complexity of punctuation without them. The semantic perspective explores the meanings that punctuation (chiefly through the mediation of grammar) is able to express. The pragmatic perspective explores the factors that cause variation and change. It's essential to use both perspectives in teaching, for each explains only half of what is going on (Chapter 34).

In relation to grammar, punctuation shouldn't be thought of as some sort of appendage. This was the problem with traditional approaches, which relegated it to a chapter at the back of a book. Rather, as Percival Leigh put it in his *Comic English Grammar* (1840), 'Punctuation is the soul of Grammar'. It's always there, awaiting a call whenever a grammatical point needs to be taught in relation to writing. So it should be spread through a syllabus. For example, sentences, in their various functions (statement, question, etc) will motivate an exploration of ending options (Chapter 16). Subordinate clauses will motivate an exploration of how they are to be linked punctuationally to main clauses (Chapter 25). Important semantic contrasts will need to be explained in their place (such as when dealing with relative clauses, Chapter 25). Ambiguities ('are you asking me or telling me?') will need to be noted when encountered (Chapter 21). There are so many points of connection that their exploration needs to be spread in a leisurely way over time. Try to avoid the trap of 'having a lesson on punctuation', without some other motivation. That should never be the routine, for punctuation is never an end in itself. It's always in the service of some other aspect of language.

Detect the limitations

In relation to oral fluency, punctuation represents the

dynamic features of the voice: intonation, loudness, speed, rhythm, and pause – what are technically called the *prosodic* features of speech – and it's illuminating to compare speech and writing from this point of view. Punctuation makes its contrasts, literally, in black and white terms. The dynamic features of speech are not like that; they are an indefinite number of shades of grey. A pitch level can gradually rise, tone by tone, until something that began as a statement ends up as a question; but a period does not gradually morph into a question mark. Information is always being left out, therefore, when speech is written down. And conversely, information is always being added when a written text is spoken aloud.

An adaptation of the old dictation pedagogy can be rewarding: a class writes down a dramatically spoken utterance, and sees what punctuation variation turns up among their responses. They then 'back translate' – reading the different versions aloud, and seeing which corresponds most closely to the original and where the punctuation has let them down. This way they learn the limitations of punctuation – that it isn't a perfect system and can't solve all problems in the graphic representation of speech. An important aim is to draw students' attention to the places where the system breaks down, and to suggest ways around the difficulties. They need to see what punctuation can't do as well as what it can do.

Speaking aloud can also draw attention to places where a wrong punctuation decision has been made, as in the case of comma splices (Chapter 22). This common error usually remains unnoticed while writing, but becomes more obvious if what is written is then read aloud. But there's a caveat: if young writers read their own work aloud they may pass over the error, as they already know the meaning of what they've written about. The problem is much more likely to surface if a child *other* than the writer reads the piece aloud.

Recognize the hierarchical system

This principle governed the central part of the book, from Chapters 13 to 29. It expresses the fact that the various punctuation marks don't all operate at the same grammatical level: some relate to paragraphs, some to sentences, some to clauses, some to phrases, some to words, and some to parts of words. But at each level, the marks work in a systematic way – even though there are exceptions and variations. Getting the idea of a system across to students is probably the most important intuition about punctuation that a teacher can convey.

To say that punctuation is a system means simply that, at any one place in a written discourse, a choice has to be made from the set of options the language makes available (Chapter 13). The important thing, therefore, is to make students aware of what the semantic and pragmatic options are. No one punctuation mark can ever be satisfactorily explained in isolation, and it should never be taught in isolation. There should always be a contrast with some other mark. To discover the function of the semicolon: replace it by something else, and see what happens (Chapter 22). To work out how to handle end-placed adverbials: reflect on the available options, such as those in the series *Come here immediately* (Chapter 25). To develop a sense of the semantic function of an ellipsis: add continuations to groups of sentences as in *It's time you went home* … (Chapter 16). This is where teaching punctuation can get quite exciting, when a class of youngsters act out the consequences of one punctuation mark being used in a story rather than another. When there are no clear-cut rules to guide usage, we need to build up students' intuitions about good practice by getting them to reflect on as many instances as possible. This can come unconsciously just from reading a lot; but the issue can be neatly focused by presenting learners with a judicious selection of examples.

Work within genres

In a pragmatic approach, it's important to ensure that the choices are presented within a single genre. It would make no sense to consider together the use of a comma in a newspaper and the use of a colon in a legal text. That wouldn't be a real choice. Rather, we need to select the punctuation options that operate *within* an individual genre, so that students can see how the system is put to work. What do journalists do? More specifically, what do journalists on a particular paper do? The trick is to find genres that are motivating, given the age and background of the students' point of view. Journalism may not be of interest, but there are plenty of punctuation-using alternatives in computer games, text messages, advertisements, best-selling stories ... What can be done with James Joyce or E E Cummings can also be done with Roald Dahl and Terry Pratchett.

Inculcating a sense of language appropriateness in different genres (varieties, styles, registers ... terminology varies) is the foundation of the modern approach to mother-tongue language pedagogy. For the teacher, the main challenge is to draw students' attention to the stylistic differences between them, and especially to the differences between standard and nonstandard usage. This is especially important in relation to genres where nonstandard punctuation is the default practice, as in several online situations (Chapter 33). For a young learner (and for older users too) the challenge is not to mix the two worlds up. The media panic is that new punctuation habits learned in the online nonstandard world will transfer to the offline standard one. This won't happen if the differences have been thoroughly explored and understood.

Highlight consistency

I've repeatedly mentioned a principle that all punctuation commentators respect: the need for an individual writer to be consistent. But how is this to be achieved when there's so much stylistic variation around? In the days when children had most of their primary education from a single teacher, the maxim would be 'Do as I do', which worked well enough. That would guarantee consistency – or, at least, a consistency that was no worse than that of their model! Today, children are taught by several teachers and classroom assistants as they progress, and are exposed to many more unofficial 'teachers' outside school, such as parents and online peers. Given that there is so much personal variation, how is consistency to be achieved now?

A recurrent message of government reports into language, from the Bullock Report (1975) on, is the role of a school language policy. This is especially important when it comes to punctuation. A situation where Teacher P insists on a comma at a certain place whereas Teacher Q insists on the opposite, without any explanation being given, is unlikely to foster a confident use of punctuation. A punctuation policy doesn't mean that all the teachers need to adopt the same pattern of use – which would be difficult to implement, given their different personal histories and the deep-rooted nature of punctuation habits – but it does mean that they need to be aware of the differences in individual practice that exist (including between school and home, or school and examining board), so that they can alert their charges to the variation and establish pragmatic guidelines. Children will never develop a consistent personal punctuational style if they don't see a coherent model around them.

Take account of the child's point of view

With young readers (and often with older ones too), teachers should be aware of what the learners bring to the literacy table. Even very young children will already have encountered punctuation marks in various settings, and will have formed some opinions about them. As I suggested in Chapter 14, we therefore need to understand punctuation from the child's point of view. This was part of the message of Emilia Ferreiro and Ana Teberosky's hugely illuminating *Literacy before Schooling* (1983), a book about all aspects of the way children think about literacy, and which included examples of what they had to say about punctuation. One of the children they studied, Mariona, age five, describes punctuation marks as 'head letters' because 'you think them but you don't say them'. Another, Alejandra, also age five, was shown two cards: THEBEAREATSHONEY and DAD KICKS THE BALL, and the authors comment:

> We ask her if she thinks it is okay and she says no. When we ask if something should be corrected, she responds, 'Here I have to put other letters,' and she begins filling in letters in the blank spaces of the sentence with the conventional separations.

This is an intriguing reverse of what an adult would expect.

The literacy hierarchy was also the motivation behind the acclaimed *LARR* test of the 1980s (*Linguistic Awareness in Reading Readiness*, by John Downing and others), which is still as relevant as ever. *LARR* assessed the extent to which a child understands the meaning of literacy metalanguage, from its most general terms ('reading', writing') down to points of detail. For punctuation, it presented short pieces of text and asked children to perform a simple circling task:

(a) Dr. Smith bought a car. [Circle each thing that is a full stop (period).]

(b) Sandy, Bruce and James ran home. [Circle each full stop (period).]

(c) Can all birds fly? Yes, they can. But can an emu fly? [Circle each thing that is a question mark.]

As children develop their linguistic awareness, they make some interesting decisions, such as circling only the second period in (a) because 'it goes at the end', or circling the comma as well as the period in (b). Engaging a child in a discussion of what punctuation is all about is always mutually beneficial. It is the message also of *Help Your Child to Read and Write, and More* (see the Interlude to Chapter 14): 'Discussion of the physical aspects of a book, including the lay-out of the pages, will help them to understand what they themselves must do as writers.' And it is the basis of the excellent *Punctuation Project*, led by Sue Sing and Nigel Hall at Manchester Metropolitan University, which is based on the belief that young children 'have the ability to talk freely about punctuation in ways that would offer insights into how they thought about it'.

One of the findings of this kind of research is to highlight the importance of choosing terms that don't confuse young learners. For example, describing an apostrophe as a 'little raised comma', won't help, as there's nothing linguistically in common between the two. And while the term 'speech marks' is fairly transparent, to express what's going on when people are speaking, it needs to be carefully watched, for (as we saw in Chapter 31) these marks are also used in quite a wide range of other circumstances in which people aren't speaking at all. It isn't a difficult matter discovering the way punctuation terms can confuse children: they will tell you themselves.

Make the task more appealing

This is definitely the teacher's domain, but authors have made a contribution too, by incorporating punctuation terms into their fiction. The ability to talk about language is known to be a critical element in the development of literacy, so anything that fosters this awareness in relation to punctuation is likely to be helpful, such as anthropomorphic or zoomorphic stories about how punctuation marks behave. Here are three:

- 'The comma that didn't belong anywhere', a short story by American writer Martha Baird, and filmed by Ken Kimmelman in 2009 as *Thomas Comma* – the adventure of a lonely comma looking for the right sentence.
- *In the Land of Punctuation* (an illustrated translation of the comic poem by German writer Christian Morgenstern written in 1905). It begins (in Sirish Rao's version):

    The peaceful land of Punctuation
    is filled with tension overnight
    When the stops and commas of the nation
    call the semicolons 'parasites'.

    (It's quite a violent story!)
- *Punctuation Bestiary*, by American writer Kiran Spees. We see the two ears of a pair of rabbits morph into quotation marks ... a frog's long tongue turns into a dash ...

Punctuation can be fun: that is the message of books like these. And there is no limit to the games that can be devised to put this principle into practice. Authors such as Cummings and Joyce show us various ways of playing with punctuation (Chapter 30). Percival Leigh rewrote famous texts – 'taking liberties' with punctuation, as he put it (Chapter 11). Thanks to YouTube, even quite young students can watch (and adapt) Danish comedian Victor Borge's famous sketch in which he gives a distinctive noise to every punctuation mark and reads out passages, with hilarious results. And there are endless opportunities to replicate the way artists use punctuation in comics and cartoons, where the marks can replace whole sentences and convey reactions in the manner of emoticons. Charles Schulz was a master of this technique. Here are four of his strips from a September 1964 punctuation sequence:

Become an MP

Teachers have to show their students how to *manage* punctuation, which means not just getting their charges to read a lot, but guiding them towards an informed awareness of the nature of the system and of the stylistic differences that exist. A good linguistically based grounding in punctuation should give students a solid understanding of what the rules are – remembering, as Kurt Vonnegut said (Chapter 22), 'Rules only take us so far' – and an appreciation of the problems to be faced when applying them. It should draw attention to the strengths and limitations of the system as a whole. The ultimate aim is to nurture the ability to 'translate' from one genre to the other as occasion demands, thereby fostering a mature and confident control of punctuational styles. We all need to become MPs – 'masters of punctuation'.

References and further reading

Chapters 1–10

Blake, N F. *Caxton's Own Prose*. London: André Deutsch, 1973.

Crystal, D. *Evolving English: One Language, Many Voices*. London: British Library, 2010.

Crystal, D. *The Stories of English*. London: Penguin, 2004.

Parkes, M B. *Pause and Effect: An Introduction to Punctuation in the West*. Aldershot: Scolar Press, 1992.

Roberts, J. *Guide to Scripts Used in English Writing up to 1500*. London: British Library, 2005.

Saenger, P. *Space between Words: The Origins of Silent Reading*. Stanford, CA: Stanford University Press, 1997.

Chapters 11–12

Crystal, D. *Making Sense of Grammar*. London: Penguin, 2004.

Sutherland, K. *Jane Austen's Fiction Manuscripts: A Digital Edition*. Available at http://www.janeausten.ac.uk.

Sutherland, K. *Jane Austen's Textual Lives: From Aeschylus to Bollywood*. Oxford: Oxford University Press, 2005.

Chapters 13–34

Barfoot, C. 'Trouble with the apostrophe: or, you know what hairdresser's are like', in I Tieken-Boon van Ostade and J Frankis (eds), *Language Usage and Description: Studies Presented to N E Osselton on the Occasion of his Retirement*. Amsterdam: Rodopi, 1991, 121–39.

Baron, N and Ling, R. 'Necessary smileys & useless periods'. *Visible Language* 45 (1/2), 2011, 45–67.

Carey, G V. *Mind the Stop* (Cambridge: Cambridge University Press, 1939; London: Penguin Books 1971).

Crystal, D. *The Fight for English*. Oxford: Oxford University Press, 2009.

Crystal, D. 'On a not very bright grammar test'. 12 September 2013 at <http://david-crystal.blogspot.co.uk/2013/09/on-not-very-bright-grammar-test.html>

Deck, J and Herson, B. *The Great Typo Hunt*. New York: Crown.

Fowler, H W. *A Dictionary of Modern English Usage* (1926), edited by D Crystal. Oxford: Oxford University Press, 2009.

Gowers, E. *Plain Words* (1948), revised and updated by R Gowers. London: Penguin, 2014.

Hale, C and Scanlon, J. *Wired Style*. New York: Broadway Books, 1999.

Houston, K. *Shady Characters*. London: Penguin, 2013.

Kay, C, Roberts, J, Samuels, M and Wotherspoon, I. *The Historical Thesaurus of the Oxford English Dictionary*. Oxford: Oxford University Press, 2009.

Ledgard, F W. *Punctuation*. London: Cassell, 1977.

Mackay, D and Simo, J. *Help Your Child to Read and Write, and More*. London: Penguin, 1976.

Miller, G A. 'The magical number seven, plus or minus two: some limits on our capacity for processing information', in G A Miller, *The Psychology of Communication*. Baltimore. MD: Penguin, 1967, 14–44.

Partridge, E. *You Have a Point There*. London: Hamish Hamilton, 1953.

Quirk, R, Greenbaum, S, Leech, G and Svartvik, J. *A Comprehensive Grammar of the English Language*. London: Longman, 1985.

Strunk, W and White, E B. *The Elements of Style*. Original edition by Strunk, 1918. Joint revised edition, New York: Macmillan, 1959.

Toner, A (ed.). *Punctuation*. A special issue of *Visible Language* 45 (1/2), 2011.

Truss, L. *Eats, Shoots & Leaves: The Zero Tolerance Approach to Punctuation*. London: Profile Books, 2003.

Appendix

Baird, B. 'The comma that didn't belong anywhere', filmed by Ken Kimmelman as *Thomas Comma*. New York: Imagery Film Ltd, 2009.

Downing, J, Ayers, D and Schaefer, B. *Linguistic Awareness in Reading Readiness*. Windsor: NFER-Nelson, 1983.

Ferreiro, E and Teberosky, A. *Literacy before Schooling*. London: Heinemann, 1983.

Morgenstern, C. *In the Land of Punctuation* (*Im Reich der Interpunktionen*, 1905), illustrated by Rathna Ramanathan, translated by Sirish Rao. Chennai: Tara Books, 2009.

Sing, S and Hall, N. 'Listening to children think about punctuation', in A Carter, T Lillis and S Perkin (eds), *Why Writing Matters*. Amsterdam: Benjamins, 2009, 189–203.

Spees, K. *Punctuation Bestiary*. Seattle, WA: Excite Kids, 2011.

User Design. *Punctuation ...?* <www.userdesign.co.uk/books>, 2012.

Illustration credits

Index